Wild Riv

Rugged mountains surround the Middle Fork country, including the Great Bear Wilderness and Glacier National Park. This vast area was one of the last drainages in the United States to be explored and settled, so the pioneer period persisted longer in the Middle Fork than nearly anywhere else in the American West. In *Wild River Pioneers*, you will find the stories of dozens of rugged pioneers, including the first Sheriff of Flathead County, his role in the hanging of Charles Black, and his 1893 gunfight with notorious train robbers along Bear Creek. You'll read about the Cattle Queen of Montana's death struggle with her mining partner, Frank McPartland, in a leaky rowboat on Glacier Park's McDonald Lake. You'll discover these stories and many more, and you'll discover the rich landscape and natural history of Montana's wildest river.

Praise for Wild River Pioneers

Because I still cherish the wildness of the Flathead that lured me here back in the 1960s-specifically to Glacier and its contiguous wilderness areas-I warmed to *Wild River Pioneers*, discovering that for several nights running, John's book was my evening compulsion.

In his title Fraley is, of course, referring to what quite arguably may be the wildest of the state's rivers, the Middle Fork of the Flathead. It's a river I greatly appreciate through some writings of my own, but one that John undoubtedly knows better than any contemporary wilderness wanderer.

He knows the area through research and from oral history interviews, and from experiences derived there as a research biologist. In some ways, then, John has lived the life of some of the book's protagonists. Through these activities John has uncovered tales of grizzly bears; of picturesque pioneer characters, such as "Slippery Bill" Morrison. Many of the tales once generated by all these players are now being diluted from our collective memories, in part because of the changing interests of a changing society.

Nevertheless, so many of us still cherish our "wild river heritage" and the people who shaped it, and must now thank John for his detailed research and the wonderful narration that has resulted. Because of these efforts John has not only preserved a vital segment of our outdoor history but he has transformed it into literature.

Bert Gildart, Author of *Montana's Early Day Rangers, Glacier Country, and Explore! Glacier National Park and Montana's Flathead Valley*

Advance Praise for
Wild River Pioneers

"Raging down through the Flathead's Continental Divide wilderness, the Middle Fork was "born wild," but the pioneers who first explored it over a hundred years ago seem equally untamed. John's book gives a spellbinding history on those daring, valiant, and sometimes "different" people. I'd buy the book just for the chapter on Josephine Doody (the Bootleg Lady of Glacier Park)."

George Ostrom, Montana's most colorful newsman, and author of *Glacier's Secrets*, and other books about Glacier National Park

"Once started on the stories, I read them all nonstop except for two lumber sales, four visitors, at least three coffee breaks, and one night of deep sleep recovering from the adventures of the Middle Fork's People. Hooked on the pace, suspense, and interest, I wanted always to see the next page. Would that my knees were once again strong enough to rediscover the sense of place of your story. I wish I were Slippery Bill at age 35..."

Bud Moore, retired U. S. Forest Service Official Emeritus, noted conservationist, and author of *The Lochsa Story: Land Ethics in the Bitterroot Mountains*

"If natural surroundings could be deliberately secretive, reclusive, inhospitable, and grandly beautiful as well, the Middle Fork of the Flathead River would be the ultimate example. Much of John Fraley's life has been shaped by the fact that as a biologist and as a curious, caring individual he has tramped those mountains, rivers, and streams, hunted, trapped, *and* sought out the life-details of the few earliest settlers, eloquently sharing them with us. Read this book and you shall be touched by the heart, not only of the author, but those whose biographical records he has so diligently sought out even to their graves.

Carle F. O'Neil, historian and author of *Muscle, Grit, and Big Dreams: Earliest Towns of the Flathead*, and *Two Men of Demersville*

"I think John has done an excellent job of capturing the aura of the Middle Fork of the Flathead River. He should be commended for having the foresight to pull all of this rapidly disappearing history together while there are still a few of us around who lived in that era. I appreciate the references to my father, Glacier Park Ranger Clyde Fauley, Sr.

Clyde Montana Fauley, Jr., Retired Glacier National Park Ranger

"I sincerely appreciate John Fraley's research and writings, which both confirmed and revealed many aspects of the life of my great grandfather, Joseph Gangner. I doubt if a true conclusion will ever be drawn in regard to the conviction and hanging of Charlie Black. Was he a terribly vicious killer who earned his fate, or rather a victim, caught up in the political struggle between Kalispell and Columbia Falls in the quest for the Flathead County seat? This event troubled Big Joe for the rest of his life. Because of the efforts of John and Sexton Mike Hamlin, a headstone will be placed at Joe's burial site in St. Mary's Catholic Cemetery in Missoula. Rest in peace, Big Joe."

Mike Dockstader, great grandson of Big Joe Gangner, the first sheriff of Flathead County

Wild River Pioneers

Adventures in the Middle Fork of the Flathead,
Great Bear Wilderness and Glacier National Park

by

John Fraley

Big Mountain Publishing
Whitefish, Montana

Library of Congress Control Number: 2008933109

Published with the cooperation of the Northwest Montana Historical Society, Museum at Central School.

Wilo River Pioneers

Adventures in the Middle Fork of the Flathead, Great Bear Wilderness and Glacier National Park

Copyright © 2008 by John Fraley

ISBN 978-0-9622428-8-5

Cover Photo: Middle Fork of the Flathead River in the Great Bear Wilderness.

Table of Contents

ACKNOWLEDGEMENTS

Wild River Pioneers became a big undertaking that spanned more than a decade of research and two years of writing. I found that each chapter became a complex story, made up of many smaller ones. Sometimes I felt that my head was going to explode and I wondered if I was up to the task.

I wrote each chapter first for my teenaged daughter, a writer in her own right, and a person I consider my most trusted advisor. I figured that if she were pleased and entertained with each story, others would be too. My daughter never tired of hearing about the intricate lives of these pioneers along the Middle Fork of the Flathead River. Thanks, Heather.

It's hard to know where to start thanking people who helped me in my research. Ann Fagre and Lon Johnson of Glacier National Park steered me to letters, documents, historical interviews, and other original sources for many of the events that took place in Glacier, and they reviewed several of the chapters. These chapters would be much less if not for them. Ann helped me locate photos in Glacier's collection and arranged for their use in this book. Deirdre Shaw, Glacier's museum curator, was a great help as always and she provided a thorough review of the chapter on George Snyder. Lon also provided a contact for Krys Peterson, the distant cousin of George Snyder, one of the major characters in the book. Krys helped locate information and records, and provided photos. Ed Amberg and Billie Homlund of the Montana State Hospital helped me get more information on George. Jodie Foley of the Montana Historical Society located and copied George Snyder's file from the Montana State Hospital. Former Glacier Park Ranger Clyde Fauley Jr., whose father was one of the Wild River Pioneers, reviewed a couple of chapters and gave me comments. Thanks to you all.

Gordon Pouliott of Nyack inspired me to chase down the stories of some of these pioneers, provided great background information, and told me how to find Josephine Doody's hideout cabin. Gordon was a Middle Fork lore master, the killer of more than a few grizzlies, a professional boxer, and a heckuva man. I wish he could have lived long enough to see this book completed. Betty Robertson (Schurr), a pioneer lady at Nyack Flats, provided photos and patiently put up with my questions during numerous interviews over the years. Other Middle Fork folks who allowed me to interview them included: Bob Robertson, Wes Bell, Velma Guy, Lewis Voss, and Tiny Powell. Sadly, these old-timers are gone now.

Dale Sommerfield, Middle Fork woodsman extraordinaire, was a companion on some of my trips in the Wild River country. Dale provided advice on the setting of the Penrose story and thoughts on the motivations of the characters. Dale and I proved to each other many times over that backcountry death marches are actually fun if you have the right perspective.

Author and conservationist Bud Moore encouraged me to reach a higher standard in my writing and helped me focus the theme of Wild River Pioneers. He reviewed an earlier draft of the book and pointed me in the right direction. I'm honored that he took the time to help.

Bill and Barbara Chilton granted me interviews about their years in the Middle Fork backcountry with the U.S. Forest Service and generously shared early photos. Bill reviewed that chapter and provided helpful insights. Pioneer Ranger Art Whitney did the same. I'm sad to say that Art has been gone for years now. Ranger Don Hauth shared some of his knowledge about the Heart of the Middle Fork as well. Flathead Forest Archaeologist Tim Light reviewed the chapter on Schafer Meadows. Backcountry guide Tim Darr passed along lore of the upper Middle Fork and spurred me on with his enthusiasm about the backcountry.

Pete Darling, the keeper of Woodlawn Cemetery in Columbia Falls, helped me locate a lost grave and talked with me about the meaning of chasing the pioneers' ghosts. The descendents of Sheriff Joe Gangner, including Mike Dockstader, Effie Dockstader, and Mary Sullivan, gave me insights about Sheriff Joe. It was an honor to meet Effie, who has lived in the Flathead for nearly a century. Mike Hamlin, keeper of Old St. Mary Cemetery in Missoula, helped me locate Joe Gangner's gravesite.

My two sons, Kevin and Troy, came along with me on many long hikes over the years through the Middle Fork's devil's club and alder while searching for clues and for the setting for some of the stories. Thank you, my sons. Doris Huffine, the subject of *A Woman's Way West*, my first book about the area, and her sister, Maxine, gave me lots of insights and contacts about the characters in this current book. Doris and Maxine have been gone for years, but I've been honored to preserve at least a little bit of their knowledge in this book. My sister, Beth McMahon, read early versions of the stories and urged me to keep it up.

Ron Wright, of Big Mountain Publishing, believed in the book and graciously brought it to publication. Historian and author Carle O'Neil, a representative of the Northwest Montana Historical Society, ably edited the manuscript. Gil Jordan of the Society lent encouragement and supported the project. The Matthew Hansen Endowment for Wilderness Studies, a Fund of the Montana Community Foundation, also helped support Wild River Pioneers.

Finally, I thank my wife Dana, who has now put up with two of my ten-year odysseys of chasing down tales of Montana's Wildest River.

PREFACE

In *Wild River Pioneers*, I do my best to bring alive the history of Montana's wildest river drainage by telling the stories of some of its most riveting historical characters. I tell a series of true stories that reflect the excitement and historical richness in this mountainous watershed. I've focused on the people and the landscape, with some natural history, biology, old-timer recollections, and my personal experience included in the mix.

I start with the pioneers who brought the railroad over Marias Pass, and end with the pioneers who settled Glacier National Park's Lake McDonald Valley. In between, there are murders, bootlegging, poaching, gold prospecting, hunting, fishing, fur trapping, grizzly encounters, shootouts, political corruption, an ice cream-eating pet bear and a hanging. It's amazing what you can find out about the history of one river drainage when you start peeking under rocks and following cold trails.

I followed three principles in writing the book. First, the Middle Fork of the Flathead River drainage is the common geographic thread for the stories. Each story relates to the Middle Fork or a pioneer who is a part of the Middle Fork's history. Second, to make the stories entertaining and lively, at times I've assigned motivations or feelings to the characters, or recreated settings for certain events. I did that based on my experience in the same area in which I've traveled extensively and regard with affection, or on interviews with people in the best position to know how the old-timers would have felt or acted. Whenever possible I talked to a relative or a friend of the character. Often, with careful looking or listening, I found treasures of detail or background in newspaper accounts or old-timer recollections. Third, I did everything I could to make sure the information is historically accurate. Most of my nearly 200 sources were newspaper accounts from the time of the events, or letters, documents, and personal interviews with old-timers and others. If I move the story into the realm of legend, I clearly identify it as such.

As I wrote Wild River Pioneers, I drew heavily from my three decades of experience in the Middle Fork of the Flathead Drainage. I served as a state fisheries biologist in the frontcountry and backcountry areas of the Middle Fork in the 1980s, and continued to take part in bull trout and furbearer surveys since then. I've also spent a lot of my personal time fur trapping, hunting, fishing, skiing, and hiking year-around in the drainage. *Wild River Pioneers* grew out of my first book, *A Woman's Way West*: In and Around Glacier National Park, 1925-1990 (Big Mountain Publishing, 1998), a book that has much of its focus on a Glacier Park pioneering couple.

I didn't set out to make this book a comprehensive history of the Middle Fork drainage and it's certainly not that. But I hope you will find it fun to read, and I hope you'll pick up some of the sense of place I've felt as I've chased the stories of these Wild River Pioneers.

PROLOGUE
Wild River Pioneers: I'm on their trail

The Middle Fork of the Flathead is Montana's wildest river. For 40 miles, from the confluence of Bowl and Strawberry Creeks, the river's clear waters rush through the Great Bear and Bob Marshall Wildernesses to join Bear Creek. Then, the river flows another 40 miles through lightly populated canyon country to meet the North Fork of the Flathead on the southern edge of Glacier National Park. No dams block the river, and only two auto bridges cross its channel. If any major stream in Montana deserves to be called Wild River, it's this one.

My love of this drainage began decades ago as I worked as a fisheries biologist along the river and its tributaries. There's something special about a stream that is so clear that you can put on a snorkel and mask, stick your head in the water, and see the blue, gray, red, and green stream-bottom rocks in 30 feet of transparent water.

The Middle Fork, surrounded and isolated by rugged mountains, was one of the last drainages in the United States to be explored and settled. The railroad, bringing with it the telegraph, didn't cross into the drainage until 1890. The pioneer period persisted longer in the Middle Fork than nearly anywhere else in the West.

An old blaze mark on a dead snag or a few log remnants of an old cabin might be the only visible marks left by pioneers on the Middle Fork's landscape. But these Wild River Pioneers left much more than that, something intangible, parts of themselves that paint the land with a sense of place. I saw some of the visible marks these old-timers left on the land, and I wanted to discover their stories. To find the stories I knew I'd have to carefully follow old trails, and dig deep into the lore and legend of the drainage. I knew it would be a big task, and I knew that it would take years. It turned out that I was right.

I found myself interviewing everyone I could find who might know something of the Middle Fork's history. I searched archives of historical information at libraries and pored over century-old newspapers until I thought my eyes would cross. I gathered information and lore, and what I found led me ever to more; the connections were endless.

But the most exciting times came when, using old tips from a cold trail, I was able to discover evidence that pointed to the truth of a story. At first, many of the stories or characters seemed more legendary than real. Then, I would find a death certificate here, a cabin log there; a lost grave, an old news story; and the stories and characters would begin to take solid shape. Now, I feel like I know these Middle Fork Pioneers intimately. Sometimes late at night I think I know some of them too intimately, almost as if I were possessed by them to tell their stories.

It's been said that the human spirit longs to be noticed and remembered. Maybe my spooky feeling has something to do with that.

On one of my discovery trips not long ago, I searched for the setting of one of the most important stories in *Wild River Pioneers*: the encounter between Philadelphia Surgeon C. B. Penrose and a great "white grizzly" high on the Middle Fork divide in the central part of the drainage. As an adventure, Penrose and two of his brothers had accompanied the first U. S. Geological Survey Party to enter the Middle Fork country.

On a sunny September day muted by haze from a forest fire, I set out with my oldest son and another companion from the South Fork side of the divide to find the Penrose site. Could we locate the site of the U. S. Geological Survey camp where Penrose and his brothers had stayed a century ago? Could we find the spot where Penrose and the grizzly tangled? We had collected plenty of clues from the topography and from early writings but the chance of success seemed remote.

We cut through the timber and followed an old brushed-in forest road for the first three miles, skirting around the bottom of Tiger Creek to the divide ridge with Margaret Creek. Once we gained the ridge at about 4,200 feet in elevation and began to climb it, I figured we were following the century-old steps of Penrose and the survey party, who had conducted Penrose and his famous brothers into the high country. According to Alvord Stiles, the lead geographer of the party, as far as he could tell in 1907 his party was the first to penetrate this remote country as they blazed their way up this ridge. As we walked along, I was thinking that the beargrass carpet and the fir and lodgepole timber probably wasn't much different than it was 100 years ago. We saw little sign of any recent human use anywhere along our track.

The ridge rises steeply at first for two miles to a little flat at 5,600 feet. On either side we could look over the drainages of Margaret and Tiger creeks stretching north to the Middle Fork divide ahead of us. We found a few old grown-in blaze marks on weathered snags still standing from a long-ago fire. Could these be the blaze marks Penrose referred to in a later description of his trip as the only signs showing that the survey party had passed this way? We continued a few miles along the ridge as it rose another 1,000 feet past a series of saddles between the two drainages. Finally, we reached the gentle saddle that led to the likely Geological Survey campsite below the notch at the top of the range. Based on topography and descriptions, this saddle must be the gateway that Penrose and Stiles passed through on their way from the camp to reach the "little glacial basin" they both later described as the site of their hunt and bear encounter.

Like Penrose and Stiles a century before us, we passed through the saddle to the northwest and headed for the base of a pyramid-shaped mountain. We crossed alpine meadows, small seeps, and ravines, looking for the spot that fit the men's descriptions. We split up and searched across the rolling alpine benches. I heard an elk bugle a few hundred yards away; it crashed through the brush and I could smell its strong, musky odor.

We joined up again and then came upon a little hidden basin: everything fit, including the stream, the "jumble of boulders" and the distance from the survey campsite. It seemed too good to be true and I wondered if I could really be standing at the spot I had tried to visualize for years as I chased this incredible story and the ghosts of these two men and the ghost of the great bear. But the topography told the tale: this had to be it.

As we swung into the basin and walked along its dry outlet, we studied the old streambed for clues. Then we saw one: lying among the gravels was a very old, almost completely oxidized cartridge casing. Over the years, melt waters had gradually transported the casing down the little stream a hundred yards or so until it came to rest here, where the stream gradient flattened. Could this really be from Penrose's encounter with the grizzly? The shell was a 7mm Mauser, made for use in the Spanish American war and later used as a sporting cartridge. On the shell's base was stamped "UMC 1900," signifying that it was made by the United Metallic Cartridge Company in 1900. Incredibly, everything fit. We had found the proverbial needle in a haystack. Elated, we kept looking.

That's the way this 20-year search along the trail of the Wild River Pioneers has been for me. I've found much more than I thought possible about these old-timers, allowing me to bring their stories alive. I've found hideout cabins, trapper cabins, and an old town site. I've found people willing to share old letters and documents and photos. I've chased the stories of explorers, outlaws, killers, lawmen, bank robbers, forest rangers, park rangers, and lady trappers. I've gotten to know Slippery Bill Morrison, the Cattle Queen of Montana, the Bootleg Lady of Glacier Park, the first sheriff of Flathead County, and the Glacier Park Maverick. I pieced together the story of a young mother who was brutally murdered and I found her lost grave.

I've tried to bring alive the history of the Middle Fork by finding and telling these true stories. Now I want to share them with you.

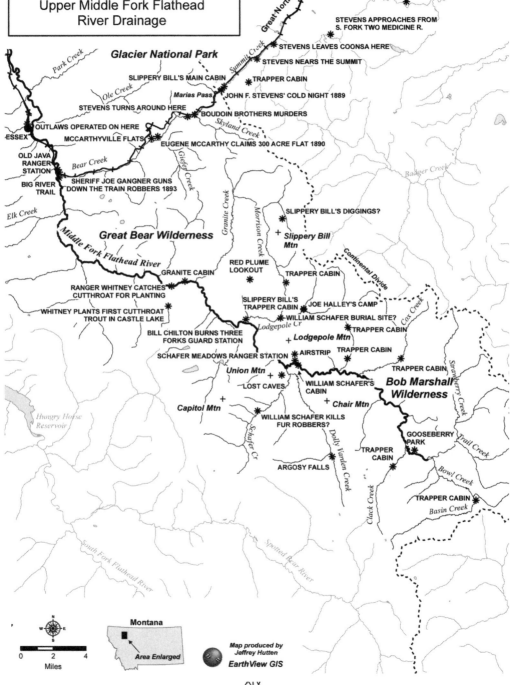

Wild River Pioneers
Locations Map

Upper Middle Fork Flathead River Drainage

Park Creek

Two Medicine River

Great Northern Railway

STEVENS SENDS MULE TEAM BACK

STEVENS APPROACHES FROM
S. FORK TWO MEDICINE R.

Summit Creek

STEVENS LEAVES COONSA HERE

STEVENS NEARS THE SUMMIT

Glacier National Park

SLIPPERY BILL'S MAIN CABIN

TRAPPER CABIN

Ole Creek

Marias Pass

JOHN F. STEVENS' COLD NIGHT 1889

STEVENS TURNS AROUND HERE

BOUDOIN BROTHERS MURDERS

Skyland Creek

OUTLAWS OPERATED ON HERE

Badger Creek

ESSEX

MCCARTHYVILLE FLATS

EUGENE MCCARTHY CLAIMS 300 ACRE FLAT 1890

OLD JAVA
RANGER
STATION

Bear Creek

BIG RIVER
TRAIL

SHERIFF JOE GANGNER GUNS
DOWN THE TRAIN ROBBERS 1893

Gifey Creek

Elk Creek

Granite Creek

SLIPPERY BILL'S DIGGINGS?

Morrison Creek

+ *Slippery Bill
Mtn*

Continental Divide

Middle Fork Flathead River

Great Bear Wilderness

RED PLUME
LOOKOUT

TRAPPER CABIN

GRANITE CABIN

RANGER WHITNEY CATCHES
CUTTHROAT FOR PLANTING

SLIPPERY BILL'S
TRAPPER CABIN

JOE HALLEY'S CAMP

Cox Creek

WHITNEY PLANTS FIRST CUTTHROAT
TROUT IN CASTLE LAKE

WILLIAM SCHAFER BURIAL SITE?

TRAPPER CABIN

Lodgepole Cr

BILL CHILTON BURNS THREE
FORKS GUARD STATION

+ *Lodgepole Mtn*

SCHAFER MEADOWS RANGER STATION

AIRSTRIP

TRAPPER CABIN

Union Mtn +

LOST CAVES

TRAPPER CABIN

Strawberry Creek

WILLIAM SCHAFER'S
CABIN

*Bob Marshall
Wilderness*

+ *Capitol Mtn*

+ *Chair Mtn*

*Hungry Horse
Reservoir*

WILLIAM SCHAFER KILLS
FUR ROBBERS?

Schafer Cr

GOOSEBERRY
PARK

Trail Creek

TRAPPER
CABIN

ARGOSY FALLS

Dolly Varden Creek

Bowl Creek

TRAPPER CABIN

Clack Creek

Basin Creek

South Fork Flathead River

Spotted Bear River

Montana

Area Enlarged

0   2   4
Miles

Map produced by
Jeffrey Hutten

EarthView GIS

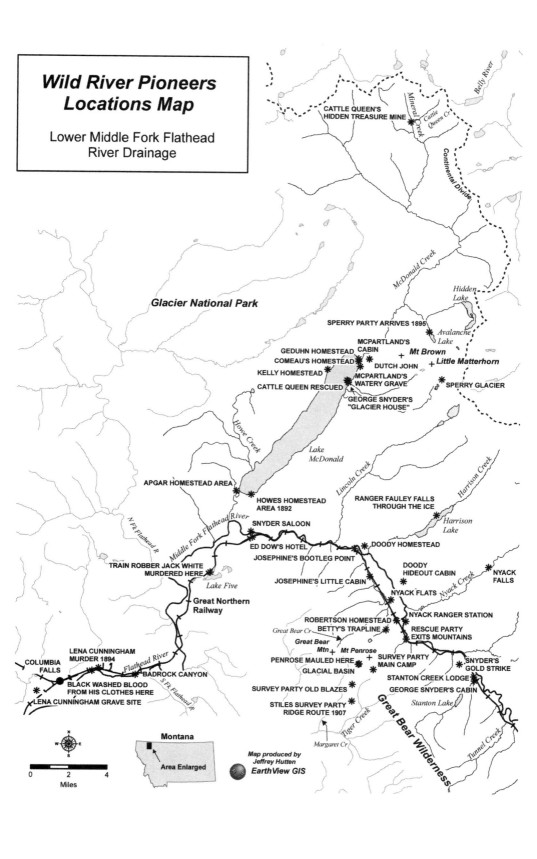

Wild River Pioneers Locations Map

Lower Middle Fork Flathead River Drainage

CATTLE QUEEN'S HIDDEN TREASURE MINE

Mineral Creek
Cattle Queen Cr
Belly River
Continental Divide

McDonald Creek

Hidden Lake

Glacier National Park

SPERRY PARTY ARRIVES 1895

Avalanche Lake

MCPARTLAND'S CABIN
+ *Mt Brown*
+ *Little Matterhorn*

GEDUHN HOMESTEAD
COMEAU'S HOMESTEAD
DUTCH JOHN
KELLY HOMESTEAD
MCPARTLAND'S WATERY GRAVE
CATTLE QUEEN RESCUED
SPERRY GLACIER

GEORGE SNYDER'S "GLACIER HOUSE"

Howe Creek

Lake McDonald

Lincoln Creek
Harrison Creek

APGAR HOMESTEAD AREA

HOWES HOMESTEAD AREA 1892
RANGER FAULEY FALLS THROUGH THE ICE

Harrison Lake

SNYDER SALOON

N Fk Flathead R
Middle Fork Flathead River

ED DOW'S HOTEL
DOODY HOMESTEAD
JOSEPHINE'S BOOTLEG POINT

TRAIN ROBBER JACK WHITE MURDERED HERE

Lake Five

DOODY HIDEOUT CABIN
NYACK FALLS

JOSEPHINE'S LITTLE CABIN

Nyack Creek

Great Northern Railway

NYACK FLATS

ROBERTSON HOMESTEAD
BETTY'S TRAPLINE
NYACK RANGER STATION

Great Bear Cr
Great Bear Mtn
+ *Mt Penrose*
RESCUE PARTY EXITS MOUNTAINS

LENA CUNNINGHAM MURDER 1894
PENROSE MAULED HERE
SURVEY PARTY MAIN CAMP
SNYDER'S GOLD STRIKE

COLUMBIA FALLS
Flathead River
GLACIAL BASIN
BADROCK CANYON
STANTON CREEK LODGE
GEORGE SNYDER'S CABIN

S Fk Flathead R
SURVEY PARTY OLD BLAZES

BLACK WASHED BLOOD FROM HIS CLOTHES HERE
LENA CUNNINGHAM GRAVE SITE

STILES SURVEY PARTY RIDGE ROUTE 1907

Stanton Lake

Tiger Creek
Great Bear Wilderness

N W E S

Montana

Area Enlarged

0   2   4
Miles

Margaret Cr
Tunnel Creek

Map produced by
Jeffrey Hutten
EarthView GIS

Chapter 1
TOUGH TRIP OVER THE LOST PASS

*John F. Stevens shows the way over Meriwether's
Marias Pass and down the Middle Fork*

The discovery of Marias Pass over the Continental Divide and the construction of Jim Hills' Great Northern Railroad opened the remote, pristine Middle Fork of the Flathead Watershed to travel and communication. The location of the pass was generally known for years, but its official discovery and description had eluded many explorers. Finally, in the year Montana gained its statehood, the location of the pass was confirmed.

An unlikely three member corps set out from Assiniboine on the east slope prairie on a quest to find the pass, and confirm its suitability for Jim Hill's Great Northern Railroad. This unlikely trio included an engineer, a soldier, and a Flathead Tribal member. Their success was one of the great feats of exploration in the American West.

The Middle Fork Drainage was a complete wilderness in 1889. A few rough trails followed the main river course but there were no paths that could even be considered wagon roads. A handful of lonely trappers and prospectors explored the drainage, but that was it. The landscape was shaped by fire because there were no means to fight fires in this vast backcountry. The high peaks and rugged, timbered slopes and valleys lay virtually untouched by humans.

As they had for millennia, waters of the cold, transparent tributary streams rushed clear and unaltered to join the Middle Fork of the Flathead River, and then continued downstream to join the North and South Forks to form the main Flathead River. The streams teemed with westslope cutthroat trout and bull trout. Bull trout migrated from Flathead Lake up the river and the tributary streams of the upper Middle Fork drainage into what is now the Great Bear Wilderness. These huge trout also migrated east up Bear Creek almost to Marias Pass itself.

As fall arrived the big bull trout spawners built their nests in Bear Creek and its tributaries. The golden larch needles fell, carpeting the forest floor. Winter was coming and the sleepy isolation of the Middle Fork was about to profoundly change.

In the mid-1880s the Great Northern Railway Company's founder, James Hill, pushed his line west from Minneapolis across the northern region of the western United States paralleling the Canadian boundary to Havre by 1887. From there a spur line was completed southwest to Great Falls, Helena, and Butte. A small siding extended four miles west of Havre by 1889. But to go further westward Hill needed a low pass through the mountains, one that would give the shortest possible route, the easiest grade, and the most maneuverable curves on to the Pacific.

Blackfeet and Flathead Indians had used such a low pass for hundreds of years, according to their elders. Also, trappers and others likely had crossed the pass many times; they just had not documented their trips. Fur Trader Finan MacDonald was thought to have crossed the pass from the west with a party of 150 Flathead Indians in 1810 on the way to buffalo country. Duncan MacDonald, also associated with the lower Flathead area, claimed to have crossed the pass from the west three times in the 1870s. Some who knew of the existence of the pass avoided crossing it to the east side because they feared Blackfeet war parties.

For many decades, in fact, a number of explorers had tried to locate the rumored low elevation dip across the mountains. In July of 1806 Meriwether Lewis and three of his most trusted men (Drouillard and the Field brothers) tried but failed to find a low pass across the Divide in the headwaters of the "noble" river he named after his cousin Maria Wood. Lewis ended his quest at "Camp Disappointment" on Cut Bank Creek, a tributary of the Two Medicine River. Lewis and his men had approached to within 10 miles of a range of the Rocky Mountains, later named the Lewis Range in his honor. Within the party's sight were the spectacular peaks of the present Glacier National Park, the Continental Divide, and the area of Marias Pass (about 25 miles distant). But if Lewis had continued, reached Marias Pass, and been able to take measurements with his chronometer and sextant, he would have been disappointed. He was searching for a pass north of 50 degrees latitude, which he believed might lead into a southern branch of the Saskatchewan River in Canada, not a westward flowing tributary of the Middle Fork of the Flathead River.

An official expedition, launched by Governor Isaac Stevens of Washington Territory in 1853, found a number of divide-crossing passes, but failed to identify the true pass. James Doty approached the pass from the east in 1854, ascending the South Fork of the Two Medicine River toward the divide. Doty stopped short, however; he climbed a mountain, looked to the west, and claimed to have seen the pass. Upon returning to his duty station at

Fort Benton, he drew a remarkably accurate map showing the pass's location, but the pass remained officially unexplored for years.

Several people, including Major Marcus Baldwin, the Blackfeet Indian Agent, told Hill that the sought-for pass could be found at the headwaters of two drainages: Two Medicine River on the east side and a large tributary of the Middle Fork of the Flathead on the west side. Baldwin told Hill that he'd actually reached the pass from the west by traveling upstream from Flathead Lake along the Flathead River and then its Middle Fork. It is unclear whether or not he had continued over and down the east side, though.

After considering all of the reports, Hill had no doubt about the existence of the pass, even though his engineers had not yet found it. In 1888, Hill had sent a Canadian engineer of the Canadian Pacific Railway by the name of Barclay to confirm the presence of the pass. Like others before him, though, Barclay's effort was disappointing. He failed to locate the low pass. Hill decided he needed a new engineer.

Chief Engineer E. H. Beckler was in charge of the rail extension for Hill. He hired John F. Stevens, an engineer with a sterling reputation of accomplishment on the Canadian Pacific Railway, to confirm the existence of the fabled pass. Beckler met with Stevens in Helena and explained the need to find the pass as soon as possible. The railroad contract had already been signed with construction companies to extend the line west to Spokane, but no one yet knew where the line would cross the Divide. The only rail line crossing the Rockies in Montana at that time was the Northern Pacific, located far to the south. Beckler explained to Stevens that the proposed northern route would pass through the Flathead Valley and then along the Kootenai River and across northern Idaho. For this route to be established, a pass across the mountains must be discovered in the north, as directly west of Havre as possible. Would Stevens be interested in finding the route?

Stevens, a self-educated, decisive and confident man, immediately agreed to the proposition.

The task would not be easy. Even today, this pass is a lonely, cold, windswept place between the more open and rocky east side of the Divide and the heavily timbered west side. Present towns on the east side such as Browning and Cut Bank are some of the windiest in the U. S. The small source streams of the major Middle Fork tributary of Bear Creek begin in willow and lodgepole flats on top of the pass. Bear Creek then drops steeply to the west through a rocky, timbered canyon.

Imagine the difficulty of locating this pass from the east side with limited information, and after so many others had failed to find it or at least document its suitability for a railroad crossing. Adding to the difficulty, Stevens set out to look for the pass in the cold of December 1889, so that construction could begin that spring.

John F. Stevens was commissioned by Jim Hill's chief engineer in 1889 to verify the existence of Marias Pass and report on its suitability for the Great Northern Railroad western route. Glacier National Park Historical Collection.

Stevens later said that he didn't at first realize the enormity and fateful importance of the task, instead just viewing it as "another engineering experience." Stevens didn't lack confidence. He was physically imposing, powerfully built and well over six feet tall, with a thick, dark mustache. He had a reputation of being a daring and competent backcountry explorer, and that reputation was about to be put to the test.

The self-assured, 36-year old engineer traveled from Helena to Havre on the existing rail line and made preparations for the expedition. At Fort Assinniboine, a few miles west of Havre on the prairie, Stevens secured a covered wagon, mule team, supplies and a saddle horse. A soldier was sent along to drive the team and return it to the fort after they reached the foot of the mountains.

The three-man corps set out for Blackfeet Agency (now called Browning) in a "light blizzard." Days and about 150 miles later they reached the agency after enduring nearly constant blowing snow.

Once at the agency, Stevens asked everyone he could find about the fabled pass. The white men there didn't believe it existed. The Blackfeet he talked to seemed to know about the pass, but feared it. They believed that the pass held an evil spirit, and that anyone who crossed it would surely die.

Stevens eventually found a Flathead Indian who was staying with the Blackfeet, after reportedly killing another member of his own tribe. Stevens convinced the Indian, by some accounts named Coonsa (or Coonsah), to accompany him by offering him a good sum of money. Stevens later said that he hired the man to go with him in case he needed to send back a messenger, but in no way did he serve as a guide.

Even though Stevens had not been told precisely how to reach the pass, he had a sixth sense that it existed. It was as if fate was pulling this confident man along towards a great accomplishment. He made last preparations to head into the mountains and climb the pass. To cope with the deeper snow he knew they would encounter as they entered the mountains, Stevens bought old pairs of snowshoe frames from a Blackfeet tribal member. He laced leather thongs across the frames to support them on the surface of the snow.

Stevens' little party left the agency and headed across the final stretch of prairie to the foot of the mountains, following the drainage of the Two Medicine River and staying in abandoned "Indian cabins" for several nights along the way. The snow deepened as they entered the mountains, and the wagon bogged down. Stevens instructed the soldier to drive the wagon and mule team back to the last cabin and to wait there for his return.

Stevens and Coonsa loaded some food and blankets on their backs and continued up the South Fork of the Two Medicine River. Stevens briefly explored two side drainages that appeared to head to a pass, but they led nowhere. Finally, he found a branch that he called a "fair prospect." Stevens and Coonsa followed the branch for a few miles and reached an apparent summit. Stevens was elated, thinking that they had reached the pass that had eluded so many explorers. But almost immediately a "sixth sense" as he described it, told him that this wasn't the true summit.

At this point, Coonsa used sign language to tell Stevens that he was quitting there and then. Stevens found some dry wood and built a fire, telling Coonsa to keep it going all night if necessary.

Wisely, Stevens chose to angle southwest to search for the pass after leaving the false summit. Unbeknownst to Stevens, the passes directly west and to the northwest over the mountains in what is now Glacier National Park got higher and more impassable. Firebrand Pass was only four miles distant but at 6,951 feet, it would have ended Stevens' quest. I've crossed it summer and winter, and it's a high, rocky, inhospitable place with a steep final approach over alpine rocks and a few alpine fir and limber pine clinging to the steep funnel of a pass. Farther north and west, Two Medicine at 7,500 feet, Dawson at 7,598 feet, and Cut Bank at 7,800 feet are even higher and more rugged. All these passes were completely unsuitable for the purpose Stevens sought.

Stevens had made his choice, guided by fate, and he headed out alone, south and west along the wide, easy gap in the mountains. The afternoon was waning. Driven by an internal fire that had pushed him all his life, Stevens pushed his makeshift snowshoes through the powder, gambling that the true pass would not be too distant. He followed the small, gentle drainage of what is now called Summit Creek, buried under many feet of snow. A few limber pines and alpine fir, along with taller willow, were all that protruded from the deep snow. Stevens must have been wondering if the approach to this elusive pass could be so easy.

Luckily, after mushing only about three miles and gaining only about 150 feet in elevation, the charmed engineer found himself standing in the legendary Marias Pass over the Continental Divide. The pass was remarkably wide and flat. To Stevens, it must have looked as if these spectacular mountains had simply parted, just for him. To his north and west, the rocky peaks of Summit, Little Dog, and Elk Mountains towered 3,000 feet over the gentle, flat pass. As he stood there, Stevens must have found it hard to believe that such a wide and easy pass had foiled other explorers for so long.

Stevens made a number of aneroid readings to confirm his discovery. He was now certain that he stood in the lowest pass across the Divide in the United States north of New Mexico. Later surveys showed it to be only 5,216 feet above sea level, thousands of feet below the surrounding peaks. It was the evening of December 11, 1889, a date Stevens would later remember as the occasion of his greatest engineering accomplishment. How triumphant he must have felt to succeed in finding the long-sought pass after so many others had failed to discover it.

But Stevens, being an engineer, liked to be absolutely sure of things. He firmly believed he stood in the true pass, but noted that "it would be an inexcusable blunder if I was deceived." So he walked on through the wide, gentle pass for about a half-mile, and then downstream along the first headwater stream that feeds Bear Creek, a tributary of the Middle Fork of the Flathead.

Almost immediately, Bear Creek dropped into a timbered canyon and the going got rougher for snowshoeing. After mushing about three miles down the drainage to near the mouth of Skyland Creek, Stevens turned back towards the pass. He was now completely certain that "the waters of the stream under the snow beneath my feet" flowed into the Pacific Ocean. He had crossed Marias Pass and he knew that it would make him famous.

Stevens had seen enough to conclude that rails could easily be laid to the pass and down the west side. He was elated; he had fulfilled the trust of tycoon James Hill, and believed he would be well rewarded.

Turning back, the engineer started snowshoeing up along the western tributary, finding it considerably steeper than he remembered the approach from the east side. His joy and adrenaline had carried him some three miles down the west side of the pass, and now, as he climbed back up the steeper, more timbered drainage, his energy began to fail. Before he knew it, darkness had fallen. After a "seemingly hopeless struggle," he reached the pass again, exhausted; he could see nothing in the pitch black and he knew that the situation could be life-threatening. It was frigid and windy, and he had no energy remaining. He decided to wait for dawn before continuing to the east, reasoning that it would make no sense to discover and explore the pass if he didn't live to report it.

A heavy blizzard settled in and prevented Stevens from starting a fire. In the dark he could find no suitable wood above the surface of the deep snow. To keep from freezing to death, he walked back and forth in his snowshoes,

Finally, about three miles from False Summit, Stevens was amazed to find himself in the broad, flat, legendary pass through the mountains. Author Photo.

packing a trail in the snow that would support his weight. He then removed his snowshoes and walked in the trail, back and forth, throughout the night, estimating that the temperature plummeted to 40 degrees below zero. He later found that thermometers had dropped to minus 36 that night at Blackfeet Agency. Stevens knew that he would surely freeze to death if he fell asleep.

The determined engineer gnawed on some bread and bacon to keep up his energy, and he kept up his monotonous back and forth trudge on the packed trail. In doing this, Stevens showed his ingenuity and brilliance. Given the conditions, this clever feat was probably the only way a man could have survived that night under those conditions.

Next morning, at "the first streak of light," happy to be alive and able to see the surroundings, Stevens put on his snowshoes and mushed back across the flat of the pass and two miles down the east side. When he reached Coonsa at what is now known as "False Summit," he found him nearly frozen because he had allowed the fire to die during the night. Stevens "beat some life back into him," and helped him warm up and get on his feet. The two men started tramping down the east slope, retracing their steps to the cabin where the wagon, mule team, and soldier awaited them. They rode the wagon back to Indian Agency, looking forward to a well-deserved warm bed and a good meal.

Stevens sent the driver and team back to Fort Assinniboine and made his way south to Helena. Proudly, Stevens reported his findings to Chief Engineer Beckler. Stevens said that it took a while for him to fully realize how unusual and hazardous the expedition had been, but the gravity of his accomplishment must have been sinking in by then.

The chief engineer reported Stevens's discovery to Jim Hill, who recognized immediately that Stevens had made him another fortune. Hill ordered all surveys underway in passes to the south abandoned and transferred to the low pass Stevens had discovered to the north. The rail line would be built almost directly west from Havre over Marias Pass. Survey parties quickly began their work and the construction crews pushed the line west as the weather allowed. Stevens had saved the railroad 100 miles in distance, and found a more direct route across the mountains through what he then thought was "the lowest railway pass in the United States north of New Mexico."

Hill retained Stevens and rewarded him well over the years for his spectacular discovery. A year later, still working for Hill's Great Northern, Stevens discovered "Stevens Pass" farther west across the Cascades. Hill promoted Stevens to chief engineer, then in 1902, general manager of the Great Northern Railroad. In 1905, because of Hill's recommendation (Hill had told Taft and Roosevelt that Stevens was the finest civil engineer in the country), Stevens met personally with President Theodore Roosevelt. Roosevelt appointed him as chief engineer on the Panama Canal Project. Stevens never failed in an assignment and this was no exception. He laid the groundwork for the successful completion of the canal. It was Stevens' perseverance and daring in discovering Marias Pass that most impressed Hill and led Stevens to these great accomplishments.

At the last stop of the Great Northern Railway Upper Missouri River Historical Expedition, on July 21, 1925, a ceremony was held on Marias Pass to honor Stevens. A 20-foot high bronze statue was unveiled showing him bundled in the winter garb he wore on that fateful day in 1889. The statue is awe-inspiring. Stevens wears heavy gloves, wool cap, watch coat, and boots. In his hand, he holds his aneroid instrument. The statue had been completed in April of 1925 by New York City sculptor Caetano Cecere and transported west by rail. The spectacular peaks to the northwest of the pass provide a fitting backdrop.

Lots of dignitaries were on hand for the event. Speakers included Montana Governor J. E. Erickson, U. S. Supreme Court Justice Pierce Butler, officials of Glacier National Park and other agencies, and Robert Ridgeway, president of the American Society of Engineers. Ridgeway praised Stevens' accomplishment as one of the "glories of the profession." Great Northern Photographer T.J. Hileman photo-documented the event and western artist C. M. Russell was there for the heck of it. A proud Stevens spoke, describing

72 year-old John F. Stevens stands with his nephew next to his statue on Marias Pass at the July 21, 1925 dedication. Glacier National Park Historical Collection.

his discovery of the pass. Stevens, now 72 with white hair, was still a physically powerful and impressive man. It's hard to imagine his emotions as he stood before what he described as his "heroic statue," near the spot where he had spent that frigid night walking back and forth in his snowshoe trail.

The ceremony meant much to Stevens, who was sensitive about some people perhaps challenging his rightful designation as the discoverer of the pass. He noted that he never claimed to be the first through the pass, but was the first to locate and describe it officially. He called the ceremony a "very deeply appreciated recognition."

The U. S. Geographic Board later gave John F. Stevens the credit for

"discovering the low pass across the Continental Divide." The canyon of Bear Creek and the Middle Fork of the Flathead from Marias Pass to West Glacier forms the present southern boundary of Glacier National Park.
The Board named this the "John F. Stevens Canyon" in a 1933 ruling, and confirmed that Stevens was indeed the first to explore the low pass, describe it, and make his discovery publicly known (his report to Beckler). Meeting these official criteria, Stevens was formerly acknowledged as the discoverer of Marias Pass.

Because of the official criteria, Stevens was credited with the first official "discovery" and recognition of the pass, even if it was acknowledged that members of the area tribes had traveled it for centuries. And there is no doubt that a handful of trappers and prospectors had used the area of the pass from time to time, even to the extent that one trapper already had a small cabin near the pass when Stevens came through. Some people point out that Stevens should not be credited with the "discovery" of Marias Pass, and that is arguable. But no one debates that, as a professional engineer, he was the first to measure its elevation, and confirm its suitability for construction of the railroad.

Stevens had accomplished what no one previously had been able to do. With his little party including a soldier and a Flathead Indian, a few pairs of snowshoes, a wagon and mule team, and great determination, he had beaten the odds and confirmed the location of the legendary pass that had escaped other explorers as far back as Meriwether Lewis more than eight decades before. Most importantly, Stevens' report to Chief Engineer Beckler gave final impetus for Hill to begin construction of the railroad.

Stevens' accomplishment set in motion the development of one of the last unsettled areas in the United States. Grading construction on the route would begin almost immediately. Soon, the rails would be pushed over the Continental Divide and down the pristine Middle Fork. The wild, untouched Middle Fork Drainage was about to be changed forever.

Chapter 2
THE MIDDLE FORK'S TOMBSTONE TOWN

*The Great Northern Railroad pushes over the divide to
McCarthyville and down the Middle Fork of the Flathead*

Now that John F. Stevens had pointed the way, the extension of the rail line across the Continental Divide at Marias Pass would radically change the Middle Fork Drainage. Mechanical transportation and telegraph communication would suddenly come to an area that had neither before.

Symbolic of this loss of innocence was McCarthyville, the raucous, lawless rail "town" that sprang up with the railroad construction over the west side of the summit. McCarthyville's founding was tentative, its existence was short and violent, and its story reflects some of the worst and best examples of human character in the Middle Fork's history.

Events were moving quickly. Stevens had discovered Marias Pass, and Hill had a route across the Lewis Range. Railroad survey and construction moved rapidly westward. The Shepard-Seims grading outfit gouged their way towards the pass. Meanwhile, E. F. Greenough, whose company provided ties for railroad construction, sent out timber cruisers along the proposed Great Northern Route. He contracted with Eugene McCarthy, a cocky young entrepreneur, to cruise the route over the summit. McCarthy was the son of buffalo hunter, and he honed his outdoor skills at a very young age accompanying his father on the hunts. When Eugene was 11, his family moved to Montana. Once in Montana, Eugene's ambition grew as big as the Big Sky.

In the spring of 1890, Eugene, just 20 years old, headed out to survey the timber from the east side of Marias Pass. Montana had just changed from a territory to a state, and Eugene was determined to be a part of its growth. On a stout packhorse he loaded enough food to last a few weeks and rode his favorite saddle horse into the mountains. The trail-less trip up the east side of the pass challenged his ability. Downed timber and the steep-sided canyon limited the number of miles he could make each day. He completed his cruising task up the east side of the pass, but was not satisfied. Looking over the heavily timbered canyon to the west, not knowing what he would find, he started down the drainage and kept going for several days and eight rugged miles.

This section of what is now known as Bear Creek plummets 80 feet per mile. The narrow canyon is loaded with boulders and it's easy to see why a man and a packhorse picking their way through without a trail would be limited to a few miles per day.

McCarthy ran out of food but he was determined to explore the new country. He lived entirely on game for two weeks. His gamble paid off in a very big way.

McCarthy retraced Stevens' path as he headed west over the pass. He passed Skyland Creek entering from the east, where Stevens had turned back four or five months earlier. Then from the west, several small streams and Autumn Creek entered Bear Creek. Still the canyon and creek bottom were narrow and steep. As the fourth tributary, now called Fielding Creek, entered Bear Creek from the west, McCarthy broke out into a level meadow. Instead of tumbling steeply over boulders, the stream he'd been following suddenly changed completely. It widened to about 30 feet, meandering lazily over smaller gravels through a beautiful, wide flat. McCarthy accurately estimated the size of the flat at 300 acres. Another pretty stream, Geifer Creek, entered Bear Creek from the east. In the next few days, he traveled several miles further downstream on Bear Creek and found it reentered a steep canyon. Some eight miles on down, Bear Creek enters the larger and even steeper canyon of the Middle Fork of the Flathead River.

McCarthy recognized the value of the flat as a site for the railroad grading camp. It was the only suitable site for many miles that could accommodate the thousands of workers of the huge rail building operation. Thinking big was not a problem for McCarthy. He decided to do anything necessary to take possession of the tract of land, knowing that if he could establish ownership, it would make his fortune. He headed back out of the mountains as quickly as he could.

Because the land had not been legally surveyed, it was impossible for McCarthy to formally file for ownership; he would have been too young to legally file anyway. So he did the next best thing: he filed a declaration of occupancy, thereby establishing "squatter's rights" to the beautiful flat.

It wasn't long before advance men of the Sheppard-Seims grader outfit made the same discovery McCarthy had made. Immediately, they disputed the young man's claim to ownership of the flat, and threatened to take him to court if he didn't cede to the company enough land to build their camp. Both parties realized, though, that the matter would take too much time

Bear Creek and the flat that McCarthyville occupied. Author photo

to settle once the lawyers got on board. So showing diplomacy beyond his years, Eugene reached an agreement with the company: he would take the northwest side of Bear Creek, the company would take the southeast side, along Giefer Creek. Eugene was clever: he got the side closest to the timbered hillside that would bear the railroad line.

It's hard to imagine how a "town" could spring up as fast as this one did. By the summer, Eugene was platting the site. But before he could complete it, businessmen who moved west with the railroad construction were demanding lots on which to set up their fly-by-night establishments. They could see the bonanza that was coming with the thousands of railroad workers and big payrolls. Gambling, drinking, and prostitution houses would draw the workers like coyotes to carrion. Speculators quickly began buying up the prime lots, reportedly making McCarthy $1,700 in the first week.

Eugene's boldness and foresight had enabled him to make more money in a week than he'd ever seen before. The new unincorporated town, McCarthyville, bore his name. And to top it off, he was unofficially elected as Montana's youngest "mayor".

In late November of 1890, McCarthy traveled west downstream along the Middle Fork of the Flathead River 60 miles to Demersville, a town preceding Kalispell, to legally establish his title to the land. He reported to the Demersville newspaper that the town already had a "population of 100 souls, six saloons, three restaurants, and one store." Eugene boasted that the town featured a "meadow of 300 acres or more with a stream of pure, sparkling water running through it which will furnish water power for electric lights, saw mills, etc." He added that he had a large tie contract with the railroad company. On behalf of the townspeople, he had petitioned for a post office.

Still, the town was really just an oasis in a vast wilderness. Residents with outdoor skills could hunt the plentiful deer and elk for food, and trap the beaver, marten and ermine for valuable fur. Among the well-known outdoorsmen and trappers were Bill Morrison and Dan Doody, both of whom went on to colorful careers as federal rangers in the Middle Fork backcountry. Bill and Dan took the opportunity to make some fast dollars working for the grading outfit and railroad while it was in their neighborhood. Eugene McCarthy was known for his love of fishing and the outdoors, and he no doubt admired these mountain men and their outdoor skills.

Fish were a ready food item easily obtained. Whitefish, westslope cutthroat, and bull trout thrived in the area's streams, including Bear, Giefer, and Skyland creeks. Eugene and the other McCarthyville residents especially must have taken advantage of the bull trout spawning run in Bear Creek. Back then, these colorful spawning fish were called Dolly Varden trout, named after the gaily clothed and painted ladies found in dancehalls. The main townsite occupied the flat where McCarthy's "stream of pure sparkling water" flowed. These men sought game and fish, and would have speared or caught these big spawners any way they could during the summer and early fall in the shallow, clear water.

Bull trout migrate all the way upstream from Flathead Lake to spawn in the stream's clean gravels. The big female bull trout sought the upwelling springs in the creek near the McCarthyville site. More than a hundred years later, dozens of these big fish still spawn in Bear Creek each year. As a biologist operating fish traps in lower Bear Creek, I observed bull trout up to 32 inches long and 15-20 pounds heading for the same old springs at the McCarthyville site. When the young fish hatch from the spawn deposited by these big adult fish, they imprint on the springs, living in the stream before migrating downstream to the lake to grow to adulthood. As 6-8 year-old adults, most return to the area where they were born to spawn and lay their own eggs. Some adult fish make the journey multiple times.

With the coming of the railroad survey and grading outfit, the Middle Fork suddenly was open to travel and commerce. The December 5 edition of the Demersville paper reported that the Miller and Ramsdell Company had the contract for supplying beef for the Great Northern crews. Another company received the contract for construction of a storehouse totaling 3,000 square feet for Shepard, Siems, and Co.

By late January 1891, Eugene reported to the Demersville paper that the

Railroad construction near Marias Pass, circa 1890. Betty Robertson Schurr collection

population had quadrupled and had been granted a post office, although no record exists of its official establishment. McCarthyville was now on the map.

Some of the businesses in the town were built of pole frame and canvas at first, but these didn't stand up to the heavy snows. Most of the buildings were built of logs, or frame with shingled roof. They were put together as cheaply as possible, designed to last for the year or two the speculators knew the town would last.

Soon, the "town" began to descend into anarchy. Rail workers poured into McCarthyville from the east, a lot of them city folk from Minneapolis. Grading and construction continued in the cold weather, and the snow caught many of the workers unprepared. They had to walk part of the distance from the end of the rails to reach the summit, then on to McCarthyville. Some of them arrived sick and frostbitten.

Asa Powell, father of western artist Ace Powell, related an experience of a youngster passing through McCarthyville about this time. The boy was sharing a room with an older man. As he bedded down, a single gunshot rang out. The boy got up to investigate, but the older man said, "Son, I wouldn't go out if I were you. Five or six shots and it's a cowboy cutting up, but one shot and it's murder."

Typical of the violence that gripped the town was a triple murder that took place just upstream along Bear Creek. In late January 1891, Joe and Pierre

15

Boudoin abandoned their blacksmith shop at Two Medicine, on the east side of the summit. Using their life savings of $1,000 they planned to get rich by opening a saloon in the new boomtown.

The brothers were camped in a wall tent that served as a "restaurant" along the creek a few miles upstream of McCarthyville. They were playing "freeze out" poker with three other men: LeBlanc, Winand, and Warner. Suddenly, two masked men stepped through the tent flap and ordered the card players to reach, and face the back wall of the tent. The masked men burst in undetected because the soft, deep snow around the tent muffled the sound of their horses' footsteps.

Pierre Boudoin turned around and one of the gunmen said, "If you look this way again I'll kill you." The other gunman said, "Kill him anyway," and they started shooting.

Joe Boudoin was shot dead and all the others were hit except Warner. When the shooting started, Warner knocked down the wooden chandelier and plunged the tent into darkness. He bolted and managed to dive under the side of the tent and get away. Winand dropped with three wounds from a .45 pistol. He crawled under a bunk and managed to cut through the back wall of the tent and crawl out into the snow, but one of the gunmen ran around the back of the tent and shot him twice in the head. Amazingly, the shots didn't kill him because they were both glancing. He was stunned and unconscious and the gunmen left him for dead.

Warner managed to make his way to McCarthyville and told the story of the gruesome murders. Word of the murders quickly reached Deputy Evans of Demersville, who happened to be in McCarthyville at the time. Evans hastily organized a posse and headed out on what they supposed to be the trail of the killers.

Eugene McCarthy, who served as both unofficial mayor and deputy sheriff, took some men and rode quickly to the Boudoin camp and found Winand near death, and Joe Boudoin and LeBlanc dead. Joe Boudoin was shot in the nose, mouth, brain, and three times in the chest. The tent was ripped and full of bullet holes; blood stained the floorboards of the tent and the surrounding snow. McCarthy supposed that the motive for the murders was robbery, but Joe Boudoin had a wallet in his pocket containing $115. McCarthy later said that it was the "coldest kind of murder."

Along the trail near the camp, McCarthy's horse shied at something and jumped off a bridge across a small tributary of Bear Creek, probably near Skyland Creek. They found Pierre Boudoin lying there with nine bullet holes in him. His blood flowed into the waters of the creek. The murderers had shot him up and dragged him around after they had killed him. The killers had gotten away with about $900, but it was clear that money was not the only motive for the slayings.

Asa Powell, left, related stories of shootouts in McCarthyville during its tawdry peak. Here, Powell (left) and some friends (left to right, Cal Tidrick, Orrie Greenwald, and Mart Sibley) reenact a "disagreement" during a poker game. Notice that the pistol is cocked. Photo from the Joyce O'Neil Collection.

Deputy Evans and the posse pursued the men through the snow east toward the summit. They had a good description of the badmen: The tallest man was five feet, nine inches tall, with a brown duck overcoat, remarkably fine voice, and slender build. The other man was about three inches shorter, younger, with a black overcoat. The posse headed over Marias Pass and trailed the men east. They overtook two men, but found they were not the murderers. Discouraged, they returned to McCarthyville, after being out three days and two nights in deep snow.

Meanwhile, word of the killings had reached Demersville; Deputy Mumbrue and another posse started up the Middle Fork towards McCarthyville. On the way, amazingly, they found one of the killers, Henry Hart, holed up in a cabin. Mumbrue arrested him and took him on to McCarthyville. Eugene McCarthy joined Mumbrue's posse at McCarthyville and acting on a tip, pursued the other badmen back over Marias Pass. Miles to the east they caught up with and arrested the ringleader, Jim Cummings, an outlaw known from Oklahoma to Canada. A third man, who had held the gunmen's horses, escaped.

When the posse returned back over the pass to McCarthyville, they found that Hart had escaped. Mumbrue secured a fresh horse and gave pursuit. Hart was arrested several days later in a boxcar far to the southeast in Helena, Montana. Mumbrue brought Hart to Demersville via Missoula.

Deputy Evans took Cummings downstream along the Middle Fork and on to Demersville. The men stood for a preliminary hearing. Afterwards,

Sheriff Bill Houston of Missoula County took them to Missoula for trial.

The number of sick men or men wounded in brawls in McCarthyville forced the railroad to establish the Great Northern "Hospital" in a log building with a low ceiling. The construction company hired a doctor from Great Falls who turned out to be, in reality, a veterinarian. A nurse, known as Big Swede, was hired to assist the "doctor." The railroad paid the men one dollar per month for each sick or injured man treated at the hospital.

Men who were not on the railroad payroll were not profitable, so they were quickly moved out with minimum care. The deplorable conditions at the medical center caused many suffering men to contract pneumonia and "la grippe." One victim asked the nurse for water at 11 a.m. one day, and after being forced to trudge through the snow and take a bucket to the creek, died within a few hours. Another man lay moaning in a cot when a piece of dirt fell from the mud roof into his eye. When someone asked the Swede to remove it, he replied that it didn't matter, because the man would probably die soon anyway.

Townspeople noticed that the Swede made regular dawn trips along Bear Creek, dragging a toboggan which bore a body wrapped in a two-dollar blanket. Once out of site of the town, the Swede rolled the bodies into a hastily scooped "grave" in the snow.

The April 1891 edition of the Demersville *Inter Lake* carried an article, "Hospital Horrors," that detailed these terrible conditions and reported that Eugene McCarthy was under fire to do something about it. Some of the citizens in the town organized and laid down an ultimatum: get better treatment of the sick or they would lynch the town's officials, including Eugene.

Earlier, a compassionate saloon girl named Josephine Gaines had seen enough of the treatment of the sick men lying on the dirt floor of the "hospital." As the story goes, she strode up to the railroad construction superintendent, leveled a six-shooter at his navel, and demanded that he get rid of the veterinarian and his "nurse." Nobody knows if Josephine's threat affected the superintendent, but McCarthy finally decided to take action without the approval of the railroad company.

He organized a posse, including Will Hardy, Mike Conley, Jack Damey, Hiram Briggs, and Ed Fox. The men marched to the Great Northern Hospital and rapped on the door. When the Swede opened the door, Hardy clubbed him and knocked him down with the butt of his rifle. Meanwhile, the veterinarian slipped through a flap that covered the back window and escaped. The townspeople were able to find a legitimate doctor and the death rate at the hospital decreased sharply.

During McCarthyville's brief existence, records show up to 200 deaths and only one birth. Bill Morrison claimed that in the spring of 1892, snowmelt exposed nine bodies around the perimeter of the town. Lots of graves (100 by one account) dotted the two-acre cemetery established for this violent town. Anticipating heavy use, residents picked the cemetery location based on the only patch of land they could find where the digging was easy. Most of the flat was conglomerate gravel washed out into the floodplain of Bear and Giefer Creeks.

McCarthyville attracted robbers and gamblers like a magnet. Probably the most well known gambler in the town was the multi-talented Bill Morrison. Morrison had squatted on some land near the summit, claiming to be living there in a small cabin when Stevens "discovered" the pass two years earlier. Bill also had a trapping cabin way upstream on the Middle Fork in what is now the Great Bear Wilderness.

Bill made his name in a poker game earlier that winter. He ate dinner in the company of about 20 men, including Eugene McCarthy. Knowing that there would be a poker game that night, Bill didn't drink whiskey with the rest of the men. He and Eugene began talking, struck up a friendship, and found out they viewed the world in a similar way. McCarthy trusted Bill and staked him twenty dollars for the poker game. It paid off. The next morning the two split four hundred dollars of Bill's winnings.

Another night, Bill sat in on a big poker game in the raucous town. He handled the cards with the hand skills of a brain surgeon. He could deal from the top, middle or bottom of the deck, and was also lucky in a straight deal. It wasn't long before Bill had several thousand dollars in winnings on

The remnants of McCarthyville, about 1916. Glacier National Park historical collection

This is the last remaining building of McCarthyville, 1990. This served as the unofficial "post office" and general store. Author photo

the table. He coolly pocketed the money, but he kept on playing until he had won another 600 dollars.

Bill knew that he would probably be shot if he tried to leave the game with his impressive pile of money. So he made an excuse to leave the table, leaving the six hundred dollars on the table as if he would return to complete the game. He slipped out of the dancehall and vanished into the night, protecting the first few thousand dollars he'd won. With this daring escape, Morrison earned his nickname: "Slippery Bill."

McCarthyville reached its peak in the summer and fall of 1891, supporting 32 saloons and more than a thousand people, including who knows how many gamblers, dancers, and prostitutes. The Great Northern Railroad did not schedule regular paydays and workers could collect their pay at any time, so people came and went at will. The Shepard-Seims grading outfit paid monthly, so monthly paydays pumped thousands of dollars and workers seeking a good time into the town's establishments. A nomadic citizenry, who moved west along with the railroad construction and money, occupied the town.

Great Northern Railroad construction continued west and by the late fall of 1891, tracks were being laid below the confluence of the three forks of the Flathead and through Bad Rock Canyon at Columbia (now Columbia Falls). By early 1892, the "golden spike" was driven as the tracks were completed to Kalispell. Mary Kimmerly, the first woman settler, and Nicholas Moon, the oldest settler, had the honor of driving the spike. For now, Kalispell would host the 30-stall roundhouse and division point for trains to continue west and on to the coast.

The completion of the railroad and its movement west sucked the life out of McCarthyville. The town was only a remnant of its boom size by the spring of 1892, and by 1893 had dwindled to a few residents.

Symptomatic of the injustices that piled up during the town's existence, the killers involved in the Boudoin murders a few years earlier ended up escaping justice. Bill Houston, the sheriff of Missoula County, had taken the gunmen to Missoula to stand trial, but by the time the courts could hear the case McCarthyville had died. The witnesses were scattered or dead; Cummings and Hart, after brutally murdering and robbing innocent men, were set free.

But this wild town didn't die without an event that brought as much notoriety to the site as had its birth. Violence came back like a recurring fever. Late that summer of 1893 McCarthyville was the site of a shootout with badmen who pulled off the most daring train robbery in Montana's history.

Chapter 3
SHOOTOUT AT BEAR CREEK
*A daring train robbery and gunfight mark
McCarthyville's colorful death*

It was late August 1893, about the time the bull trout were running thick in Bear Creek. The few McCarthyville residents, including Great Northern section foreman William Bracken, were enjoying the warm evening in the lonely remnant of the town. Who knows, maybe William had just finished a dinner that included a big bull trout he'd caught in Bear Creek earlier in the day.

Hundreds of miles to the southeast along the Northern Pacific rail line, a gang of badmen was hitting Northern Pacific Train number four. Little did Bracken know that it would soon affect him in a big way.

Plans for the train holdup began when four ranch hands decided to try for a big payday. They first planned on robbing a bank in Big Timber, west of Billings, but decided to hold up a train instead. Their decision led to gunplay, bloodshed, bravado, intrigue, and death on a 400-mile chase that ended up leading to McCarthyville.

The four men held up an eastbound Northern Pacific passenger train at a small town along the Yellowstone River. The daring crime attracted attention all across Montana. The September 1 edition of the *Kalispell Inter Lake* called the holdup a "cool piece of villainy, admirably planned and systematically executed...in a manner that does credit to the road agents' nefarious avocation."

The robbers were heavily armed; each of them carried two revolvers and a Winchester rifle. They wore masks and they carried out their plan perfectly.

Two of the badmen jumped on the train and slipped past the train crew into the baggage compartment. Once the train reached full speed, they crawled over the engine tender to the cab. The train engineer heard the rumble of coal sliding down the tender and turned around, only to have a six-shooter thrust into his face. The other gunman covered the train's fireman. The first gunman addressed the engineer: "If you make a suspicious move it will be your last. Run the train like we tell you. Pull this train down the road until you are flagged with a signal light and stop, and God help you if you don't."

Soon a lantern came into view. The trainmen stopped the train and climbed down as ordered, and met the other two masked members of the gang. The robbers demanded entry into the express car, but before they blew the door, the express messenger opened it from the inside. The robbers ordered the messenger to open the main safe, which reportedly held $60,000. The messenger told them the safe was timed to open in St. Paul, and he couldn't open it even if his life depended on it.

"Let's blow it," said the gang's ringleader. The bandits brought out a sack containing "giant powder"

Albert Babcock, a member of the first Montana Legislature, was on the train when it was robbed. The outlaws collected only $4 from him. Montana Historical Society.

and began to rig up the safe. But the robbers had trouble with the operation and recognized they didn't have the firepower to open the safe. Knowing that a freight train was not far behind them, the robbers abandoned the big safe.

To appease the gang members, the messenger produced $50 from a small safe and several wads of money he had concealed before he opened the door.

The robbers walked the trainmen at gunpoint to the rear Pullman car. As they opened the door, the porter fired a shot through the window. The bandits fired a volley into the end of the car and ordered the porter to open the door.

As they entered the car, two of the badmen covered the terrified passengers with leveled Winchesters. The other two robbed the passengers one by one, without regard for age or gender. They intimidated and robbed a preacher and an elderly woman, treating each of them roughly. As they moved from car to car, the number of trainmen they held at gunpoint increased. The employees were marched ahead of the gunmen, and were forced to watch the plundering operation. The masked men threatened anyone who ignored their order to "shell out."

After all the robber's big expectations they were annoyed at their lack of booty. A. L. Babcock, a banker from Billings and a member of the first

Montana Legislature, only produced $4. When a robber asked him for his watch, Babcock replied, "I never carry it when I'm away from home." The badmen didn't believe him, but Babcock escaped with a cussing rather than a beating.

The robbers ended up disappointed: they netted only about $2,000 in cash and valuables. The holdup lasted about 50 minutes. The robbers then slipped into the darkness, mounted horses, and fired wildly at the train as they rode north.

Unknown to the robbers, the brakeman ran back up the track and met the approaching freight train. The crew cut the engine loose, backed up to the Greycliff station, and telegraphed news of the holdup to Billings. Early the next morning after train number four arrived, men at the Billings depot prepared a special train to carry a posse to the holdup scene. The Sheriff of Yellowstone County brought horses, provisions, and 12 men. Another group of lawmen met them at the holdup site.

The combined posse set out on the trail of the robbers. The lawmen learned that the robbers were traveling northwest, day and night, stealing fresh horses along the way, maybe headed for Canada. It wasn't long before the badmen left the posse far behind, so the lawmen gave up the chase.

The badmen they were chasing were accomplished horsemen and hardened criminals. Jack White, an outlaw from Laurel, had come up with the idea to rob a bank in Big Timber. But when a one-armed member of his gang fell in the Yellowstone River and drowned, he abandoned that idea. The gang included Englishman Jack Chipman, a tall, slender man known as the "dude cowboy." Sheepherders Sam Shermer and Charlie Jones were recruited with promises of a big payday.

Even though the gang had easily eluded the pursuing lawmen, one posse member wasn't ready to quit. Sam Jackson, the sheriff of Livingston and now granted an appointment as a federal marshal, was a big man. He was good-natured, but determined to see the robbers brought to justice. He convinced the superintendent of the Northern Pacific to help him to continue chasing the robbers. Jackson knew ranchers around the state and he had the full run of the rail system, including the cooperation of the Great Northern Railroad, where the bandits seemed to be heading.

Using his connections, Jackson learned that the robbers had traveled north to the Missouri River, then to a ranch near Wolf Creek. He trailed them north past Augusta, then about 100 miles to Blackfeet Station, near the east slopes of the Continental Divide where the prairie meets the mountains. So far, Jackson had been on the gang's trail for more than 300 miles. He talked to restaurant owner Henry Schubert, who some say helped the robbers but then had second thoughts. Jackson learned that the gang was turning west towards Midvale.

When the gang arrived in Midvale, Shermer recruited Jimmy Moots into the gang to bolster their numbers for yet another planned robbery. So, just 30 miles short of the Canadian Border and safety, the badmen stopped going north. They suddenly took a sharp turn to the west, heading for the safety of the rugged, timbered mountains of the west slope. It was almost as if the remnant of the bad town of McCarthyville was drawing the outlaws as the lawless town had done with others during its short heyday.

In fact the gang had brazenly decided to rob a Great Northern Train, as it slowed down at Bear Creek Station near the McCarthyville town site. Jimmy Moots had convinced the other gang members that they could hold up the train at that remote location and avoid pursuit by taking to the trails that he knew across the mountains. He planned on guiding them down the Middle Fork and on south to old Demersville, where he knew someone who would help them hide out from the law.

Jackson organized a posse with the help of the Blackfeet Indian police, then sent Dick Kipp and another Blackfeet to follow the outlaws and report on their location. The Blackfeet trailed the robbers west to a cabin along the Two Medicine River, and then they returned east to inform Jackson.

The next day, October 2, 1893, Jackson and the posse boarded a special Great Northern train to Midvale. There they unloaded their gear, mounted horses, and rode to the cabin. They untied the badmen's horses and led them away. Jackson strode to within 30 feet of the cabin door, and ordered the robbers to throw up their hands and come out.

Jack Chipman threw open the door and the robbers fired into the posse. A bullet shattered the shoulder of Duck Head, one of the Blackfeet. Schubert, the restaurant owner who had joined the posse, was mortally wounded. Perhaps the gang members focused their gunfire on him when they saw they had been betrayed. The posse returned fire. A bullet struck the rim of outlaw Sam Shermer's hat, but none of the gang members was wounded.

After an intense exchange of gunfire, the badmen escaped into the woods. Jackson rushed Schubert back to Midvale to find a doctor, but the badly wounded man died on the way. It was obvious that the lawmen were up against a hardened, resourceful group of men who were skilled gunslingers. Jackson realized that he needed more men and greater firepower. He telegraphed west to Kalispell and requested help from Flathead County.

Sheriff Joseph Gangner (pronounced "Gon-yer") of Kalispell, the Sheriff of Flathead County, responded immediately by telegraph and agreed to join the manhunt. The 32-year-old Gangner, of French-Canadian descent, migrated from eastern Canada to western Montana in the early 1880s. Joe was a big man, a superb horseman, handy with a gun and good in a fight. These qualities led to his appointment as Flathead County's first sheriff.

Gangner was a controversial figure in Flathead County. No one questioned his bravery or skill with a gun, but many citizens, rightly or wrongly, had accused him of corrupt management of the sheriff's office. Over the coming months Gangner would be on a roller coaster ride of grand jury indictments and trials.

For now though, the sheriff of Flathead County responded with bravado and professionalism. He collected a posse of 18 men and saw to it that they were well armed. He convinced his friend Judge E. C. O'Donnell to join the posse. Gangner packed his 45-90 Winchester, his side-arms, and plenty of ammunition. Based on the information in the telegram, he knew that the robbers would be desperate and that the lawmen might end up in a shootout for their lives.

Gangner arranged for a special Great Northern train to transport him and his posse of 18 men east. The train passed through Columbia Falls on the Flathead River at 5 p.m. Columbia Falls, located below the mouth of the South Fork of the Flathead River, was in a heated competition with Kalispell to become Flathead County's seat. The town's newspaper, the Columbian, would soon be leading the malfeasance charges against Gangner and the county commissioners. For now though, the paper's editor noted the passing of the special train carrying the sheriff and posse and was following the effort to capture the train robbers.

The special train carrying Sheriff Joe and the posse headed up the Middle Fork, crossed Marias pass, and arrived at Midvale that night. The Lewis and Clark County Sheriff also arrived. The combined posse, including the Blackfeet, now numbered at least 45 men. The men set out by train east over Marias Pass in the morning, with trackers following the robbers' trail in the snow dumped by an early October storm.

The resourceful badmen had made their way through the mountains over Marias Pass and down out of the snow to McCarthyville. They had now been on the lam for more than a month, riding nearly 400 miles across Montana with their loot, only to reach what had become little more than a ramshackle ghost town with a few hangers-on residents. A year or two earlier, they could have blended in with the large, lawless population. Now, there was no place to hide. The fact that they planned on getting away with another train robbery at this little railroad siding reflected their lack of respect for the lawmen who had been chasing them.

Amazingly, the badmen believed they could quickly hold up the Great Northern train, and then disappear into the backcountry to hide their loot and wait until the law gave up the chase. It's clear that they grossly underestimated the effort that would be mounted against them.

Now that October had arrived, the larch trees had shed their needles, and the alder and willow had dropped their leaves along the Bear Creek bottom. Cover was thinner, winter was coming on, and the outlaws were running out of luck.

The train bearing the posse traveled east over the pass and down to McCarthyville. At the town site members of the posse were surprised to see one of the robbers dash from one building to another. The train immediately slowed down and dropped off groups of posse members several hundred yards apart. When the last

Sheriff Joseph Gangner and Deputies O'Donnell and Chambers encountered the outlaws near here in an evening shootout. Author photo.

of the posse was dropped off, the train stopped. With that, the robbers knew the jig was up and they dashed into the timber.

Knowing the gun skills of the outlaws, the posse members advanced slowly in skirmishing order. After more than an hour, the lawmen closed in and a gun battle began. The lawmen exchanged about 35 or 40 shots with the robbers. Because of their respect for the badmen's marksmanship, the posse members kept their distance and did not try to rush them. Again, even outnumbered nine to one, the robbers escaped.

But the gunfight was not without effect. Badman Jimmy Moots was shot in the leg during the long-range exchange of gunfire. Moots, who had joined the gang at Midvale and had encouraged the gang to rob a Great Northern train, by now must have realized his mistake and regretted it.

The posse members cautiously spread out and hunted for the train robbers. By evening, Sheriff Gangner and two posse members had worked their way west towards the railroad siding at Java Creek. Sheriff Joe, his friend Judge E.C. O'Donnell, and Harry Chambers walked along the tracks on the chance of running into the robbers, who they reasoned must be exhausted and hungry.

Gangner, the more accomplished and experienced rifleman of the group, had prepared well. His 1886 lever-action Winchester in the 45-90 caliber was considered the most powerful and accurate repeating rifle then in existence. Winchester had built the rifle's action sturdy enough to accommodate cartridges as powerful as the ones fired by the large single-shot rifles of the time. Multiple cartridges were loaded into a tubular magazine through a slot on the right side of the receiver portion of the action. The large, 300-grain lead-alloy bullet was propelled at about 1,400 feet per second. The impact of this bullet would knock down a man, and any shot to a major part of a man's body would usually prove fatal.

The sheriff and the two posse members moved cautiously over the uneven ground. Suddenly they heard one of the robbers shout, "There's a man!" Another replied, "Give it to him, then!"

Gangner's worst fear was realized as the robbers fired rapidly and the lawmen were caught in a surprise ambush. Bullets whizzed by the lawmen as they dropped to the ground. In the sheriff's mind, several bad scenarios might have been playing out. Would he see his wife and young children, including 8-year old Annie again? Would he have to inform O'Donnell's wife that her husband had been killed?

But the lawmen stayed cool. Gangner, O'Donnell, and Chambers took aim and returned fire as the bullets passed over their heads and snapped into the underbrush around them. Gangner's experience and courage served him well as he fired his 45-90 Winchester over and over to great effect.

One of the badmen dropped like a sack. Jack Chipman had been shot in the head and was killed instantly. The "Dude Cowboy's" career was over. A bullet ripped through Sam Shermer's thigh and lodged in his hip.

Suddenly, the outlaw's guns were silent. Jimmy Moots, who knew Gangner from earlier times in the Flathead, called out, "Don't shoot, Joe," and surrendered. The small town sheriff and his two posse members routed the gang that had thwarted dozens of lawmen led by a federal marshal.

But one bad guy gave the posse the slip. During the shootout, Charlie Jones escaped down the steep side of the canyon into Bear Creek, or perhaps into the Middle Fork of the Flathead River. The canyon of Bear Creek is steep and rocky. The Middle Fork at Java Creek is precipitous and narrow; the railroad bridge across it is more than 100 feet high. It's amazing that Jones, weak after being pursued across the mountains, survived after stumbling down the side of the canyon and maybe suffering a dunk in the frigid water. By October, the water temperature had plummeted to the 40s, just the right conditions to bring on hypothermia in a hurry.

The relieved Sheriff Joe, Chambers, and O'Donnell made their way to the railroad tracks with Chipman's body, the wounded Shermer who was losing blood and could not walk, and Moots, who had been wounded less seriously near McCarthyville the afternoon before. They waited along the tracks until 10 p.m. when they flagged down a westbound Great Northern train. The train transported the lawmen and their "game" four miles west to the Great Northern siding of Essex.

At Essex, a doctor from Midvale operated on Shermer. The 300-grain, 45-90 bullet that hit Shermer passed through his left thigh, into his right thigh, and flattened against the bone into the shape of a silver dollar. The impact of the bullet caused great trauma to the outlaw's lower body, and it was clear that he likely would not survive for long. The doctor also tended Jimmy Moots' less serious leg wound.

Meanwhile, Charlie Jones, the outlaw who escaped over the canyon side, was still at large. He had worked his way back to the east, hoping to vanish into the mountains above McCarthyville. But with the rugged landscape full of lawmen, Jones' freedom was short-lived. The next morning, William Bracken of McCarthyville noticed a white handkerchief on the woodpile outside his cabin. When Bracken stooped to pick it up, a cold and

The bridge downstream from McCarthyville, near Essex. After the shootout, Sheriff Gangner and the other lawmen loaded the outlaws on a train and transported them here. At this railroad siding a doctor operated on Shermer. Betty Robertson Schurr Collection

bedraggled Charlie Jones sprang from the woodpile, thrust a Winchester into Bracken's face, and ordered him back to his cabin. As Jones ate the food he had demanded, Bracken decided to try a bluff and said, "Partner, the country is full of men looking for you; there's anyway 200 men on your trail. You ain't got a chance to get away."

Bracken asked Jones to hand over his rifle and pistol, and Jones complied. The daring bluff had succeeded. Bracken took the outlaw to Jackson, who along with most of the posse was camped at Bear Creek station and McCarthyville. Jackson had made it known that a $500 reward was offered for each outlaw still at large. Bracken handed over the fugitive, and filed for his reward. Bracken's decision to stay on in McCarthyville had finally paid off nicely for him.

The fifth gang member, Jack White, was still at large. He had managed to elude nearly 50 lawmen with great resources at their disposal. At this point, there were no leads as to his whereabouts.

Jackson, Gangner and the other lawmen took Jones, Shermer, Moots, and Chipman's corpse into Kalispell on the Great Northern train. The outlaws were put "behind the bars" in the Flathead County jail awaiting further action.

Coroner G. D. Cummings held an inquest in Kalispell that day and the next regarding the October 4 killing of Chipman and the shooting of Sam Shermer. The jurors determined that Sheriff Gangner and the two posse members acted in self-defense when they killed Chipman and wounded Shermer as the badmen resisted Sheriff Joe's attempt to arrest them.

There was considerable doubt as to whether the men brought in were really the train robbers, but Jackson was positive that they were, having trailed them for over a month. Shermer removed most of that doubt a few days later in a deathbed confession in the Flathead County jail.

Shermer weakened rapidly in the days following his arrival in Kalispell. On October 8 he decided to confess to the train robbery and identify his accomplices and their roles in the robbery and subsequent shootouts. He identified Chipman, Jones, White, and himself as the train robbers. He explained that Jimmy Moots joined the gang later, in Midvale. He admitted that they were preparing to hold up a Great Northern train when they were surprised in McCarthyville. He identified Jones as the shooter who killed restaurant owner Schubert at the Midvale shootout.

Shermer, under the influence of opiates to relieve his great suffering, died at 3 p.m. shortly after completing his confession.

Coroner G. D. Cummings held an inquest regarding Shermer's death the next day. Six jurors were appointed to examine Shermer's body and reach a verdict regarding his death. According to the inquest report filed on October 10, the jury found that Shermer died from "a gunshot wound by him received on the 4th day of October near Java Station on the line of the Great Northern Railroad... while resisting officers who were lawfully endeavoring to arrest him and others upon charges of train robbery and murder. That at said time said Samuel Shermer died from the effects of said wound at the County Jail of Flathead County, Montana on the 8th day of October A. D. 1893." The jury could not positively say who shot Shermer, but it's probable that Gangner's bullets found their targets in Shermer and Chipman.

Federal Marshall Jackson and other lawmen took Jones and Moots to Helena to await a federal grand jury indictment. Legal wrangling for them would go on for more than a year.

Plans were to bury Chipman and Shermer in Kalispell, but not before dozens of people scrambled to get a look at the robbers. Eva Randolph, a young girl at the time, couldn't resist the temptation to look at the bodies. "Shortly after the shooting of the bandits near McCarthyville," Eva began, "I remember a schoolmate by the name of Edna Bradley, whose father was coroner and undertaker, told me that the dead robbers were in a shed behind the undertaking parlors, and we both decided to go and see what they looked like. My mother had no knowledge of this, as she would not have allowed it. We went into the shed and pulled the covers from the robbers' faces and took a look at them. They had heavy beards and were tough looking, all right. As I remember, we did not linger long."

Only one robber, Jack White, remained at large. Unbeknownst to the lawmen, he had traveled downstream along the largely unsettled Middle Fork to the confluence with the North Fork of the Flathead River. He lived on wild game and kept a low profile.

Sheriff Gangner and his deputies were interested in finding White, but no one knew if he was still in the area. Also, Gangner's concentration was drawn away from the manhunt. The October 19 *Columbian*, in large letters on the front page, proclaimed: Rotten to the core! Bribe-taking, corruption, and perjury charged against officers of this county." The county commissioners were accused of corruption. Gangner was accused of splitting a $5 fine with the jailer and pocketing the money, lying about expenses incurred to bring various witnesses and prisoners to Kalispell, and general malfeasance in regard to his handling of the sheriff's office and county jail. Why the press would go after the sheriff after his bravery and effectiveness in bringing men to justice is a mystery; less than two weeks earlier, *Kalispell Inter Lake* headlines proclaimed that Gangner and his posse "acquit themselves credibly" in the shootout that ended the train robbers' run from the law. Gangner's legal problems would play out in the newspapers over the next five months.

The last gang member, Jack White, was hiding out northeast of Columbia Falls along the Middle Fork of the Flathead River. In late October, John P. Gensman, a resident of the area, ran into White in the hills above the river. The two men had traveled together in the past, and recognized each other immediately. White trusted his old friend and asked for help. White acknowledged his connection with the train robbery, which by now had become sensational news across Montana. Perhaps White promised to give Gensman some of the loot from the train hold-up. The two men agreed to meet several days later near Lake Five, and plan White's escape.

But Gensman betrayed his friend, probably reasoning that reward money was a sure bet, while the train robbery loot was not. He returned to Columbia Falls and telegraphed to find out the price on White's head. When he found the bounty was $500, it made his decision easy. On October 23, Gensman returned to the meeting place at the agreed-to time, taking along his friend John Fitzpatrick as a backup man.

White acknowledged Gensman, and then approached him, but Gensman ordered him to reach. According to Gensman, White dropped his Winchester

Judge Hiram Knowles sentenced badmen
Jones and Moots. Montana Historical Society.

but then reached for his pistol. Gensman then shot White through the heart. Coroner Cummings, not satisfied with Gensman's story, held him over for a grand jury investigation.

The coroner found that Gensman owed White a large sum of money. He believed that Gensman had killed White for the reward and to avoid paying the debt. Several witnesses were called. Gensman testified that after initially meeting White, he asked lawyers in Columbia Falls if he had the right to take White in, and was told that he did. Gensman said he could not obtain irons to restrain the robber, so he had to kill him in self-defense. The backup man confirmed Gensman's story, although he had not seen Gensman shoot. Because of lack of evidence and witnesses, Gensman was released, and White was buried in Kalispell.

In December, the federal grand jury in Helena indicted Jones and Moots on charges of murdering restaurant owner Henry Schubert near Midvale. Neither man could afford an attorney, so Judge Hiram Knowles, a former U. S. attorney of sterling reputation, appointed two attorneys to defend them.

In court, the conductor of Northern Pacific train number four took the stand and identified Jones as one of the train robbers. Members of the Blackfeet Indian posse and others testified about the gunfight near Midvale and Schubert's death. None of the witnesses could say who shot Schubert, but confidentially, Moots told lawmen that Jones was the shooter. The jury convicted Jones of first-degree murder. Moots pled guilty to being an accomplice and was sentenced to two years in the penitentiary at Deer Lodge.

But the legal process wasn't over yet. Jones's attorney appealed on technical grounds and Jones got a new trial. After spending a year in jail, Jones took the stand at the new trial and flatly denied he had shot Schubert. The jury reached a split verdict: two for murder, five for manslaughter, five for acquittal. Finally, they agreed on manslaughter.

An eloquent, angry and blunt Judge Knowles finally sentenced Jones, saying, "As far as I can find out you have undertaken a life of crime. Instead of working for an honest living, you have tried to filch from others. As I understand it, you have a respectable father and mother, but they were unable to do anything with you. You came to this country and joined a band which had for its object robbery, a band which had for its object plunder and killing." Knowles sentenced Jones to 10 years in the penitentiary and fined him $100. Based on his stern reproach, it is likely that Knowles would rather have sentenced Jones to hang.

The only known photo of Sheriff Joe Gangner taken years after the shootout. Mary Sullivan Collection.

I could find no records on the fates of Moots and Jones after their release from prison. The grave markers, of Chipman, Shermer, and White if they ever had them, have disappeared. The ranch hands turned bandits, who pulled off perhaps the most daring train robbery in Montana's history, have nearly vanished from memory.

Lawmen never found the several thousand dollars in loot and the booty of jewelry and gold watches that the robbers lifted in their holdup of the Northern Pacific train. For years, though, there were lots of rumors about its whereabouts.

So, a manhunt and shootout proved to be the last notable events in McCarthyville's existence. That seems fitting. The town was born in violence, bathed in violence, and died in violence. After all of McCarthyville's notoriety it's hard to find any mention of it in the newspapers of the area after the badmen's trials were over.

But some of the McCarthyville characters scattered along the Middle Fork, enriching the drainage's quirky history. Before the town died, Dan Doody kidnapped a saloon girl and took her down the drainage to Nyack to "dry her out" and keep her for his wife. Slippery Bill Morrison stayed in the area he pioneered, and even headed up into the more remote portion of the Middle Fork into what is now the Great Bear Wilderness.

Some say that Slippery Bill might have found the stolen loot and jewelry that the train robbers never coughed up.

Maybe he did, maybe he didn't, but that's another story.

Chapter 4
BLACK MURDER ON THE RIVER
After a sensational trial, Charles Black is hung for the murder
of a young mother

By 1894, Jim Hill's Great Northern Railway had brought goods and vigor to the Flathead Valley and the town of Columbia Falls. This scenic lumber town sits in a prime location where the collective waters of the of the North, Middle, and South forks of the Flathead River burst through Badrock Canyon and spill into the broad Flathead Valley.

Unlike McCarthyville, Columbia Falls' three-year existence thus far had been peaceful. That spring, as the townspeople enjoyed the warming weather, they had reason to think that it was a safe place to raise their families. But one April day that feeling of safety was shattered by one of the most brutal murders in Montana's history.

Columbia Falls perches amid an abundance of natural resources, most important among them being land, timber and water. Prime agricultural land was going for prices ranging from $5 to $30 per acre. Lumber milled from the area's vast timber resources filled the expansive yards of the Great Northern Lumber Company. Coal and limited oil reserves had been found up the North Fork Drainage. And the town was served by the *Columbian*, a little newspaper with a big voice that continually promoted the attractions of the community and surrounding area.

The Montana Legislature in 1894 passed a bill officially establishing Flathead County, carving it out of Missoula County. In the elections later that year, voters selected Kalispell, 15 miles downstream from Columbia Falls as the county seat. J. W. Pace, the editor and publisher of the *Columbian*, had conducted a spirited campaign to have Columbia Falls anointed the seat of Flathead County, but much to his chagrin, the effort failed.

Badrock Canyon, a defining geologic feature of the town site, forms a narrow funnel through which the Flathead River flows before emerging into the wide floodplain of the Flathead Valley. The canyon narrowly divides the terminus of two mountain ranges. Two mountains stand as sentinels above the canyon: Columbia, of the Swan Range to the south, at 7,234 feet and Teakettle, of the smaller range to the north, at 6,306 feet. The Columbia Falls town site sits 4,000 feet below these summits, giving the effect of being in the mountains' shadows.

Badrock Canyon took its name from a ford just upstream of the canyon mouth. Blackfeet Indians moving west on raiding parties and Flathead Indians moving east to the buffalo country crossed the Flathead River at this ford. At times, warriors from one tribe ambushed the warriors of the other tribe as they waded the ford. Because of this strife and death, the place took on a bad feeling and reputation, thus Badrock.

April 28th, 1894, was a beautiful early spring day and Sheriff Joseph Gangner was on duty at the Flathead County Sheriff's Office in Kalispell. It had been an eventful year for him. The fall before, he had spent weeks chasing the Northern Pacific train robbers all over the Middle Fork country. Gangner's success in bringing the badmen to justice had earned him fame and the respect of many citizens around the Flathead Country. He'd had to shoot several of the train robbers, something he didn't like to do and wasn't proud of. But the small town sheriff and two posse members had ended the careers of three badmen who had eluded a federal marshal and up to 100 lawmen for more than a month. The last badman at large had been shot under questionable circumstances by a citizen northeast of Columbia Falls above Badrock Canyon. Gangner didn't like the look of death and hoped he wouldn't have to deal with it again for a long while.

The Sheriff was still stung by a campaign that had begun the fall before to remove him from office. The negative notoriety he received must have brought great concern to him and his family. A grand jury indicted him on perjury, theft in connection with pocketing fines, and for charging for trips that weren't actually made to transport prisoners and serve subpoenas. He was also charged with general malfeasance and incompetence in running the county jail, which included being too friendly with the prisoners and allowing them to be supplied with whiskey. As an added insult, the sheriff's bail was set at $3,100, which was raised and provided. The county commissioners had also been charged with a number of offenses. Judge Dubose had overseen the indictments but he brought in a different judge to conduct the trial of the county officials.

Gangner and his many supporters considered the affair a witch hunt, brought on in part by the jealously of Columbia Falls residents who had been campaigning for their town to become the county seat. They considered Kalispell's domination of county affairs almost a form of taxation without representation.

The charges against the sheriff played out in the *Columbian* through the fall and winter calling him and other county officials "rotten to the core," and prompting the *Kalispell Daily Inter Lake* editor to call the *Columbian* a "weekly howl." The *Columbian* was obviously biased against Gangner. When the sheriff had shown courage and professionalism in a shootout with the train robbers, the *Columbian* didn't mention his involvement, but emphasized the work of the federal marshal on the case.

The sheriff's case had finally gone to trial in late January. The only charge for which he was tried was perjury in lying about the alleged trips he didn't take. It didn't take the jury long to acquit him of the charge. When the jury announced their verdict, the courtroom audience applauded. According to the *Columbian*, the judge admonished those in attendance calling the outburst of support "outrageous." Maybe the judge had a smile on his face when he said it though.

Even with all the venom spewed at Sheriff Gangner in the *Columbian*, he didn't hold a grudge against the citizens of Columbia Falls. That's lucky for them, because they were about to need him very badly.

That Saturday afternoon in April, Lena Cunningham was getting ready to walk to Columbia Falls from the land she homesteaded with her husband, John W. Cunningham. The Cunningham homestead was located a little over a mile northeast of Columbia Falls below where the South Fork joins the Flathead River, which is five miles downstream from the confluence of the North and Middle Forks. The ranch sat on the west side of the river just downstream from Badrock.

Lena, 33, the center of her unusually happy home, grew up in Germany. John had brought her to the U. S. to be his wife. Just a month earlier, Lena and John had celebrated their 14th wedding anniversary. The citizens of Columbia Falls noticed that the couple got along especially well, and they, along with their children, were highly respected as a successful family. It was hard not to like Lena with her engaging accent and a disposition that people described as "sunny."

Lena, a strong and attractive woman, walked to town often, and she enjoyed it. She kept in shape by walking everywhere and raising her three children: Edith, age 10, William, 9, and Bertha, 6. The children demanded a lot of attention, and Lena loved to dote on them. Even so, Lena probably considered it a nice break to walk to town alone that afternoon and have some time to herself. This day she was in no hurry. She had plenty of time because the days were noticeably longer, stretching out to 14 hours of daylight.

Lena had an important errand in town. She planned to pick up her husband's paycheck from his job and then trade at Main's Store selecting, among other things, a gift for each child. Her husband stayed at home doing chores and keeping an eye on the children. Lena started for town. She assured John and the children that she would be home for dinner.

Taking along her parasol, Lena walked along the tote road that followed the tracks. The Flathead River was beginning to swell with late April runoff from the melting snows up in the forks. Colorful westslope cutthroat trout from Flathead Lake were migrating in large numbers up the river following the surge of runoff. These native trout, called "mountain trout" by the locals, were heading for spawning grounds in tributaries of the Middle, South, and North Forks of the Flathead. Townspeople were no doubt having success fishing for the vibrant and tasty fish along the riverbanks on the edge of town. The *Columbian* carried drawings of anglers floating down the river in rowboats, fishing with long poles.

Everything around the young woman spoke of spring, leaves were springing out from the willow brush, and the first buttercups, trillium, and skunk cabbage flowers were showing their yellow colors.

Lena arrived in town, picked up John's pay, and did her shopping. After she was finished at the store, she had just $2 left over. She stuck the bills in her purse, gathered her parcels containing the children's presents, and started for home. Lena nodded to Henry Spence as she walked past Kennedy's stable.

At the north end of town near the schoolhouse, Lena ran into family friend Robert Saurey, who was driving a wagonload of lumber to town. Saurey was one of the town's original residents. He had even camped along the river with his young wife and infant daughter two years before the town was officially established. Saurey and Lena chatted for 10 or 15 minutes. In his side vision, Saurey saw Charles Black, whom he considered a drifter, walking on the road east of the schoolhouse; but Black ignored them. Saurey and Lena said their goodbyes at about 5 p.m. As Lena started up the tote road towards home, Saurey saw Black about 200 yards away going toward the depot. Lena walked up the tote road and out of Saurey's sight.

About an hour later the Cunningham's neighbor, Ernest Miller, had been taking a walk along the road not far from the Cunningham ranch. He'd been searching for a few missing cattle. Stopping along the road he noticed signs of a struggle in the dirt and leaves and, at the same time, heard pitiful groans coming from the timber east of the road. Investigating, he followed splashes of blood along a drag-trail to a brush pile where he found a young woman, still breathing but unconscious. Miller gasped when he recognized the woman: it was Lena Cunningham face down in leaves, partly covered by brush. She was lying just off the edge of the road at a point where it wound through the timber along the tracks. Horrified, Miller jumped on his horse and galloped to the Cunningham ranch to get Lena's husband.

Back at the Cunningham homestead, John and the children waited for Lena's return. John expected her by about 5 or 5:30 p.m., but it was already

The Flathead River near Columbia Falls. The murderer washed Lena Cunningham's blood from his clothes at about this location on the river. Badrock Canyon is to the right of Teakettle Mountain in the background. Author Photo, 2007.

after 6 p.m. Finally, the family heard hurried hoof beats outside the farmhouse door. John looked out and saw that it was Ernest Miller, who owned a nearby ranch. Miller breathlessly described the location and told John to go quickly because Lena had been badly hurt. John mounted Miller's horse and galloped to the spot where Lena lay dying. Miller followed on foot.

When Miller arrived back at the scene, Lena was still breathing, but obviously near death. Horrified and in shock, John held his wife, who had been badly beaten and whose head was covered with blood, dirt and leaves. Miller mounted his horse and galloped back down the wagon road towards town for help.

Miller arrived in Columbia Falls about 6:30 p.m. He searched desperately for a doctor, and informed Justices Scully and Smith about the crime. Scully wired Sheriff Gangner in Kalispell. Word spread quickly about the brutal attack, and enraged townspeople prepared to accompany lawmen to the scene.

The justices hurried to the site accompanied by a doctor and a number of town residents. When the party arrived at the location, they found John Cunningham leaning over his wife. Lena had died minutes after Ernest Miller started for town.

An inquest jury was immediately impaneled and the inquiry began. Doctor Piedalue examined the young mother and found that the murderer had struck Lena's head seven times with a heavy object, each blow breaking her skull. There was a terrible gash on her temple and her forehead was horribly bruised. Her skull was so badly crushed that the "brains were oozing out," according to the report.

The entire party was abhorred by the brutality of the attack. Death was not unknown to these men, but such a horrible beating of a young woman was too much for them.

The doctor noted that a 40-foot trail of blood led from the road where she had been dragged east to a clump of trees. The searchers found the small end

Searchers found the murder weapon not far from Lena Cunningham's body. The murderer clubbed Lena with a coupling pin, similar to this one at the old McCarthyville site. Author photo.

of a coupling pin lying 40 feet south of the body. The 5-inch long pin was covered with blood and had hair sticking to the broken end.

Lena's purse still held the $2 she had placed in it after completing her shopping in town. This led officers to speculate that the murderer's motive may have been rape rather than robbery, and the murderer had killed her during the struggle or to cover up the crime. Lena's parcels, marked with blood, had been tossed into the brush near her. Her blood-covered parasol was found nearby.

Lena's body was transported to Earnest Miller's house, and the doctor began a detailed examination. He described the various wounds and skull fractures made by the murderer wielding the coupling pin, noting that the blow to the forehead had shattered the entire frontal bone of the skull, and that the brain protruded from other skull fractures. The doctor found no sign of strangulation on the woman's neck.

Looking for signs of rape, the doctor noted that the buttonhole of the waistband of Lena's undergarment had been ripped out and pulled down about six inches; the other part of the waistband was fastened under the corset and had not been pulled out. There was no sign of pulling or tearing on any other part of her undergarments, which were of thin muslin. The doctor concluded that rape could not have been committed with Lena's clothing in this condition and no sign of violence on the lower part of her body. One thing that was certain from the doctor's examination, evidence at the scene, and the multiple blows to her head: Lena had put up a terrific struggle and thwarted any attempt by the murderer to violate her.

While the doctor examined Lena's body, other members of the party followed a man's deep tracks marked with blood into the timber, across the railroad tracks, and down to the Flathead River bottom. By the river was a place where the party guessed the murderer had washed his hands and clothes. The footprints then led along the river into Columbia Falls.

Next morning, on Sunday, officers and townspeople continued the investigation, now led by Sheriff Gangner and Deputy Seth McFerran who had arrived from Kalispell. Seth McFerran served as the sheriff's right-hand man. Young and popular, even in Columbia Falls, McFerran never missed a dance in that town, according to the *Columbian*.

The sheriff and his deputy were grim and determined, knowing that they had to catch this murderer or the womenfolk would never feel safe. The party took exact measurements and retraced the murderer's trail, collecting evidence.

Sheriff Gangner was particularly silent and sullen that day. His family had been among the first to settle in the Flathead Valley in the early 1880s. As part of the law enforcement community, he looked forward to seeing the communities of the valley prosperous and peaceful. This murder was a big step backward from that view. On top of that, Gangner had a wife and a young child and he could feel the grief and horror that John Cunningham must be experiencing.

Justice Scully released a warrant for the murderer and sent a telegram to Governor J. E. Rickards in Helena describing the heinous murder of the young mother of three children. Handbills signed by Sheriff Gangner and the Governor, included as a notice in the *Columbian*, offered a $300 reward for information leading to the conviction of the killer.

Lena's funeral was held on Monday afternoon, two days after the murder. First, a private viewing was held where John led his three children to the coffin to have their last look at Lena. Then Lena's body was transported to the funeral hall. A third of the town's residents paid their respects. More than 200 people attended, and fully 100 could not fit into the building. To show the town's grief and support, all 84 grammar and primary school children of Columbia Falls marched in a body to the hall. The town choir provided inspiring music, and the Reverend Richard Wrench gave the service. After the service the hall was closed, and people were permitted to view Lena's corpse. The wounds of her forehead were covered with plasters and people marveled at how her beauty seemed untouched.

At the cemetery, John Cunningham and the three children stood by while Lena's body was lowered into the ground. Mingled with his feelings of grief, John must have been wondering how he was going to give the children a proper life without the strong support of his wife. He was heartened, though, by the tremendous show of support from the townsfolk. In the *Columbian* a few days later, he published a thank-you on behalf of himself and his children, saying, "if anything could lessen the horror of my wife's death, it is the knowledge that I am among such kind hearted, generous people."

Meanwhile, an inquest panel of six Columbia Falls citizens conducted a preliminary inquiry calling Dr. Piedalue and a number of other witnesses who were in the investigating party to come forward with information. Within a few days officials arrested Charles Black, a young painter. Robert Saurey had reported to Scully that he saw Black, who folks considered a drifter, acting suspiciously at the north end of town while Saurey and Lena visited.

Drifters were common around the Flathead. Columbia Falls was still a frontier town, even with the advances of the railroad and telegraph. A person could walk a few miles north and be on one of the forks of the Flathead River. The drainages of the North, Middle, and South forks were all still largely wilderness in character. This combination of convenience with wilderness at the back door drew people who wanted to spend time in the woods most of the year and avoid people, but still work nominal jobs to get by.

Charles Black was one of these men who had come from Minnesota on the rails to Columbia Falls to live on the edge of the wilderness. He had arrived in town about a year earlier. He painted houses during the summer and trapped and hunted during the rest of the year. People noticed that he sometimes ice-skated on the river in winter to get around. If the ice formed just right, the skater would have smooth sliding and could even look through the clear ice and the Flathead's clear water and see the rocks on the river bottom.

Black may have looked suspicious to some, but from the beginning he denied that he had anything to do with the murder.

An inquest was held for Black, and the Justice demanded that he give a description of his activities the day of the murder. Black said that he played a ball game on Saturday afternoon, but he couldn't come up with a corroborated story of where he was in the late afternoon and evening, especially around 6 p.m. which was the estimated time of Lena's murder. Black admitted that he knew Mrs. Cunningham. He had met her and talked to her at the "Odd Fellows' Dance" at Christmastime and at a spring dance a few weeks before the murder.

Investigators pointed out that Black's shoes closely fit the tracks found at the murder scene, and traces of what appeared to be blood were found on his pants. Black claimed that the stains were made by paint and forcibly denied any part in the murder.

Meanwhile, the indignation of the residents of Columbia Falls had reached the boiling point. The *Columbian* indignantly proclaimed that the murder was the first serious crime in the town's 4-year history. Information began circulating that the citizens were enraged about the sheer, pointless brutality of the murder and the fact that three young children were now without a mother. Convinced that Black was the killer, some began forming a lynch party to hang him. One member of the lynch mob reportedly noted that "Black made a picture of a typical thug with his low brows, small black eyes closely spaced, and medium intelligence." Word was that many people had no doubt that Black murdered Lena, and they wanted to kill him as fast and violently as possible to pay him back for what he did to the young mother, her family, and the town.

Sheriff Gangner could see what was about to happen, and he wasn't going to allow it. If anyone in his county were going to hang, it would be through the legal system, not by a lynch mob. So the sheriff rounded up two fast horses, mounted one, and forced Black to mount the other. "Ride like hell to Kalispell," Gangner told Black. According to the *Columbian*, the story of the lynch mob was overblown. Nevertheless, Black was quickly locked up in the Flathead County Jail in Kalispell.

Black sat in jail for more than three months while officers gathered evidence against him. J. H. Schumacher, a St. Paul detective from the Pinkerton Agency, spent several weeks in the vicinity of the crime collecting evidence. Schumacher then posed as a criminal and was placed in Black's cell in an attempt to gain Black's confidence and build a case against him. Black remained stoic about the murder, but he did talk some with Schumacher about his checkered past. He repeatedly and strongly denied having anything to do with the murder of Lena Cunningham.

County Attorney Sidney Logan, assisted by W. J. Brennan, prepared an elaborate case against the accused killer. Black had no money, so the court finally appointed defenders Henry Heideman and C. H. Foot to defend him. The defense lawyers complained that they didn't have enough time to prepare their case. Judge Dudley Dubose denied their complaint.

Jury selection had gone smoothly. On the first day, forty potential jurors were questioned and 12 were accepted by the defense and the prosecution. Jurors included Louis Blanchet, Thomas Manuel, H. Christianson, John Eccles, William Dewar, T. Widdowson, D. Carpenter, Charles Smithers, Alex LeBeau, Robert Bohart, and the prominent John Weightman. Thomas Collins served as jury foreman. The judge was surprised that of the first 24 potential jurors examined, not one was disqualified on account of being prejudiced against hanging.

The trial commenced August 6 in a frame building with no windows on First Avenue West in Kalispell. The atmosphere was sweltering. The prosecution called the first witness. Columbia Falls resident Harry Pence testified that he saw Black going toward the schoolhouse after he saw Mrs. Cunningham walking past Kennedy's stable on her way home about 5:30 p.m. Pence recognized Black by his walk and by the dark coat Black wore.

Next, the prosecution called Robert Saurey to the stand. Saurey said he saw Mrs. Cunningham coming from town and met her about 75 yards south of the schoolhouse. Saurey described how he and Lena talked for a while, and then he saw Black walking down the road towards the depot in the general direction of the murder scene, acting suspiciously. Even though Black knew Saurey, he did not acknowledge him.

James Rattan testified that he was in the blacksmith shop about this time and also saw Black walking towards the depot. But inexplicably, Rattan said Black wore a suit of light corduroy, not a black coat. Rattan's conflicting testimony created the first opening in the prosecution's case against Black.

Then, in quick succession, C. F. Sully, Dr. Piedalue, and D. Smith testified about the condition of the body, the murder scene, and the discovery of the coupling pin a short distance from the body. Their descriptions of the young mother

Photo by Inglis.

Calvin J. Christie, alias Chas. J. Black and Chas. J. Adams, hanged at Kalispell Dec. 21, for the murder of Mrs. Lena Cunningham April 28, 1894.

Rendition of Charles Black by a local artist. The drawing was published in the Kalispell Graphic the day of the hanging.

face down in the dirt and blood with her skull crushed made a powerful impression on the jury and the others in the courtroom. John Cunningham was called to the stand and testified as to the condition of his wife when he arrived at the scene. The murder weapon was circulated among the jury for their examination.

Next, County Attorney Logan presented some of the most damaging evidence against Black. Comparisons had been made between Black's shoes and the tracks found at the murder scene and along the river. The tracks were a match, right down to the heels. The heels on Black's shoes were notched to fit a pair of ice skates; the murderer's tracks bore identical notches in the heel area. Plaster casts of the murderer's tracks and Black's shoes were displayed and compared.

Prosecutors also claimed that minute traces of blood had been found on Black's shoes, overalls, and left sleeve. They brought in an expert who claimed that the blood found on Black's shoes corresponded to the blood found on the coupling pin which, if true, linked Black directly to the murder. But it's hard to say if the technology available at the time could positively correlate blood traces as described by the blood expert.

Now it was time for the defense to present their case. Heideman and Foote were confident that they could present an effective case on Black's behalf, but they doubted that Black could get a fair trial given the obvious hatred towards him on the part of most people in the courtroom.

The defense called their first witness. James Haller testified that Black passed through his saloon at 5:50 p.m. that evening, headed for his cabin. The defense lawyers claimed that Black could not have killed Lena along the tote road, because the estimated time of the murder was 6 p.m., and Black was still in the saloon just 10 minutes before that. They also pointed out that witnesses' testimony conflicted regarding what Black wore that evening. How could they be sure that the person they saw was Black and not someone else?

Then the defense refuted the evidence of the notched heel marks in the murderers tracks. They produced other shoes from townsfolk, showing that many shoes bore similar notches designed to fit skates. This was a brilliant piece of work by these public defenders who had little time and resources to prepare their case. However, on cross-examination, the notches were shown not to be exact fits; also, none of the men had ever walked in these shoes along the river near the murder scene.

The third and fourth points made by the defense team also were persuasive. They explained that Black accompanied Ed O'Brien and Harry Raymond to the murder scene the night of the murder when many townspeople searched for evidence. Would Black have helped search for evidence if he had been the murderer? They further claimed that if blood was found on Black's boots, it was picked up from the scene as Black helped follow the murderer's tracks.

Because of the complexity of the evidence, the jury was transported on the train to Columbia Falls to see the places mentioned by the witnesses. The jurors retraced the supposed path of the murderer and examined the crime scene. The jury also returned to town via the circuitous path of the river. They spent three hours in the area.

The next day, back at trial, Black took the stand in his own defense. A young man of 22 years, he looked neat and cleanly dressed. According to the *Kalispell Daily Inter Lake*, Black was "cool and collected during his examination and bore the trying ordeal without flinching…He appeared totally oblivious to his situation or the shadow of the awful crime hanging over him." Black appeared to be either a hardened criminal, or he believed in his innocence.

Black told his story matter-of-factly. He said that he played in a baseball game the day of the murder. He left Heller's Saloon and walked to the river bottom east of town looking for signboard, then went to Bachman's cabin where he stayed for a short time before returning to town about 7 p.m. Then he heard of the murder and joined the townspeople headed for the crime scene.

The prosecution had a devastating trick yet to play. They biased the jury by bringing up previous convictions they had learned about through Schumacher's jailhouse conversations with Black. On the stand, Black admitted to having been convicted of a felony and sentenced to a penitentiary in Minnesota. He feigned insanity and was sent to an asylum. Then he escaped and came west. He admitted that he used an acquired name, his real name being Calvin Christie. Other crimes and convictions came to light under questioning. As a teenager, Black was heavily involved in crime with street gangs in St. Paul.

Throughout his cross-examination, Black strongly denied talking to Lena Cunningham or having any contact with her on the day of the murder. In all, Black spent four hours on the stand.

Two damaging admissions Black made in the previous inquest in Columbia Falls months before were not allowed to be introduced in this trial. First, Black had admitted that he met Lena Cunningham at two different dances held in Columbia Falls, the second time only two weeks before the murder. Also, an acquaintance of Black testified that he and Black had discussed how easy it would be to rape certain women when their husbands were away for a time. It's unknown why these points weren't allowed in the current trial, because they certainly would be damaging to the defense.

At the close of the testimony, W. J. Brennan addressed the jury for the prosecution. He slowly reviewed each piece of evidence against Black. C. H. Foot followed for the defense, pointing out the weak points in the prosecution's case. Foot's address was called "brilliant and logical," but nearly the entire Columbia Falls community and most residents of Kalispell thoroughly believed that Black was guilty.

Henry Heideman followed Foot and spoke on Black's behalf. It was clear that both defense attorneys believed Black was innocent. Heideman summed up his case dramatically, making a "splendid effort," according to the *Kalispell Daily Inter Lake*. Heideman used "pointed, telling words, growing eloquent as he proceeded." The defender pleaded for Black's life, noting that substantial doubt remained as to who really killed Lena Cunningham. People in the courtroom listened to Heideman with "breathless attention."

County Attorney Logan closed for the prosecution, focusing on two effective points. He emphasized the brutality and senselessness of the crime. And, he reminded the jury that Mrs. Cunningham left behind three children.

Both sides had presented their arguments effectively. But, even as the local paper noted, the defense was laboring under a disadvantage from the start. They had little time to prepare their case, while the prosecution had worked on their case for more than three months.

Judge Dubose instructed the jury, passed along to them a 17-page typed version of these instructions. The instructions included: definition of reasonable doubt, rules of evidence and circumstantial evidence, degrees of murder, notes on Black's criminal history, witness credibility, and details on the nature of rape. "As the court has instructed you before," this section began, "all murder which is committed in the perpetration or attempt to perpetrate rape is murder in the first degree. The state's theory is that the man who killed Mrs. Cunningham...killed her in the perpetration or attempt to perpetrate a rape. Rape is defined by the statute as an act of sexual intercourse with a female, not the wife of the perpetrator...where the female resists but her resistance is overcome by violence or force...If you believe from the evidence beyond a reasonable doubt that this defendant in the perpetration or in the attempt to perpetrate rape upon Mrs. Cunningham killed her, you will find the defendant guilty of murder in the first degree."

After the instructions were read, the jury members retired to a room to deliberate. To the surprise of the defense team, the jury members returned after about only 30 minutes of deliberation. The jury announced their hasty verdict: Charles Black was guilty of murder in the first degree. Black took no interest in the verdict and displayed no emotion that would lead one to believe his life was at stake. He appeared unconcerned as the judge polled each jury member. He joked with the guards on the way to the jail.

On Monday, August 20, officers escorted Black into court to receive his sentence. Spectators filled the courtroom and fell silent to hear Judge Dubose pronounce Black's sentence.

First, Dubose ordered Black to stand and then listed the charges and the conviction for murder in the first degree. Dubose asked Black if he had any cause to show the court why judgment should not be pronounced against him.

Black replied, "I never killed Mrs. Cunningham or anyone else."

Dubose then said, "Black, on an occasion like this when we are almost in the presence of death itself, it seems to the court that whatever it might say regarding the enormity of your crime would have no effect...any man who maliciously, willfully, and premeditatedly takes the life of another shall suffer death. Thus you have broken the law, and thus you will suffer."

Again, the judge asked Black to make peace with himself by admitting that he murdered Lena Cunningham, but Black said nothing.

Dubose then delivered the sentence: "It is therefore ordered, adjudged, and decreed that you, Charles J. Black, be taken to the county jail of Flathead County and that you there be kept in safe custody by the sheriff of said county until Friday, the 28th day of September A. D. 1894, and that upon that day and between the hours of 9 o'clock in the forenoon and 5 o'clock in the afternoon of that day, you be taken hence…and hanged by the neck until you are dead, dead, dead, dead, and may God have mercy upon you."

According to the *Kalispell Daily Interlake*, Black listened to the sentence with no apparent reaction, stating, "Black retains his composure and will no doubt meet his death calmly and without flinching."

A few days later, the editor of the *Columbian* proclaimed the prosecution was "well and quickly done," noting that the county attorney and prosecuting lawyers did a marvelous job of linking the circumstantial evidence together in an airtight case against Black. The town's loathing of Black is obvious in the article, in which the editor writes that

BLACK IS DEAD

The Murderer of Lena Cunningham Executed Friday.

DIED WITHOUT CONFESSING

An Unnatural Nerve Made the Murderer Defy Grim Death.

THE HAPPIEST DAY OF HIS LIFE

The *Columbian* proclaims the execution of C.J. Black.

"Calvin Christie, alias Charles Adams, alias Charles J. Black, the fiend in human form, will atone for the murder of Lena Cunningham on the 28th of September next, in so far at least as the surrender of his worthless life on the gallows will amount to an atonement."

Work on the gallows moved forward in preparation for the hanging. From the window of his jail cell, Black could hear the nails being hammered.

Black and his lawyers filed a motion for a new trial in the District Court. The 11-page, typed motion, filed by Heideman and Foot, was thorough and persuasive and focused on three main areas. First, they alleged that the witnesses were compromised, being improperly informed by the defense outside the trial. Second, the lawyers claimed that the map of the murder scene and the presentation of it to the jury were in error. Finally, they claimed that the evidence putting Black at the murder scene was false and spurious. They had also submitted an affidavit, signed by Foot and by Black himself, protesting the testimony of Dr. Bullard, the medical expert brought in by the state.

Judge Dubose denied the motion for a new trial, so Black's lawyers appealed the case to the Montana Supreme Court. This action would delay Black's execution date until at least October 26, unless the Supreme Court granted him a new trial. Two further delays followed, each announced by an official respite of execution signed by Governor Rickards. The Court took months to reach a decision.

Finally, on December 10, the Honorable Wm. Y. Pemberton, Chief Justice of the Montana Supreme Court, signed a final judgment finding in favor of the State of Montana and against Black and his lawyers, noting that "the defendant has been granted a respite by the Governor until the Twenty-first day of December 1894…it is therefore ordered that the judgment of the court below be executed on that day." This judgment cleared the way for Black's writ of execution to be carried out.

Under the headline "Black Will Swing", the December 14 *Kalispell Daily Inter Lake* reported that the Supreme Court had denied the motion for a new trial. The article declared, "The case of Black is one in which the people of the Flathead are especially interested, and the sentence imposed on him is just…unless executive clemency interferes in the matter, Black will solve the mystery of the great beyond on the 21st of the month."

Three citizens of Kalispell were appointed to a "death watch." It was the duty of these men to ensure that Black didn't commit suicide. They also watched over the cell to prevent anyone from killing Black before the execution. The hatred towards Black was so intense that lawmen considered an attempt on his life a real possibility.

In the meantime, a movement was underway to save Black from the gallows. Black's mother, Mrs. Albert Brimley, had arrived from the Midwest and had been circulating a petition asking Governor Rickards to commute Black's sentence to life imprisonment. People who thought Black was innocent and those opposed to capital punishment signed the petition; some signed out of sympathy for Mrs. Brimley. She was able to collect 160 signatures in Kalispell, but not a single signature in Columbia Falls. Mrs. Brimley was not an old woman, but her hair was pure white. She stated that each white hair was a result of the "waywardness of that boy."

Both newspapers admonished those who signed the petition, noting that Black had a fair trial, his peers had found him guilty, and the Montana Supreme Court had upheld the finding of the lower court. The article also pointed out "there is the side of the bereaved husband and helpless, motherless children of his victim to be considered." The article then went on to imply that Black would be lynched anyway if the Governor granted him clemency, stating that the "indignation of the people has been held in check that the law might take its course, but the feeling against Black is very bitter."

Black's mother pleaded for her son's life for two hours before Governor Rickards. Rickards listened attentively, then eloquently explained to the grieving mother why he could not grant her request.

"I deeply sympathize with you in this deep affliction," Rickards said, "and God knows that were it a personal matter I would not hesitate to lift this burden from your heart; but, Mrs. Brimley, it is my sworn duty to see the laws of the state are faithfully executed. Your son was respited three times and given every advantage possible under the law to profit by any circumstances in his favor. Every legal remedy was exhausted in his behalf…under such circumstances, I cannot, in deference to my oath of office and my duty as governor of Montana, interfere with the decision of the courts. Nearly

Montana Governor J. E. Rickards was personally involved in the Lena Cunningham murder case. Rickards showed compassion when he met with the mother of Charles Black, but the Governor eloquently denied her request for her son's clemency. Courtesy of the Montana Historical Society.

every man under conviction of crime has some loved one, a mother a sister or a wife to plead the cause of affection with the argument of the heart; and were I to be governed by my sympathies, executive clemency would be my daily occupation. Painful as this occasion is to me, I must do my duty as God gives me to see the right and in doing this duty I am compelled to withhold my hand and permit the law to take its course."

Black mostly maintained his indifference as he waited for his execution date.

Many people stopped by the jail to gawk at the youthful murderer. He sat sullenly or paced the floor, puffing on a cigarette. The editor of the *Columbian* stopped by and asked Black if he had anything to say to the people of Columbia Falls but Black replied that he had no statement to make.

Deputy Seth McFerran talked often with Black. The two probably had met at the Odd Fellows Dance the winter before and grew to know each other well during Black's stay at the jail. Black didn't admit any connection to Lena Cunningham's murder. But he did infer to McFerran that he was involved in burning down the Columbia Hotel in Columbia Falls in October. This was the first fire in the brief history of town, and only "heroic action" had saved the lives of two young girls and an infant. Losses topped $10,000. Word of Black's possible connection to this disastrous fire didn't get out until after his execution. If it had been known, it would have been even harder to protect Black from lynching.

Reverend George Fisher, a large and kindly man, visited Black often in his cell, and Black finally accepted the consolation of religion. One night he received a letter from a young woman with whom he corresponded in St. Paul. After reading it, he covered his face and grated his teeth for ten minutes with tears running down his cheeks. Black tried to sleep but couldn't, repeatedly saying he did not wish to be hanged.

On December 20, the evening before the execution, Black's mother visited him, although she was not allowed inside his cell. He was deeply moved, telling her to keep up her courage and pray for him. He told her that he was saved, and thanked her for all her efforts to gain his clemency. She said to him, "Charlie, I wish I had been a better mother to you." He replied, "Mother, you have always been a good mother to me."

His mother bade him goodbye and kissed him. She fainted and the jailers carried her away.

Black walked to a corner of his cell and cried, leaning against the wall for support. He made a desperate attempt to control himself, clutched the clothes over his heart and said, "I will conquer, I will conquer." The jailer asked Black to finally make a statement about the murder, but he replied, "No, what I know I will take with me."

The next morning, a fresh snowfall blanketed the Flathead Valley. Sheriff Gangner woke Black from a sound sleep at 6:30 a.m. Black dressed himself and ate his last meal. He'd requested six raw oysters, six fried oysters, two eggs, coffee, and a bottle of wine. He ate heartily, and then rose from the table, stating, "I don't need any wine to keep my nerve up." At 7 a.m. Gangner entered the cell again and read the death warrant and the rejected respite papers. Reverend Fisher arrived and stayed with Black until the execution.

By 8 o'clock people began arriving at the jail and they could hear the clank of the condemned man's chains as he paced the cell. Black's pacing became more rapid as the hour of the execution approached. At 9:45 everyone invited to the execution, including John Cunningham, filed past the cell door into the yard where the gallows waited. It's hard to imagine the hatred John must have felt as he looked at Black in the cell.

At 9:50, Gangner opened the cell door, saying, "We are ready, Charlie," and removed the irons from Black's ankles. Black put on his coat and announced that he was ready. With the sheriff supporting him, Black passed along the corridor of the jail and shook hands with the other prisoners. Reportedly, he maintained a smile as he went from prisoner to prisoner.

Sheriff Gangner and Deputy McFarren led him through the snow to the scaffold, with Reverend Fisher, Undersheriff Hickernell and Deputy Bellfleur following. Within the gallows enclosure more than 100 people had gathered to watch the young man hang. Black was composed and his step was firm. The procession mounted the scaffold and Black stepped up on the trap door. He brushed the snow from his trousers and shoes, and then stood quietly while the men placed the straps around him. Seeing someone he knew in the crowd he said, "Hello Jack."

Gangner tightened the straps around Black's body, first pinning his hands to his sides. Gangner tightened the straps around Black's waist, and Black joked, "That's too tight, Joe. You'll throw up those oysters."

Gangner strapped Black's feet together, and then prepared to place the noose over the condemned man's head. The same rope had been used not long before to hang a murderer in Fort Benton. Gangner said, "Charley, do you have anything to say?"

Black straightened and thrust his head forward and said: "This is the happiest day of my life. I would not trade my faith in Jesus Christ for all the gold and pardons that could be stacked in this jail yard. I trust you may meet death with as little fear as I do…" Black then recited a prayer, and finally said, "Let her go."

Gangner tightened the noose around Black's neck and placed a black hood over the convicted killer's head. As the sheriff pulled the hood tight Black remarked, "Let me have air while I am alive," and Gangner pulled the hood forward away from Black's mouth.

Reverend Fisher stepped forward as a black curtain was lowered between Black and the lever. Fisher recited a prayer, and as he spoke "Amen," the sheriff pulled the lever and the trap door fell. Black's neck snapped audibly as the rope jerked tight and his head almost touched his right shoulder.

The trap dropped at seven minutes and ten seconds past 10 o'clock; Black's pulse beat for four minutes. Six minutes later, Black's body was taken down and placed in a plain coffin. Black's neck was broken completely, with the narrowed noose wedged in between the ends of the broken vertebrae. Only skin and flesh held the head to the body. The crowd showed little emotion during the hanging. John Cunningham was in the crowd but didn't react as Black dropped and Black's neck broke.

Reverend Fisher took charge of the body for Mrs. Brimley. Reportedly, Black had left six letters with Fisher with instructions to deliver them six days after the hanging. No record remains of the contents of these letters.

Black's hanging was completed 237 days after Lena Cunningham's April 28 murder. Flathead County's first legal hanging was now history, and the first sheriff of Flathead County had performed brilliantly. The next day, Sheriff Joe Gangner completed his duties on the case, with a handwritten cover page on the writ of execution. Joe wrote, "In obedience to said writ I did therefore on Dec. 21st 1894, between the hours of 9 oclock a.m. and 5 oclock p.m., to wit at 10 oclock a.m. conduct the said defendant Charles J Black to a private enclosure, annexed to the county jail, and having complied with all the provisions of law I hung him by the neck till he was dead."

Black's trial had lasted 10 days and involved fifty witnesses. The trial, 8-month incarceration, and execution had cost the county $7,000, an enormous sum for the time.

Doubts remained in the minds of some as to whether the right man had been executed. Despite all the efforts to persuade Black to talk about the crime, he had refused. In confidence he had accurately listed and admitted to all his past crimes, but would not confess to the murder of Lena Cunningham. Reverend Fisher repeatedly had tried to get Black to save his soul and confess, but Black repeated over and over that he was innocent. Either he really was innocent, or he had convinced himself that he was.

Mrs. Brimley decided not to have her son's body embalmed and brought back to Minneapolis on the train because of the cost. Maybe she also thought about what Black had been convicted of and didn't want his grave close by to remind her of it. Black's body was buried in Potter's field, a plot of ground just south of the town's cemetery, not far from where Lena's body rested. Potter's field is the "poor house" equivalent of a cemetery. Black's grave marker vanished.

The *Columbian* noted "no hanging in the west called forth as little sympathy from those present as did that of Black."

Was Black the murderer? Despite Black's convincing denials, most of the townsfolk of Columbia Falls were certain that the guilty man had been hung. Black's hanging haunted Sheriff Joe Gangner the rest of his life because he doubted that Charles Black was really the killer. But according to the legal system justice had been served to the killer who had sullied the river with Lena Cunningham's blood and decimated the springtime peace of Columbia Falls.

Three days after the hanging, Lena's three children and her devastated husband spent Christmas Eve without her. Nothing could make up for the awful murder and shattered lives of the remaining members of the Cunningham family. But in the minds of most people, Lena Cunningham's murder had been avenged.

Chapter 5:
SLIPPERY BILL'S GOLD

The enigmatic Bill Morrison finds brown gold in the Middle Fork backcountry

Slippery Bill Morrison woke before dawn and prepared to restart a fire in the tiny stove in the quiet wilderness cabin. Although there were a handful of other trappers scattered around this remote backcountry, today Bill was all alone in every way. In the 1880s before the railroad, the big snow country of the Middle Fork was hauntingly silent during the winter. Like other early trappers, that was just the way Slippery Bill liked it.

He struck a match to some small shavings from lodgepole pine chunks dried by the stove the night before. If anything was in plentiful supply in the Morrison-Lodgepole drainage it was lodgepole pine. But even using dry pine the fire sputtered, and the little 12 by 12 foot cabin began to fill with smoke. Bill knew what must have happened. Outside, the stovepipe was buried under three feet of snow from last night's storm. He laced on his snowshoes, went outside in the frigid, predawn darkness, stomped a path up to the snow's new surface, and dug out the pipe. He slid down to the entryway and reentered the tight, dark cabin. The stove drew well, and soon Bill was enjoying its warmth.

Near the stove, Slippery Bill had placed several frozen marten and ermine from yesterday's take along the wilderness trapline. For wilderness trappers, each day of running a trapline was like Christmas morning. A trap set over a week before could hold a furbearer as valuable as a gold nugget. When the trapper approached a set and found a marten, an ermine, or even a lynx hanging there, he felt a sense of success and wildness. As he reset his trap, anticipation began to build for the next time he would check it days later. And if fresh furbearer tracks ran by the set, so much the better. This excitement of looking ahead drove the trapper from set to set day after day through the deep snow.

As the marten thawed, Bill ate a meager breakfast of beans and coffee by the light of the flames from the open door of the stove. Now he needed

Slippery Bill Morrison, here in his 50s, reads on the porch of his base cabin near Marias Pass. Glacier National Park Historical Collection.

more light. He lit a tallow lamp he'd packed into the cabin along with other supplies the summer before. He laid the first marten on its back across his lap and carefully made a long slit from one of the furbearer's rear paws, and along the underside of the legs to the other paw, the slit crossing the anal opening. He could now free the pelt from the rear of the animal and pull the thin bone out of the furry tail. After the tail was free, Bill pulled the pelt down to the head like turning a sock inside out. All that remained was to make a few small cuts to free the ears, eye areas, and nose and the pelt was free. Bill stretched the pelt on a flat narrow board with the skin side out. He could probably "board" a marten in about 20 minutes. After the pelt dried by the stove for a half-hour or so, he pulled it off the board and turned it fur side out. He then placed it over the board again for final drying and soon had a fluffy, dark brown pelt of silky fur sought around the world for making luxury sable coats and fur trim. In like fashion, Bill pelted the rest of the marten and the smaller snow-white ermine.

After the big dump of snow the night before, the sky had cleared and the sun rose, illuminating ice crystals in the frigid air. Like other trappers, Slippery Bill had to feel in his chest the incredible burst of freedom and wildness of the wilderness trapline. After closing up the crude but serviceable little shelter, he strapped on his snowshoes and headed to the next cabin on his line, checking traps, removing furbearers from successful sets and rebaiting as needed. In his 30s, Bill was tough and rangy, standing over six feet tall. He could mush along on snowshoes all day through the Middle Fork's forests and along its ridges and watercourses.

Like other old-time trappers, Bill probably used a combination of baits to attract marten and lynx to his sets. In late summer he likely speared bull trout or "salmon trout" in Bear Creek below his Summit headquarters or in Morrison or Lodgepole creeks. He then rotted the fish in a barrel to make "bunkum." This concoction could draw in furbearers from miles away if the winds were right. For bait, Bill also likely used chunks of fish and scraps from deer and elk carcasses and even carcasses from the marten he skinned. This kind of recycling made a lot of sense.

The lives of Slippery Bill and the other old-time trappers in the Middle Fork were tough, but they had a lot going for them. First, this was and still is some of the finest furbearer habitat in the lower 48 states. Second, there was plenty of game to supply them with food and with trapping bait. Bill's creek (Morrison Creek) still supports bull trout spawners that run 100 miles or more upstream from Flathead Lake. One October day in 1995, I counted 25 large bull trout nests in a 3-mile stretch of Morrison Creek near the mouth of Lodgepole Creek. Imagine the density of these huge fish which were up to three feet long and 25 pounds in this section of this small creek. During low flow in the fall, Morrison Creek only averages about 30 feet wide and one or two feet deep. In 1993, I found a bull trout nest in tiny Whistler Creek within 20 yards of the trapper cabin site near the junction of Whistler and Lodgepole Creeks. Lodgepole Creek itself supports good runs of bull trout, as does Granite Creek which joins the Middle Fork about five miles downstream. In all these small creeks big bulls are easily visible in the crystal water and vulnerable to a crude spear or a well-thrown rock. It's likely that Bill, like the Native Americans before him, took advantage of this bounty for food and, yes, for making trapping "bunkum."

Even though it seems lonely and harsh, the lives of these trappers were specifically chosen by them: this was just the way they wanted it. If this life was easy, many others would be doing what they were doing; and the main ingredient of their lives, solitude, would be lost.

For these and other reasons most of these trappers lived their entire lives as bachelors and hermits. Like other trappers, Slippery Bill probably smelled a bit like his bait during the trapping season. Also, he probably provided a home for lots of fleas and ticks from the furbearers he skinned. Even if old-time trappers sought a civilized life, these factors would repel potential mates like "deet" repels mosquitoes.

Back then, Bill and other trappers used steel foothold traps and maybe even deadfalls to catch furbearers. Often, the trapper would place the foothold trap on a pole, limb, or notch in a tree situated so the animal had to step on the trap to reach the bait. When the animal was caught, it hung down by the trap chain and was suspended above the snow surface, out of the reach of rodents or other animals that could chew on the fur. Marten caught in this manner quickly expired through exposure and freezing. With a deadfall, the trapper attaches bait to a trigger stick that props up a heavy log. When a furbearer grabs the bait, he trips the trigger and is pinned by the log.

The advantage of trapping marten and ermine is the ease of handling their fur, the nearly weightless dry, silky pelts, and the relatively high fur value. These mustellids, or members of the weasel family, are so hyperactive that they have little fat reserves; thus their pelts come off nearly clean of any fat or flesh. They must hunt squirrels in trees, hares on the snow, or rodents in snow tunnels all winter long to maintain their high metabolism. Once, on a winter furbearer track survey deep in the Middle Fork backcountry in the Lodgepole Creek drainage, I watched a red-backed vole run down a lodgepole pine and disappear into the narrow space around the tree's trunk, heading for a "subnivian" (under snow) tunnel. I wondered if a marten would grab the vole, since I had just counted several sets of fresh marten tracks. And I wondered if Slippery Bill over a century before had watched voles descend into snow tunnels at this very spot, especially because I was just a quarter mile from an old cabin site near the mouth of Whistler Creek that some believe was his.

But Bill and others in the upper Middle Fork were not limited to marten, ermine, and lynx. Counting bull trout nests in Morrison, Lodgepole and Granite creeks nowadays is like running a gauntlet of beaver dams. These dams block migration of the big bulls swimming upstream to spawning areas. Bill and the others probably served as the bull trout's pal by keeping these dam builders cropped down and keeping the "salmon trout's" migration routes open.

Bill Morrison had a reputation of knowing a good opportunity when he saw one, and he recognized one in the upper Middle Fork. But, contrary to some legends, it was most likely this brown gold of fine marten pelts and heavy beaver fur, not yellow gold, gambling, or stolen loot that drew Bill's attention and effort, especially when he first arrived in the 1880s from back east.

Few if any people trapped the rich fur region of the upper Middle Fork when Bill arrived. The dense moist forests of spruce, fir, and pine provided superb habitat for valuable furbearers, especially lynx and marten. These pelts were in high demand and worth big money on the fur market. Middle Fork marten sport some of the darkest brown fur of any marten in the lower 48 states and so were particularly valuable. A good winter's take of marten would bring today's equivalent of a year's wages.

Bill apparently had a handful of trapping partners or acquaintances, and they focused some of their early effort on the Schafer Meadows area in the heart of what is now known as the Great Bear Wilderness. Information on Bill's trapping operations is hard to find, and there's a good reason for that.

Any trapper, just like any prospector, knows an important key for success. The way you thrive in the trapping business is to find an area rich in fur and then keep it to yourself and maybe a few trusted partners. It's just natural: the only way to keep your secret is to not tell anybody what you are doing or where you are doing it.

Trappers saw the wilderness and potential dollars in a marten hanging in their well-placed trap sets. This marten was trapped along the Middle Fork in the Great Bear Wilderness.

To illustrate Bill's tight-lipped attitude, consider this story. One summer, a Great Northern train stopped at Bill's siding at Marias Pass at the top of the grade after the railroad had been established a few years. Bill was popular with the trainmen and he had his own rustic "bar," so they often stopped and gave Bill some trade. A lady passenger reportedly asked Bill how people made a living way out here in the middle of nowhere. Bill replied, "Lady, we make a fine living out here by minding our own business."

If you plot old cabin sites rumored to be Bill's and other old-timers in the Marias Pass and upper Middle Fork in the Morrison and Lodgepole creek drainages, and in the river above Schafer Meadows, you soon see a pattern that looks very much like classical traplines. Back then trappers designed their traplines around strategically spaced cabins. Each cabin was about a day's snowshoe apart and, taken together, the cabins formed a rough loop. The trapper would travel from cabin to cabin, setting traps on the way. When he arrived back at the first cabin in the loop, he had completed setting the trapline. The next morning he was ready to check traps. Rising early, the trapper set out for the next cabin, eager to see what was in the sets he'd made days before. He spent all day pulling furbearers from the successful trapsets, and resetting and rebaiting the traps as he traveled to the next cabin. When he arrived, tired and wet, he built a fire in the stove or rock fireplace, thawed out the marten or other furbearers, and skinned them that night. If the trapper was exhausted, skinning had to wait until the next morning. Then he was on his way along the trapline to the next cabin. This way, the trapper made the trapline loop over and over during the long 5-month winter and piled up the fur.

At certain points along the trapline, the old-timers set "spur lines" up along promising drainages. The Schafer Meadows area, in the center of the upper Middle Fork, is just the right jumping off place for these secondary lines.

At Schafer Meadows, the Middle Fork of the Flathead River drops out of a long canyon which it enters 15 miles upstream at Gooseberry Park. The river gradient changes from a drop of about 50 feet per mile to practically flat for a couple of miles. The perfect suitability of this site drew the U. S. Forest Service to establish their main base of operations for the Great Bear Wilderness here by about 1934. But Bill and other old-time trappers discovered Schafer Meadows much, much earlier.

Very early (in the 1880s) one way to reach Schafer Meadows was by a rugged route along the Middle Fork of the Flathead, 24 miles upstream from the mouth of Bear Creek near Java. Two other routes were also possible: from Summit up the South Fork of the Two Medicine River and Badger Creek, over the Divide and down Lodgepole Creek to Morrison Creek; or from Summit up Skyland Creek, around Slippery Bill Mountain, and downstream along Morrison Creek, or downstream along Granite Creek. From the mouth of Morrison Creek it's a quick four miles upstream along the Middle Fork to Schafer. A trapper could also swing up Lodgepole Creek, over a divide, down Calbick Creek to the Middle Fork, and then three miles downstream to Schafer Meadows.

Slippery Bill and his trapping partners or loose associates, one of whom was said to be William Schafer, would have been foolish to not take advantage of these fur-rich routes. The demand for fur was high and unlike the uncertainty of prospecting or gambling, trapping marten and other furbearers that filled these rich habitats was a sure thing.

Once established at Schafer Meadows, great fur possibilities opened like spokes on a wheel. Dolly Varden and Schafer Creeks enter the river at Schafer Meadows and offer relatively gentle canyons full of prime furbearer habitat. Calbick and Cox Creeks are just upstream, and Lake Creek and Three Forks are just downstream. All of these areas support bountiful numbers of marten even today, so imagine the marten bounty that Bill and his partners enjoyed, being the first to lay steel traps in these drainages and seek these most valuable members of the weasel family. Good numbers of lynx are found there in recent times. In 1998, we counted 43 sets of lynx tracks in a 3-day furbearer track survey using Schafer Meadows as a base. Likely, lynx would have been even more numerous well over a century ago. In recent times, marten hotspots have been Dolly Varden Creek, Morrison Creek, and

These marten pelts were taken in the Middle Fork of the Flathead backcountry. This is the valuable "brown gold" that Slippery Bill Morrison and his partners sought in the Middle Fork's mountains. In Slippery Bill's time, a good winter's take of marten could yield enough cash to buy a small farm. Author photo.

Lake Creek. On 6-mile ski runs using Schafer Meadows as a base in 1998, we counted 43 sets of marten tracks along the Dolly Varden Creek trail and 50 sets of marten tracks from the Middle Fork upstream a few miles on Lake Creek. Any trapper would "kill" to lay steel in country boasting these fur densities.

Some say that Schafer and other old-time trappers may have been competitors rather than partners with Slippery Bill. They reason that, in the search for brown gold just like for yellow gold, partners tend to fall out and resent each other. It may have been that Bill was centered in Morrison-Lodgepole, Granite Creek, and the Middle Fork downstream from Three Forks, while William Schafer's territory was the Schafer Meadows, Dolly Varden, and Schafer Creek drainages. Later, Allen Calbick, who may have been a young protégé of Slippery Bill's at one time, and others may have ranged upstream from Schafer in the Calbick, Cox, and upper Middle Fork to Gooseberry Park.

It's said that Slippery Bill told friends that he had enough loot buried in caves near Schafer Meadows to last him through any hardship. Those rumors, and the long periods of time Bill and his partners spent in the backcountry, led some to speculate that Bill had robbed a train, found the loot from the Northern Pacific train robbery, or struck it rich in placer gold in the upper Middle Fork and then hid his treasure. There is no evidence supporting any of these stories, although there are several caves in the Schafer area that have not been thoroughly explored. Besides, one good winter's take of marten, ermine, and lynx would have produced more loot than Jack Chipman and the gang lifted when they robbed the Northern Pacific number four.

There are diggings on the southeast side of Slippery Bill Mountain, and it's likely that Bill did some prospecting there and in other places. Bill and the other old-timers undoubtedly tried panning and placer mining in the Middle Fork's creeks, but there is very little mineral potential there and they probably didn't find much. But there is physical evidence of Bill's cabins, and place names that reflect his travels and haunts and those of at least a couple of his trapping partners or competitors. And most telling, there's written proof that Bill considered himself first and foremost a trapper: he directed county officials to write "Trapper" on his death certificate as his occupation.

Trappers in the upper Flathead and other areas trapped right on through March, and then brought their furs to Demersville, or prior to that, south to the Northern Pacific line. There are a number of mentions of trappers arriving in Demersville or Columbia Falls or Kalispell with a winter's take of fur. One article in the *Demersville Inter Lake* in 1890 specifically mentions that Dan Doody, who Bill probably met in McCarthyville, and his partners brought in a big load of furs. Dan and his partners had snowshoed 100 miles to come out from their trapping area and reach Demersville.

There are also some exaggerated claims in some of these newspaper reports, including one mention of six trappers attempting to bring in 2,700 marten pelts that may have been lost in a rafting accident in the South Fork of the Flathead River. You might be able to trap that many muskrats, which reproduce like typical rodents, in a lower valley drainage in a winter. But for a number of reasons relating to the nature of marten populations—they maintain territories and have a low rate of reproduction—taking this number of marten would be impossible.

Just like reports of gold and other minerals, reports of fur takes could be "hyped." The fact is though that the Flathead was an extremely rich fur area late in the 19th century and early in the 20th when Bill and his partners were active. The upper Middle Fork of the Flathead was one of the last areas in the lower 48 states to be explored by Euro-Americans. Bill and his partners were the first to enter it and the first to lay steel (place traps) along its watercourses and ridges.

According to at least one story, bad blood existed between Slippery Bill and his former trapping partner, William Schafer. This may have led to Schafer's death under mysterious circumstances.

Slippery Bill Morrison at Marias Pass, ca 1930. In his prime, Morrison was tall and powerful, able to walk all day over the trackless Middle Fork backcountry. Glacier National Park Historical Collection.

Slippery Bill, even with his dubious past, was hired by the Forest Service as the first ranger in the Summit-Essex-Schafer Meadows area in the spring of 1898. He provided his own "headquarters" at Summit. Slippery Bill had a reputation of being tough and an excellent woodsman who knew the Middle Fork better than anyone else. Bill's designated territory was the entire Middle Fork Flathead Drainage of the Flathead and Lewis and Clark Forest Reserves. Bill's guidelines were few, and he did pretty much as he pleased. He was expected to patrol his vast district, look for fires, maintain trails, and keep an eye out for illegal activities (except his own). Like other early rangers, he probably mixed in plenty of personal business such as trapping, hunting and prospecting.

Typical of the early U. S. Forest Service, rangers were usually the toughest, backcountry-savvy locals that could be found in the area. They were not necessarily law abiding or "respectable" before or after they were hired. Bill Morrison was a classic example, serving as a ranger in the upper Middle Fork in the early 1900s. Like rangers in other areas, these mavericks probably trapped in their districts to pick up extra cash. Salaries for early rangers amounted to only about $60 per month (about the equivalent of one decent day's trapping take), and they had to provide their own bedrolls and food from this pay.

Bill did well enough as a ranger to be rehired multiple times. In May 1901, Forest Ranger Moser submitted a list of names he recommended for appointment to the forest superintendent, noting that they would make "first class Rangers." Listed as number 17 of the 23 names was William H. Morrison. That year Bill was listed as the ranger for the Upper Middle Fork District at Java. Nine years later, Allen Calbick, Bill's younger protégé or trapping partner (or was he?), was the ranger at Java.

Bill was born in Massachusetts in 1852 and probably reached the Flathead country in Montana in the early 1880s. Bill likely worked as a trainman on his way across the country and perhaps for a time in Canada. In his 30s, Bill was already a seasoned outdoorsman and trapper when he arrived in Montana. He established squatter's rights on a quarter section at Marias Pass and used his cabin there, among other things, as a base to access the backcountry of the upper Middle Fork of the Flathead River.

An enigmatic character, Slippery Bill was well educated and articulate. According to Charlie Shaw, a Forest Service Ranger who knew him, Slippery Bill was a trapper and prospector first, and a train conductor second.

John F. Stevens, credited by the Great Northern with the first successful survey or "discovery" of Marias Pass, spoke at the dedication of the Stevens statue at Summit on July 21, 1925. Slippery Bill , then 73 years old, was in the crowd listening to the speech. This was fitting, seeing as how Bill had donated the land for the memorial and the proposed Theodore Roosevelt Memorial Highway. Stevens told the people assembled at the dedication about the hardships he faced in searching for the pass over the Divide in the teeth of a blizzard. He explained how he had almost given up and nearly perished in the cold. According to old-timer Charlie Shaw, Slippery Bill spoke up at this point, saying, "Why didn't you just come over to my cabin? I was living right over there." He pointed in the direction of his cabin, still standing not far from the memorial.

Bill had been granted occupancy rights to a quarter section and more at Marias Pass, and for years had claimed rights to all the useable land in the area. Bill was one of the few residents in the area prior to McCarthyville's existence. His claim is roughly described as "unsurveyed townships 29 and 30 North, Range 14 West." When Bill reached 77 years of age, he agreed to donate his land and cabin to the U. S. Forest Service. Bill retained .14 acre, including his cabin and outbuildings until his death, at which time it would revert to the U. S. Forest Service. The transfer was made through Deed Record No. 206 notarized on June 27, 1930, by G.I. Porter in the presence of Slippery Bill at the Flathead County Courthouse. In the document, Slippery Bill is described as an "unmarried man of Essex, Montana." The document also described in detail the location of the .14-acre parcel that Bill retained until his death.

Bill stayed good friends with the railroad men, often riding in the engine cab 10 miles west to Essex and back from his cabin near the tracks at Summit.

During the last years of his life, Slippery Bill spent much of his time in Essex. Some say he traveled to Kalispell on the train from time to time to gamble or to stake other gamblers. According to Essex residents, he never seemed to lack money.

This could be the remnant of Slippery Bill's trapper cabin in the Lodgepole Creek Drainage near the mouth of remote Whistler Creek. Author Photo, 2006.

On Christmas Day in 1931, Bill fell seriously ill and was transported by train to Kalispell General Hospital. Dr. Albert Brassett diagnosed Bill as having cancer of the pancreas. After battling the disease for a few months, Bill died with his boots off at 11 p.m. on March 6, 1932.

The informant listed on Slippery Bill's death certificate was Mrs. Tom Armstrong of Summit, a confidant who obviously knew Bill as well as anyone, talked with him during his illness, and assisted officials with his vital information.

On March 8 at 2:30 p.m., funeral services were held for Slippery Bill in Kalispell. Even though Bill had never married, he seemed to have some female admirers. The two hymns in the service were sung by Miss Agnes Calbick and Mrs. B. L. Beaman. Obviously, he was on good terms with his old trapping protégé and Forest Service colleague, Allen Calbick. Miss Daisy Dubois played the piano. Slippery Bill's casket was banked with flowers. The pallbearers were mostly railroad men that Bill knew from Summit and Essex, along with a Forest Service supervisor. The *Kalispell Daily Interlake* carried his very brief obituary on March 9.

Bill's "cabin" along the tracks at the top of the grade at Summit had been well known by trainmen and others as a place to drink, gamble, and chat with the mysterious Slippery Bill. Bill had a redwood bar 14 feet long, 30 inches wide, and 1-1/4 inch thick. When Bill's cabin was torn down after the government acquired his land, Charlie Shaw took his bar and made it into a clothes chest. Imbedded in the bar were one .45 bullet and some shot.

So, when it was all said and done, Slippery Bill kept most of his secrets even from his closest associates. Did he ever hoard stolen loot or strike gold? There's no evidence that he did. Did he amass a big fortune from gambling? Probably not. In the end, Bill could be described by the name assigned to a creek in the headwaters of Morrison Creek: Puzzle.

But Bill's final act shed light on what he considered his essence. Among the vital facts he gave officials while he was dying was his profession/ vocation. For the record, on his death certificate, Slippery Bill's trade or profession is summed up in one word: "Trapper."

Chapter 6
HEART OF THE MIDDLE FORK
Early fur trappers and rangers find adventure in the remote region of Schafer Meadows

Renegade Fur Trappers and Early History

In the heart of the Middle Fork sprawls a lush meadow bisected by a wild river. The place is so special and so remote that old-time fur trappers fought for it and killed for it and died for it.

Schafer Meadows owes its name to a renegade trapper who was murdered there. The Meadows straddle the drainage 26 miles upstream from the mouth of Bear Creek. Old-timers like Doris Huffine and others called Middle Fork upstream from Bear Creek the "Big River," maybe to set it apart from the large creeks that join it at Three Forks, Schafer, and Gooseberry.

Like an oasis, 1,000-acre Schafer Meadows receives the clear waters of the upper Middle Fork of the Flathead River as it emerges from its steep, 15-mile long canyon. The rocky, rushing river originates at the junction of Bowl and Strawberry Creeks, and then drops 50 feet per mile to Schafer Meadows. Here, the river suddenly changes into a lazy, gravel-bottomed stream meandering back and forth through the Meadows between Lodgepole Mountain to the north and Union Peak and Chair Mountain to the south. The rounded river gravels on the stream bottom originated in crazy geologic formations. The gravels come in a myriad of colors, ranging from green to blue to black to brown and colors in between.

After flowing a few lazy miles, the Middle Fork spills out of Schafer Meadows and drops through canyons and gorges for 26 miles to Bear Creek. Then the canyon continues for 25 miles before taking another gradient breather at Nyack Flats.

Schafer Meadows also receives the waters of two major Middle Fork Tributaries, Schafer and Dolly Varden Creeks. This union of waters forms a major draw for bull trout, formerly called Dolly Varden trout, migrating more than 100 miles upstream from Flathead Lake. These cold, shallow tributaries are full of excellent spawning gravels with upwelling groundwater, and have long been known for their abundant, big bull trout spawners. Dolly Varden Creek bears the former name of these huge fish, reflecting the creek's reputation.

Back in the late 1800s, men like William Schafer and Slippery Bill Morrison fell in love with this remote, fur-rich country. When these men trapped here, they were separated from access to civilization to a degree we can't imagine today. That was precisely why they were drawn to this beautiful flat.

William Schafer lived and trapped in the meadows for years. He shunned civilization and spent his life living off the bounty of this wildlife-rich area. Not far from his cabin door, Schafer could spear bull trout in Dolly Varden and Schafer Creeks for food and trapping lure. He could shoot moose in the beaver ponds and meadows on the north side of the river. He could take elk and deer in the conifer forests and ridges.

In this trapper's paradise, Schafer had all the high quality trapping bait he could use. Scraps from butchering a moose or elk would supply enough bait for a winter's trapping. Schafer likely rotted big bull trout that he speared in Dolly Varden Creek to produce fragrant and powerful bunkum, fish oil that could draw in mustellids such as marten and wolverine from miles away to his trap sets.

Most importantly, he could trap the highly valuable marten, wolverine and lynx in a virgin area. Schafer was likely the first Euro-American to trap in this remote valley, and the furbearer densities must have been eye-popping.

The meadows supplied the perfect base camp for Schafer's trapping operation. Not only did he have superb fur country right at his cabin, he could lay steel up Schafer and Dolly Varden Creeks south to the divide with the South Fork of the Flathead River. On backcountry furbearer surveys in recent times, I've counted dozens of sets of marten tracks along Dolly Varden Creek trail upstream to the falls at Argosy Creek. I've had lynx cross my back-trail. Imagine what the numbers must have been like when Shafer arrived, probably in the early 1880s or before.

In his one visit to civilization each year, Schafer would pack out his furs and trade them for a year's supply of necessities and probably lots of extra cash. Remember, this was a time when a trapper could buy a small farm with proceeds from a single winter's successful fur take. Old-time rumors hint that some of the money Schafer made from trapping is still hidden in a cave, somewhere above the meadows

Schafer likely ranged upriver to Calbick Creek, Cox Creek, and Clack Creek. Upstream from there, Chick Grimsley, another old-time trapper who came into the Middle Fork from the east side of the Divide, had headquarters in Bowl Creek. Remnants of small trapper cabins in these areas are still visible and may have been used by the old trapper as line camps.

Schafer was in hog heaven as far as fur was concerned. That was good, but Schafer's big fur takes may have attracted notice when he brought them out for sale to the few fur buyers in the Flathead Valley, or perhaps earlier to other buyers east of the Divide. Schafer and other early trappers like Grimsley and Morrison likely divided up the area and mostly stayed out of each other's way. Schafer, though, had

Looking upstream to Schafer Meadows. Here the Middle Fork widens and flows through an extensive bottom. This is some of the country that William Schafer and Slippery Bill trapped and patrolled. Jim Williams photo.

the prime grounds. And like a prospector bringing out a load of gold, his fur takes may have built curiosity and jealousy in the few other trappers in that part of northwest Montana during this period.

A legend that seems to point to this conflict circulated through old-timers' networks and among the early U. S. Forest Service Rangers. As the story goes, Schafer was minding his own business along the trapline one spring. When he returned from one of his traplines or line cabins, he found his home cabin at Schafer Meadows had been ransacked. Robbers had made off with many of his supplies and his furs. There was enough light snow on top of the snowpack that he could follow the tracks of the perpetrators. He caught up to them at an open avalanche slope along Schafer Creek near the Capitol Mountain trail junction. There, Schafer got the drop on the two men and "dry-gulched" them, shooting them both dead. If this story is true, these two badmen didn't just stumble on to Schafer's cabin. Given the remote location, these men must have had prior knowledge of the cabin's location and Schafer's trapping operation.

Another story that supports the notion of conflict between frontiersmen and trappers involves Schafer's mysterious death more than a century ago in the meadows, and the story has spawned an intriguing legend. In about 1908, Slippery Bill Morrison, who trapped mostly downstream from Schafer's area in Morrison and Lodgepole Creek and Three Forks, reportedly came out from the meadows and contacted Deputy Standford in Kalispell. Bill reported that Schafer was dead in his cabin at the remote meadows. The deputy accompanied Bill and others into the backcountry and indeed found Schafer dead in his cabin along the Middle Fork upstream from the mouth of Dolly Varden Creek. Stories differ as to the circumstances of his death. One account says that he was shot in the back, with the murderer intent on robbery. The other story is that Slippery Bill told the deputy that Schafer had killed himself. The deputy examined the body, and found that the bullet wound was inconsistent with suicide, unless Schafer had figured out a way to shoot himself in the back.

Any Flathead County records made by Deputy Standford about the investigation have been lost, reportedly destroyed in a fire. Standford, Morrison, and whoever else accompanied them reportedly buried Schafer on Morrison Creek near the confluence of Lodgepole Creek. Perhaps the deputy and his party planned on taking him out of the backcountry then decided after four miles that it would be better to leave the old trapper in the area he loved. Others believe that he is buried near Whistler Creek in the area of the trapper cabins there. Still others thought he was buried at his cabin site at Schafer Meadows.

Another account places Schafer's death at about 1904. The details of this account are similar. The investigating party found Schafer dead in his cabin. The furs he'd been piling up were gone. The investigating party suspected foul play and robbery, but let it go. Similar to the other account, Schafer's body was buried near Lodgepole Creek. According to old time Ranger Charlie Shaw's account, Slippery Bill was the main suspect in Schafer's death because he'd been spending time and trapping near the Meadows. When approached, Slippery Bill supposedly said to the investigators, "I killed him. Now I told you, now you prove it."

I've spent time looking around the mouth of Lodgepole Creek for traces of Schafer's grave. If consistent with other graves of that era in the backcountry, it should appear as a mound of rocks and might still be visible. Much of the area burned shortly after the supposed year of Schafer's death, so the vegetation is mostly lodgepole pine with little underbrush. I haven't given up. I will keep looking.

But physical evidence of Schafer's cabin remained for many years. Old-time Schafer Meadows rangers Art Whitney and Bill Chilton saw what was left of Schafer's cabin in the 1930s-1950s, often riding or hiking by the site on their way up Dolly Varden Creek. The cabin had been small and humble, formed from 8-inch logs, and measuring 10 or 12-feet on a side. Bill says that Schafer's cabin was on the south side of the river near the trail where it crossed the river and headed up Schafer Creek. He said the backcountry phone line that ran over the divide to Spotted Bear used to be suspended just below that trail. The cabin was on the same side, downriver, 50 feet from the trail.

Schafer had built his cabin just on the edge of the bench along the river, maybe so he could let the river's music put him to sleep each night. With this location, he could throw a line from his doorstep into the river for a big bull trout or cutthroat trout. He could watch the reddish-orange glow of the sunset on the river's surface. But the cabin's location was its undoing. The great flood of 1964 washed away the logs and the small mark Schafer had made on the landscape.

Like many others, Bill knew that Schafer was found dead in his cabin, but he didn't hear how the party "disposed" of him after he was found. "Bill Morrison was a prime suspect," says Bill. "He was a part-time ranger, when Glacier Park was part of forest reserve land. It's hard to tell what really happened or who really killed him. There were a number of those renegade trappers."

An enigmatic early trapper, Schafer's story is mostly legend with precious little fact. Schafer's grave, death certificate, and sheriff's report on his likely murder have all been lost. Only second-hand oral history remains. There could be something left by Schafer in the lost caves at the base of Union Mountain, a mile or so from his cabin site, but until someone finds and explores the caves, we'll never know.

Schafer was *the* pioneer in the upper Middle Fork. It's too bad he didn't live long enough to see Schafer Meadows and Schafer Creek eventually bear his name.

Prior to Schafer's death in the early 1900s, the Forest Service occupied the Java Ranger Station, located far downstream near the mouth of Bear Creek and along the railroad line. At first, this served as the Forest Service administration center for the upper Middle Fork District. The first district ranger listed at the station for 1901 was William H. Morrison. This was prior to the Middle Fork being officially added to the Forest Reserve in 1903. Morrison was followed by Phillip Giefer (Giefer Creek bears his name, 1902-04), Fred Wyman (1905-06), and Richard Shields (1907-09).

But not long after Schafer's death, Forest Service rangers moved in to the upper Middle Fork. In 1910, Upper Middle Fork District Ranger Allen Calbick and a helper or two built a cabin at Three Forks, 22 miles upstream on the banks of the Middle Fork near the mouths of Morrison Creek and Lake Creek. On a small bench above the station site, Calbick selected trees and whip-sawed the lumber to build the station. The Three Forks cabin served as a convenient waypoint for rangers traveling to Schafer Meadows and on upstream to Gooseberry Park. It had long been a rendezvous site, being a crossover point for Indian trails connecting the Flathead Valley, through the South Fork and Middle Fork drainages, upstream along Morrison and Lodgepole Creeks and over to the east side of the Continental Divide. Several arrowheads were found in the Three Forks area, rumored to have come from a battle between several tribes at this strategic point.

Even with the new ranger station at Three Forks, a series of district rangers

The Forest Service crew at the Schafer Meadows Station in 1938. Schafer became the center for the Upper Middle Fork District in 1934. Photo courtesy of Art Whitney, who is third from the right.

continued to serve at Java (A.E. Havens, 1911-12; Ellis Hoke, 1913-18; James Adams, 1919-21; Thomas Wiles, 1922-25; and C.L. Pierce, 1926-27).

In 1927 the district headquarters for the Upper Middle Fork was moved upstream to Three Forks, reflecting the increased importance and attention paid to the backcountry. J. R. Hutchinson served as district ranger there beginning in 1928, and continuing until 1933.

Seeking to open the vast upper Middle Fork to better and more timely transport, Hutchinson supervised the construction of the first airstrip in the Flathead on a plateau 3/4 mile south and across the river from the Three Forks Station. The airstrip, located about 200 feet in elevation above the river, was carved out of the young lodgepole pine forest that grew there after the fires 20 or so years earlier. The airstrip turned out to be impractical for several reasons. First, it lay across the Middle Fork from the Three Forks site, adding a layer of difficulty for accessing it during high water, although a cable crossing was eventually built. Also, anything flown in for use at the station had to be packed nearly a mile after it was unloaded from the plane. Finally, the approach and takeoff opportunities were difficult. The Forest Service never officially opened it for administrative use. One adventurous pilot from the private Johnson Flying Service landed a Travelaire plane there in 1932, but that was it.

By 1933, rangers recognized that the Schafer Meadows area would be a much better headquarters because of its central location and topography.

Bears and Caves and a Ranger's Romance

The next year, official headquarters for the Upper Middle Fork District was established at Schafer Meadows, with John "Jack" Root, the first Schafer

Forest Service employees Maude Bally, Ranger Jack Root, and Katherine at Schafer Meadows in late summer 1938. The ranger arranged for the two ladies, who worked at the Forest Service office in Kalispell, to visit the ranger station to meet some of the men they talked to on the radio. Photo courtesy of Art Whitney.

Ranger serving from 1934-1938. Schafer Meadows headquarters started out as a tent camp while "Big Vic" Homlund, a Swedish immigrant and master log craftsman, built the main Schafer cabin (called the multi-purpose building by Art Whitney) and ranger residence. Some of the lumber the men used to build the station was brought by rail to Essex. If you look in the rafters at Schafer, you will see some of the boards that bear the address, Fred Neitzling, Essex. Fred was the ranger at Essex in the late 1920s. Ranger Jack Root supervised Art Whitney, who helped finish building some of the structures at the Schafer Station and several lookouts, and helped with the Schafer airstrip construction. Art also served as the ranger alternate when Root was away.

Art's skills fit his job with the Forest Service. His father and older brother, Ralph, built log cabins. Ralph had built some structures for the Forest Service. Art had helped them, and he was very experienced even in his early 20s with backcountry construction.

Young, enthusiastic, and in love with the Middle Fork, Art worked hard and long. "I inspected lookouts, worked with trail crews, and did trail work," he said. "I walked a lot of it, but I rode a helluva lot of horse. I was assigned a saddle horse and pack mule. I did a lot of maintenance and worked on the

Maude and Katherine show off about a 12-pound native bull trout caught in the Middle Fork of the Flathead River near Schafer during their 1938 trip. Photo courtesy of Art Whitney.

buildings. We ate fish a lot, we had army rations, and had lots of canned food. The whole thing was interesting."

Art found out right away that dealing with bears was a fact of life at Schafer. On patrols upriver to Gooseberry Park, he would sometimes see five or more black bears in a day, maybe a grizzly, and had no problems with them. But around the station, things were different. Grizzlies rarely bothered the station crews, but black bears were a nuisance. "I never had bad encounters with grizzlies, though I saw lots of them," Art said. "The only thing that ever went after me was a black bear and the only thing that ever bit me was a black bear."

Art attributed the behavior of the black bears to the fact that they had been allowed to get food rewards, and in some cases well-meaning station workers had actively fed them. Even small bears could be dangerous if they began to feel the station grounds and buildings were theirs.

"They'd get brave," remembered Art. "Once I went down to bring canned food out of the basement, and as I came up the steps, a small bear that had come into the station grabbed my wrist. He pushed my hands together, and pried at one of my fingers and jerked it away to make me drop the cans, then grabbed one and bolted out of the station. I didn't mess with him."

One weekend Art was relaxing in the station building, enjoying some time off. He was sitting in a chair at the doorway of the station building with his feet across each other and legs extended, looking out over the station clearing, when "a bear came up and put his head out over my legs and let out a hiss. I didn't move; I didn't want to move. The bear stepped right over me and went in and grabbed the bacon--they used to get bacon in great big slabs and had clothesline rope through the top to hang it on the wall."

Holding the bacon slab in its jaws, the bear turned and started back out of the station building. Art stood up and got his back along the frame of the door. "When the bear was right even with me," Art continued, "I saw the rope loop and I grabbed it and gave it a jerk. The bear jumped down the stairway, so I saved the bacon."

Art was perplexed at the bear's boldness and level of habituation. He was convinced that someone had fed the bear regularly. "He went inside the station," said Art. "Right in broad daylight. He stepped right over me while I was sitting in the doorway. And this was a big black bear.

"Think about it, if a bear came up and put his head over you, you wouldn't move much, would you? He just put one foot over me, then the other foot. He knew I was there, but he could smell the bacon. I think it was one of the bears that was being fed, maybe by the cook."

A black bear steps off the porch of the Schafer Station. Art Whitney cautioned against feeding bears because of the danger they could pose, but some workers at the station fed bears anyway. Photo courtesy of Art Whitney.

Another incident illustrated that bears find bacon so irresistible that they quickly learn what they have to do to swipe it. At Schafer in the 1930s, one bear rose above the others with his ingenuity. The station workers, who were staying in a tent camp, repeatedly lost food, especially their favorite bacon, to marauding bears. Bacon, especially, tastes superb in the backcountry and it supplies a lot of calories from fat. So the workers devised what they thought was a clever and foolproof way to secure their bacon from bears. A long pole was cut and its balance point was positioned just right over a pivot. To one end of the pole, the men lashed a wooden food box containing the prize sides of bacon. To the other end of pole the men fastened a heavy box of rocks. This ingenious "teeter-totter" suspended the bacon 12 or so feet off the ground, yet all the men had to do to get the bacon was pull down on a rope, take what they needed from the box, then allow the weighted lever to pivot on the fulcrum and re-suspend the food cache.

The workers felt confident that they had invented a foolproof method of securing their bacon from bears, until a new bear arrived in the area. This bear was frustrated at first; he climbed the leaning pole, passed over the fulcrum and rode the lever down as the bacon box descended to the ground. But when the bruin hopped off the pole to get at the box, the lever sprung up and lifted the bacon out of his reach. After several tries, the bear apparently gave up and ran off. The men were smug and confident. The bear had made a great try to get the bacon, but the clever device had thwarted his efforts.

Amazingly, though, the bear soon returned, accompanied by a second bear. The first bear climbed the pole and lowered the bacon box to the ground. The second bear grabbed the bacon out of the box. The two bears ran off with the bacon, snapping at each other over their prize. It seems hard to believe, but it actually appeared that these two bears somehow communicated enough to plot this clever heist.

Encounters with grizzlies were rare, but Art did have several. One fall, Art headed into Schafer alone with a packstring. He planned on packing out extra supplies before the winter snows closed off access to the station. After the long ride, Art was happy to arrive at the station grounds.

"I came in late," he remembered. "I went in the bunkhouse and got a lantern and started for the combination building (the ranger station proper). I saw a flickering shadow cast in the lantern light, and I thought it was the shadow from the ladder. I thought, well gee, I pulled that. But the second time I looked, all I could see was a bunch of teeth coming at me. I beat him back to the bunkhouse."

Another time Art took a packstring up to the Green Mountain Lookout, on top of the divide between Schafer Creek and Spotted Bear River in the South Fork of the Flathead drainage. A crew had been fighting a fire there for about a week and Art would be packing out some of their camp after they mopped up their operations. The men at the camp were uneasy about a grizzly that had been coming in to their garbage pit. Art explained that if they kept the bear from getting at the garbage, he wouldn't keep returning.

"I cut some big logs and laid them over the pit," Art said. "I hadn't had much sleep over the past week so I just laid out my bedroll right up against one of those logs and went to sleep."

Art was stunned the next morning to find much of the garbage gone and grizzly tracks all over the place. The bear had rolled some of the logs off the other side of the pit and grabbed the garbage. Art had slept right through the bear's visit. Art was surprised the bear didn't bother him because he "probably smelled stronger than the garbage."

Art was ahead of his time in his attitudes about managing bears. He was careful not to let bears get food rewards and urged trail workers and station workers not to feed them. But he was dealing with a long-standing bear-feeding tradition that was commonplace in the backcountry. Art kept his advice simple to his co-workers: "All you have to remember is: don't feed them, don't let anyone else feed them, and don't let anyone put any garbage out, because they get to owning the place and they're dangerous. They like the food, but they don't like the people."

Even with all these brushes with problem bears, Art actually respected and feared moose more than any other animal. "I learned to stay clear of moose, they are more dangerous than the bear," he remembered. "They would go out there and feed in the swamp out by the airport. You couldn't get too close to take pictures, you'd see their hair stand up." Art was right. The only station worker ever seriously injured by an animal was a victim of a moose, years after Art served at Schafer.

Art was something of an amateur geologist, and he recognized early on the special geologic nature of the Middle Fork drainage and what would later become the Great Bear Wilderness. He spoke in an awestruck tone about guiding a small group of naturalists, which included a German geologist and a botanist, on an early survey in the upper Middle Fork. According to Art, the objective of the party was to document the special features of the area and advise the National Park Service as to its suitability for inclusion in Glacier National Park.

The geologist asked Art to guide them to Pentagon Mountain in what is now known as the Trilobite Range. The party started out from Schafer and rode across the Middle Fork, up Dolly Varden Creek trail, then on up the switchbacks for a total of five miles, climbing 2,200 feet in elevation. Finally, they reached the top of the windswept Chair Mountain.

Art had been waiting to show the party some of the rocks he'd seen there. He picked up a piece of rock that he called "conglomerate" and showed it to the German.

Art described the man's surprised reaction. "The geologist said, 'I've been to every mountain in the world, and I knew this existed, but I've never seen it'," related Art. "It was right there. I pointed it out to him. I said, on top of that Precambrian limestone is quartz, that doesn't happen, it's just not right. The German said, 'I'll tell you all about that tonight at the camp.' That night he told me, 'What you were looking at was the top of the earth's old crust, that mountain had turned completely over.'"

The geologist had recognized the unique overthrust belt, where, about 70 million years ago, some of the oldest sedimentary rocks in the world slid 50 miles or so over the top of younger deposits. The geologist told Art that he should be able to find caves in the limestone reefs, and Art told him that, indeed, he'd found a few.

The next morning the party broke camp in the little alpine basin in which they spent the night. Art guided the party another six miles through eye-

Young Art Whitney at a camp in the back country. Photo courtesy of Art Whitney.

popping alpine country along the spine of the Trilobite Range, gaining another 1,000 feet, to 8,200-foot Trilobite Peak.

Art continued: "And then I took him up to Trilobite Peak and showed him thousands of fossil shells, like oysters. At Trilobite lakes we found trilobites along the lakeshore. I'd seen pictures in National Geographic of what an old ocean bed looked like, and I could tell this was it." Art was thrilled to be able to examine these features and have them explained by a professional geologist.

Art didn't say if the party reached their original goal of Pentagon Mountain, another four miles along the spine of the Trilobite Range. But whether they did or not, they explored and documented the geology of some of the most spectacular high elevation, open country in the entire area which was to become the Bob Marshall-Great Bear Wilderness Complex.

On the trip back to Schafer, the awestruck geologist told Art that this was the most remote place he'd ever been to. He said it was the most unique natural area he'd ever seen and it should be left that way. Art felt good about the trip because he'd shared the area with someone who felt the same way he did about it, and who was as excited as he was about its unusual geology.

One of the mysteries that intrigued Art Whitney and other rangers at Schafer Meadows was the cave on Union Mountain, located across river a couple miles southwest of the station. Rumors about the cave are varied. Some say it offered a hiding place for William Schafer to stow his furs, or proceeds from his furs or prospecting. Others say it holds missing loot from a train robbery, gambling, or other valuables secured by Slippery Bill Morrison. Still others scoff at these stories, or even question the cave's existence.

The cave has not been found or visited by many, and it's never really been explored or searched. I've talked to two people (Art Whitney and Bill Chilton) who were actually in a cave at the base of the mountain, and

I've read Charlie Shaw's account. These visits were in the late 1930s and 1940s. I've talked to other rangers who were stationed at Schafer in more recent years who tried to find the cave, but failed. Descriptions of the cave differ. From what I've gathered, there may be more than one cave. This might make sense given the fact that the limestone ridge is subject to cave formation by groundwater and surface water flow, and multiple caves can easily form.

When a young Art Whitney started with the Forest Service at Schafer Meadows in the mid-1930s, he was fascinated by rumors about the cave. He could see the remnants of Schafer's cabin and other signs of Schafer's presence around the meadows. Schafer had died only about 25 years earlier. Acting on the description passed down in legend, he spent time exploring the Union Mountain area, looking for a cave. Finally, exploring the area with his dog and two men from the station, he succeeded.

Art described the cave's location as a ways up the Schafer trail, up on the ledge of rock at the base of Union Mountain where a mountain creek comes down. He says he walked right along the edge of this ledge where the ground was bare dirt, and found the cave almost at ground level. He said that others couldn't find it because they weren't looking in the right place, and that there's brush growing around it and it couldn't be seen unless you looked at just the right place.

"I found the cave and crawled in there," Art began. "I crawled on my belly until I came into a kind of dome shaped room. It was just about all you could do to crawl through."

The men who were with Art stayed in the outside area of the cave in a depression in the cliff that looked like the mountain had caved in. Art's dog, part shepard and part coyote, dug excitedly trying to reach Art after he'd entered the cave. Art had a flashlight and quickly examined the dome-shaped room. Then he turned around and began working his way back out.

"I could hear my dog digging and he could hear me; he was digging where I could see daylight. So I worked in that direction. The fellows grabbed me one on each wrist and pulled me out into the entrance. Up on top where it flattens off, I was walking there and found a hole and I dropped a rock in a hole and it fell straight down into the cave."

Bears, mystery caves and wilderness solitude all appealed greatly to a young ranger like Art Whitney. But in the late summer of 1938, Art found something even more appealing.

Maude Bally worked for the Forest Service in Kalispell. Art had talked to her by radio from time to time when he called out of Schafer on the wilderness phone lines. Maude asked Jack Root, the lead ranger at Schafer, if she and the supervisor's secretary, Katherine, could be escorted through the wilderness to Schafer Meadows to see the country and meet some of the rangers and others that they had talked to on the radio. This was the stated purpose for the trip, but I wonder if someone may have thought that it would be a good thing if the attractive, intelligent Maude met the tall, handsome, quiet bachelor stationed 24 miles into the backcountry. Root quickly arranged to take them to the wilderness outpost.

When Maude rode into the Schafer Meadows station she stole Art's heart immediately.

"I'd talked to her on the radio before," Art remembered. "Maude was a year behind me in high school, and I knew who she was because she played the flute solo at assemblies at Flathead High, where we both went. She took first in the state in the flute."

Fortunately for Art, his interest in the Union Mountain cave unexpectedly enabled him to endear himself to Maude and, as it ended up, changed both of their lives.

Maude and Katherine set up in the bunkhouse. Art's stories about the caves had intrigued Jack Root and he had mentioned them to the ladies. They all decided that it would be a good idea to go explore them.

Art, Root, and the two ladies mounted and rode up the main trail upriver, then turned and crossed the Middle Fork. They rode right by William Schafer's old cabin site and on up the Schafer Creek trail. After the short, 2-mile ride, the four explorers left their horses and climbed to the entryway of the caves. Art recognized the special nature of this trip to the caves when he described it:

"I had Maude right behind me when I crawled in there," he began. Jack was behind Maude, and Katherine was behind him. I got part way in there and I was wearing a 22 Colts automatic. It was so tight that I got kinda stuck and had to work my way back. I could tell Jack was nervous, and he said, "What's the matter, what's the matter!" So I finally got my arm back and got the gun pushed out of the way, and then I pulled on into the inner chamber. That's the second time I'd been in there. I was in there alone for a short time. Maude then came into the cave with me. I knew Maude was nervous. There was an echo sound. The cave chamber was not large, smaller than my living room. The ceiling was packed with gunk from bats, smelled a little musky. This was the first day I'd met Maude, knew right away she was something special. I got in there and I could tell she was nervous and I put my hand on her and I said, look, everything's okay."

Art said that at that moment, in the cave, on the first day they'd met, Art decided she was the woman for him.

And at the same time, Maude saw Art's courage, steadiness, and compassion, and the young woman came over to his side.

In his understated way, Art added, "I think she had a lot of faith in me after we visited the cave, because I know she was nervous."

The next day, Art took Maude and Katherine fishing for bull trout. There were some big bull trout caught, including a 12-pounder, but Maude had made the biggest catch. Art and Maude began dating that winter when he came out from Schafer Meadows. In the summer of 1940, Art asked her to marry him, and a few months later they began a special partnership that lasted almost 60 years.

Back in the 1930s when Art was in the Great Bear, rangers could just about write their own job description, and sometimes it included hands-on wildlife management. Most backcountry lakes were originally fishless, because trout from the Middle Fork or South Fork couldn't negotiate the steep outlet streams to reach and colonize the lakes. Art admired Castle Lake, which perched about a mile and a half and 800 feet in elevation above the Middle Fork. On his patrols and trail maintenance trips, Art often rode past the mouth of Castle Creek, about 11 miles downstream from Schafer Meadows.

"There were no fish in the lake," remembered Art, "and I thought, gee I'll bet that would be a good place for them."

So one day in the summer of 1938 or 1939, Art uncased his fly rod and fastened a dry fly on the end of his leader. He made casts quartering upstream in the gentle chop water in the river at the base of a run near the mouth of Castle Creek. The westslope cutthroat rose eagerly to the fly and soon Art had caught about a dozen of the black spotted, native trout.

But Art didn't keep these fish for dinner, or release them back into the Middle Fork. He put the dozen or so trout in two buckets and, with care, packed them up to Castle Lake. He spilled the buckets into the shallows at the north end of the lake, and watched the pioneering cutthroat swim away into unexploited water full of bugs, crustaceans, and other fish food.

"There were no fish in the lake before that," Art said. "I viewed this as something I could do to provide fishing in a beautiful place."

Art's founding members of the Castle Lake native cutthroat population thrived and reproduced in the new environment, and many anglers would have thanked him if they knew he'd originally packed them in. Helping make more fisheries for people to enjoy made Art feel good. And, in fact, if you are going to stock fish into a new environment, you couldn't do better than Art did for Castle Lake. He introduced native fish from a population from the nearest available water. This is now called the "nearest neighbor" approach to genetic cutthroat conservation, and Art may have been one of the first to practice it in the Middle Fork.

In 1940, Art packed cutthroat in milk cans on mules into Tom Tom Lake over in the South Fork of the Flathead drainage. These fish were probably nonnative hatchery-raised cutthroat. For better or for worse, Art was part of the "Johnny Appleseed" approach to fish management practiced by early rangers and others that resulted in many of the mountain lakes in the Great Bear and Bob Marshall being populated with trout. I'm glad there are fish in these lakes, but I wish everyone had the foresight Art practiced for Castle Lake, and packed in only native fish.

Art rarely had any trouble with lawbreakers in the Middle Fork. Fur trapping was off limits during the period, so he spent time looking for people who may have sneaked in to trap. From time to time, he'd also see evidence of poaching of moose or elk.

One of the primary outlaws in the Middle Fork was Joe Halley, who had a camp up Lodgepole Creek near the mouth of Whistler Creek, where some say Slippery Bill Morrison had a trapping cabin. The likable Halley had probably improved on Slippery Bill's old trapping base. Halley came into the Middle Fork from the east side of Marias Pass, probably following the same route used earlier by Slippery Bill.

"I first met Joe Halley down by Three Forks, alone," remembered Art. "I saw a moose track and a man track came in on it. It was Halley, and I knew he was in there poaching moose. He was an old fox. He had trapped in here for years and was probably still running a hidden trapline. I was in my 20s. He was probably in his 40s."

Art never caught Halley red-handed and never had enough evidence to charge him with anything, although other rangers did catch up to old Joe.

When Art left the Middle Fork in the early 1940s to move on to other Forest Service assignments, he left part of himself in this special country. "My time in the Middle Fork was an experience any young man should have, but not many do," said Art. "I hunted in there, but not too much cause it was quite a job taking game out. There were a lot of elk, and I killed some especially on the natural mineral licks above Schafer around Cox Creek. I saw up to 30 bulls in the spring working those licks."

Not only did Art see and experience things that almost no one else has, he even found the love of his life in the heart of the Middle Fork. Not a bad combination.

A Newlywed Ranger Finds Grizzlies and Adventure at Schafer

About six years after Art left Schafer Meadows, another tall young bachelor filled in where he had left off, also becoming part of the story of Schafer Meadows. In his 20s Bill Chilton, on horseback wearing a cowboy hat looked every bit like John Wayne, right down to the ruggedly handsome face and long, lean 6-foot-4-inch frame. Bill liked to joke that he was "5-feet 16-inches tall."

Like Art, Bill was kind of a jack-of-all-trades. He did a lot of trail maintenance, and soon became the ranger alternate. After the early 1950s, he was the alternate ranger in charge. Schafer had been designated as a subunit of the Spotted Bear Ranger District over the Middle Fork-South Fork divide. Charlie Shaw, who had been at Schafer a few years earlier, was the district ranger at Spotted Bear. Bill says he was the first official "wilderness ranger" as the job is defined now.

But one of his specialties was packing. Bill was a master with a packstring, something that backcountry folks considered a fine art.

On one job, Bill and Chuck Harrington, a remount packer, hauled up materials for a new lookout at Red Plume Mountain. Red Plume was an important lookout because it was the only one overlooking the upper Middle Fork drainage. There was an old lookout structure, but the Forest Service planned on replacing it with a standard lookout, 14 feet x14 feet with railing all around. Amazingly, they packed all the lumber from the old Java Ranger Station 21 miles downriver. It was a difficult pack because some of materials were long.

At the time, the Java ranger station consisted of a bunkhouse/warehouse, little hayshed and a few corrals. The station perched on a high bank above the Middle Fork of the Flathead River downstream from the mouth of Bear Creek, where the Great Northern tracks crossed the river on a high trestle. The station served as the jumping off point for Bill's trips into the upper Middle Fork.

"Ranger McConnell at Java cut up some of the lumber so we could pack it in," said Bill. "From Schafer, we'd ride downriver on Monday and on Tuesday, return loaded to Three Forks. We'd rest the stock on Wednesday, and then Thursday and Friday we'd round-trip it again. The remount packer, Chuck Harrington, had come up from Perma to help out, so we had two strings running steady."

This was one of the biggest packing jobs conducted in the Middle Fork at the time. All told, Bill and Chuck packed about 140 loads. Although Bill describes this matter-of factly, it is much harder than it sounds to pack this much big material 21 miles one way along a backcountry trail without crashes or rodeos. At one time, Bill says the Schafer district had seven lookouts, the materials to build all of which were originally packed in.

The packers got all the materials in to Three Forks, but they had to wait a few weeks to take it to the Red Plume lookout site because the snow was too deep. Later in the summer, they came downriver from Schafer and packed it all five more miles and 3,400 feet in elevation up to the site. Counting their return trip to Schafer, this was a 20-mile round trip and they made it many times to get everything up to the top of Red Plume. Bill and Chuck were satisfied with the lookout when it was completed. They must have built it well, because it withstood the high elevation winds and heavy snows for decades. It was last manned in 1973 and finally blew down in a windstorm sometime after that.

As a member of the army reserve, Bill was called up to duty at Fort Lewis

Bill leads his string along the Schafer Meadows airstrip in the fall of 1954. Bill was admired by many as a master packer. Bill and Barbara Chilton Collection.

from 1950 to 1952 during the Korean conflict. Bill yearned to return to the Middle Fork, and he did so in the late summer of 1952. But the assignment in Washington state proved to be a lucky one because while he was there he met his future wife, Barbara. Bill recognized the special qualities of the intelligent young woman right away and it didn't hurt that the attractive redhead looked like Maureen O'Hara.

"I was a city girl," she remembered. "I'd never been on a horse until I came over to Montana and spent Christmas with him in 1952. We got married the 2nd of January, 1953."

Bill bought Barbara a horse and saddle and in the late spring, the newlyweds planned on heading into the backcountry at Schafer Meadows where Bill had his old job back. Bill was 25 and Barbara was 21. "When you are in love, and you want to stay together, you do what you have to," she said. "I'm glad I did because it was a great experience."

In May, Bill headed in to Schafer to open up the station. At the end of May, he rode out to meet Barbara at the Big River trailhead near Java. The newlyweds mounted up on the first of June, and, with another Forest Service employee, began the 26-mile ride to Schafer. They rode the Big River trail that snaked along above the Middle Fork.

Bill and Barbara's life together was becoming an interesting backcountry story, kind of like a movie script. In fact, someone hiking or riding along the trail that day who saw the pair might have thought that John Wayne and his costar were heading into the wilds of Montana to film a movie.

Everything was peaceful on the beautiful spring day trail as the small party rode along. The flowers and bushes were vibrant, and the larch needles were bright green. The runoff-swollen river churned along below them. Finally, after 17 miles, they reached Granite Cabin perched on the rock ledges above the river near the mouth of Granite Creek. Barbara had done well on her first long horse ride. At the cabin, though, an unsettling sight greeted them. A bear had torn into the cabin, and its contents were strewn all around the clearing. On his ride out to meet Barbara, Bill had noticed that a bear had damaged the cabin, so he was looking for the bear. But he was surprised and annoyed by the size of the mess the bear had made.

Bill looked over to the open slide near the cabin and immediately saw the perpetrator. A small bear perched on the rocks, holding a sack of sugar in its teeth.

Without hesitation, Bill got off his horse and shot the bear.

"Then we started cleaning up the cabin," said Bill. "What a gosh-awful mess. There wasn't a can he hadn't bit into, and sugar and flour were everywhere. The bear had tipped over a large cabinet and it took all three of us to set it back up. He tore the bottom off the door and banged a hole in it, then crashed through a window on his way out."

It took the travelers four or five hours to clean up the mess the bear had made. They patched up the cabin the best they could.

This was the first bear Barbara had ever seen in the wild, and it was her first day in the backcountry. It was a jarring introduction to the Middle Fork, and she must have been uneasy. But it turned out that this little black bear was like Booboo compared to the bears they encountered later at Schafer Meadows.

Bill and Barbara continued their ride up the Big River trail towards Schafer. When they reached Three Forks, they stopped to look over the old Three Forks Guard Station. Heavy snows of the previous winter had caved in the roof and "pretty well ruined the cabin," according to Bill. It seemed like everywhere he looked, Bill saw projects that needed his attention. Maybe that's why he worked 15 hours a day, 7 days a week while he was at Schafer. "We'd be lucky if we could get him to take off a few hours on a Sunday afternoon," Barbara said.

During that first summer, Ranger Earl McConnell's wife came in for six weeks, so the Chiltons lived in a wall tent out behind the ranger dwelling. The tent rested on a wooden floor, with 4-foot wooden walls. Barbara had a cookstove and water bucket to work with at mealtimes. Barbara never saw another woman that summer after McConnell's wife left.

Bill and Barbara took advantage of the angler's paradise around Schafer. Westslope cutthroat trout eagerly rose to nearly any fly or lure. Live bait worked well for mountain whitefish. These large-scaled, silvery fish became active in the fall when they began their spawning runs. Once everyone in the station crew had their limits, they would load them 120 at a time in the smokehouse on chicken-wire racks. A 5-gallon can attached by stovepipe to an old tin stove supplied the heat and smoke that cured the fish.

Big bull trout offered the most exciting fishing. Five or six-pounders were excellent when fried or baked, while larger ones tasted better smoked. The best spawning streams were Dolly Varden Creek, Schafer Creek, and Morrison Creek. Bill says the bulls ranged from smaller, "jack" bulls 15 to 20 inches long to behemoths weighing more than 20 pounds. The big bulls were visible in deep holes in the Middle Fork upstream and downstream from the station.

Bill pointed out one big bull in the river near the mouth of Schafer Creek that weighed well over 20 pounds to members of a study crew that was beginning to track the movements of these big migratory fish. The crew couldn't catch that fish, but they did catch others with hook and line and by using a trap far downstream near Java. The crew marked the bulls at first, using a metal jaw tag. Bill noticed, though, that the metal tags were hard on the fish and the crew eventually stopped using them.

One of the last jobs Bill needed to finish as the summer of 1953 came to a close was to do something about the wrecked Three Forks Ranger Station. The Three Forks station was only five miles from Schafer and was really no longer needed to manage the wilderness, according to Bill. Rather than watch the place turn into a packrat paradise, Bill and Ronald "Red" Rogers, the Schafer station guard, decided to torch it.

On a wet day in late September, Bill and Red mounted up at Schafer and rode the five miles to the Three Forks site. Bill didn't decide to burn the cabin on a lark, because he respected the history of the site. The building had stood watch along the river for 43 years, since Allen Calbick built it from whipsawed logs he cut on the bench above the station area. Bill said that when it was first built, the flat surrounding the station had 90 acres of bunchgrass pasture. By 1953, Bill said there "weren't any acres of bunchgrass pasture," and lodgepole pine had claimed most of the openings around the station area. A cable crossing the river had deteriorated (it eventually went in the 1964 flood), and the area was little used in general.

The two men inspected the building. A poured concrete foundation had supported the walls. Amazingly, Calbick and his crew had packed all those sacks of concrete mix into the area in 1910. The roof was high and steep, and Bill was surprised the building had lasted as long as it had. The 20-foot rafters had collapsed into the center and brought a lot of the building crashing down with them. On the north side of the building was a shop and fire cache; on the south side was a kitchen area. The upstairs had been a bunk area. Bill and Red salvaged usable lumber and lathe from the building and stacked it well away from the wrecked building. They would return with a string and pack these materials to Schafer for future use.

After the men had salvaged what they could, they piled everything else inside. Bill entered the front door and "crawled over all that junk, spreading kerosene over everything." Bill exited the old building at the back door.

"I yelled at Red to touch 'er off, and we lit both sides of the building at once," Bill said. "Talk about burn! It wasn't five minutes to where you couldn't get close to that place. It burned so hot that it killed quite a few trees around it."

Bill, Barbara, and the station crew closed up the buildings at Schafer in late October and left the station to the winter snows. On November 26, 1953, their first child, Carol Ann, was born in Kalispell. The following spring, the couple bravely took their 6-month old daughter into Schafer to raise her in the wilderness.

The doctor had given Barbara various medicines and first aid supplies to take in for the infant. But nothing would prepare the baby and mother for what happened next. On a beautiful spring day, they loaded her collapsible high chair, crib and other baby furniture in a Cessna along with other supplies. Family friend Bob Robertson, a Nyack resident who made flights for the Forest Service, piloted the plane.

Everything was fine as the small plane flew up the Flathead River. The pilot and passengers enjoyed the view of the river below them, the green mountainsides, and snow capped peaks. They continued up the Middle Fork to Bear Creek and into the canyon of the upper river.

Then things went very badly very quickly.

"We left sunshine and 70 degrees," said Barbara. All of a sudden, we met a terrible snowstorm and blizzard. Bob just hung 'er low, following the river. We were already committed. We couldn't turn around."

Robertson piloted the plane just above the ground level, hugging the river. At times they couldn't see a side of the canyon only a hundred yards away. The plane pitched up and down, and the baby got sick. Finally, the weather opened enough for the pilot to locate the airstrip at Schafer and they landed safely.

"It was an ugly trip," said Barbara. I was never so happy to see the ground in all my life." After that, Barbara never again looked forward to getting in a small plane. Decades later, at Bill's Forest Service retirement party, Bob Robertson joked that Barbara's finger nail marks were still in the plane's dashboard.

Nail-biting flights and scary take-offs and landings into Schafer were not unusual. The Schafer Meadows airstrip is the only operating airstrip within the Bob Marshall Wilderness Complex. The airstrip is short and difficult, stretching about 800 yards when it was built in the 1930s.

The airstrip has a history of tragedy. Clearing for the airstrip was underway in 1934 when the first accident struck. Workers were clearing timber and snags for the strip using horses and a drag. A root sprung up from the ground and knocked one man down, shattering the bones in one of his legs. He was loaded on a horse and packed 11 miles downstream to Granite Cabin. Tragically, he died there that night, either from blood clots, the stress of being moved, or maybe hypothermia.

A number of planes have crashed on the airstrip. In one double crash, the pilots were likely watching moose on the airstrip and collided, one plane cutting the tail off the other. This took place in the fall of 1951 when Bill was in the army. One member of the hunting party who had been flown in earlier with the gear was waiting at the station. He saw the crash and rushed to the airstrip.

The man found one plane, with two people dead, about half-way down the airstrip just into the lodgepole on the strip's north side. The plane's tail had been sheared off and it crashed almost straight into the ground without breaking any trees. On the fuselage, he also noticed the fabric from another plane.

The man returned to the station. Using the phone mounted on the outside of the Schafer station building, he called Spotted Bear and told the Forest Service dispatcher that there had been a crash. He was told to break into the station so he would have a place to stay, and go see if he could find the other plane. He searched into the timber at the far end of the strip and found the other plane, which had struck a large spruce, slid right down it, and crashed into the swamp. He reported that there was little left of the pilot.

A Forest Service Ranger, the Sheriff and several others started in by horse that night from the trailhead to investigate the crash, a foolish move according to Bill. "Why they had to rush in the middle of the night, I don't know," said Bill. "None of them knew the country. They could have flown in there the next day to do their business." Bill said it took the officials all told about a week of "messing around" before they were done investigating the crash and retrieving the remains of the three men.

The next year, Bill and the remount packer collected some aluminum from the crashed plane. They melted it down and fashioned several sets of spurs from it to use for their horse wrangling.

To improve safety for approaches and take-offs, the Forest Service later lengthened the strip to about 1,000 yards. Bill said that to lengthen the airstrip, the Forest Service "walked in" a D-7 Cat from the east side.

"Jerry Rose, the ranger who followed me at Schafer, asked me how to get the Cat in there and I suggested they come from the east side to the top, then down Whistler-Lodgepole Creek because the country was flat enough to avoid problems," said Bill. "When they reached Morrison Creek they knocked out a few windfalls and went right into Schafer." Rose and the crew had good luck on the route, only once tipping over the "can" or pull cart attached to the dozer. Whether or not they knew it, they followed a similar route pioneered by early trappers like Slippery Bill Morrison, who likely entered the Middle Fork from the gentle east side way.

Barbara and Carol Ann (age 10 months) in the Schafer Guard Station in the fall of 1954. Each day, Barbara called out the weather to Forest Dispatchers. Bill and Barbara Chilton Collection.

The work crew removed downed trees from the east end of the airstrip and filled it in, removing a fence from a "wrangle pasture" Bill had built for horses. On the west end they filled in a gully that had caused a few problems. These improvements lengthened the airstrip out about 200 yards.

The improvements helped, but the airstrip still presents a challenge to pilots. I've had a number of spooky flights into Schafer not unlike Barbara's first flight. We've hugged the river during blizzards, and rumbled through mountain passes in rough weather with the plane only a hundred yards from the cliffs on one side. I watched members of my fisheries crew being flown out of Schafer when their plane cleared the top of the lodgepole at the downstream end of the strip by only a few feet. That gave me something to think about while I waited for the plane to return for me and some of our gear.

Although that first flight in was not a good start of the year for Barbara and Carol Ann, the young child thrived at Schafer. Luckily, she never got sick while she lived there. Raising her in the wilderness did present a few difficulties, though, especially during the next few years when the child became mobile.

"She was out playing in her sand box," Barbara began. "I was washing dishes, and all of a sudden I realized that the rocky sand wasn't making noise anymore. I went out the door, and Carol Ann was gone."

Barbara rushed from the ranger's residence over to the ranger station and told the station guard she couldn't find 3-year old Carol Ann. Barbara stayed around the Station grounds, searching frantically for her daughter.

The station guard trotted downriver on the trail looking for the little girl. Amazingly, he came upon the toddler just past the river junction trail. He "snapped up" the young girl, grabbed a stick, and "love-tapped" her all the way back to the station.

"I was just frantic," remembered Barbara. "The first thing you think of is the river. Thank goodness she went the right way on the trail. If she would have gone the other way she would have headed right for the river." Barbara sternly chastised her daughter.

It turned out that the crew had been cutting wood upriver by the spring. They had come in for lunch, and when they returned to the work site, the toddler must have followed them back upriver on the trail. Bill believed that the little girl had been attracted to the noise of an old tractor (flown in earlier on a C-47 transport plane) that they used to power their wood saw. In a stroke of luck, the Chilton's dog, Copper, had stayed with Carol Ann.

"We didn't think much of it when we saw her," said Bill, who was with the work crew. "When we saw her coming up the trail, we expected Barbara would be right with her. But that's when Red showed up and started switching her to get her to go home."

After learning that lesson, the couple grew even more watchful of the toddler, especially given the frequent visits by bears, both grizzly and black.

Bill's philosophy about bears was simple: he respected them greatly but he didn't hesitate to shoot bears that became too bold and threatened the station crew. As it turned out, he had to kill several bears that left him no alternative.

"A grizzly started coming around the station," Bill began. "He had a route, I guess. Every Wednesday, about 11 or midnight he'd show up. The first night we heard him out there, I got up to see what was going on. I went up to the window and looked out, with my face close to the glass. My eyes focused and I saw that the bear's nose was right against mine on the other side of the glass."

Bill and the grizzly were looking eye to eye, with only a thin pane of glass separating them. They were both surprised. The grizzly ran off.

As time went on, the big bear got bolder. "The next week he smashed our garbage can and tore things up," Bill continued. "The week after that, we heard the screeching of nails at about two in the morning on the front porch by the window."

The grizzly was tearing apart the wooden cooler and ransacking its contents. "I thought he was coming through the window," Bill said. "He opened up that wood box like a box of Cracker Jack, turned it over, and ate everything that was in it, including the butter and bacon."

The grizzly had been visiting the station regularly for four weeks when Bill finally decided he'd had enough. Bill was returning from an overnight downriver patrol and spotted the bear's tracks in the mud in the trail. He followed the bear's tracks for four miles, right up to the station. When Bill reached the station, Barbara told him the bear had come in about 6 a.m. that morning and woke her up. From their ranger's residence Barbara had called the station guard on the phone. The guard grabbed a gun and came out to take a look, but he retreated quickly

This is the massive grizzly shot one night outside the ranger residence at Schafer Meadows. The bear ran off into the brush east of the ranger station. About a week later, the smell from the bear attracted Bill Chilton to this carcass. Bill and Barbara Chilton Collection.

back into the station building without firing. He called, saying, "He's too big for us."

That night the grizzly came around again and "hammered" the Chilton's garbage can. Bill grabbed his rifle and fired a warning shot to scare him away. Bill came back to bed. "That will take care of him," he told Barbara. "He won't be back." But just as Bill laid his head on the pillow, the couple heard the grizzly smash the garbage can again.

The couple felt threatened and Bill's patience towards the bear ended. Bill jumped out of bed and grabbed his rifle, a 30-40 lever-action Winchester short saddle carbine, made during the Spanish-American war for cavalry. Bill hoped the 180-grain bullet would be enough to put the bear down if he had to shoot it. He armed Barbara with a flashlight and told her not to hold the light on the bear, but on the gun barrel so he could sight down its length. The couple was tense, but ready.

Bill opened the door, and then the screen door. Barbara snapped on the flashlight. "That grizzly was standing with his front feet on the porch," Bill said. "I shot him behind the head and down into his chest. He stood up on his hind legs and went over backwards. If he would have fallen forward he would have been in the house and I don't know what we would have done then."

Barbara froze. Bill jerked her back in the residence and kicked the door shut. He held the rifle and they both listened for movement.

"We knew it was hit," Barbara said, "because he let out the most blood curdling roar I ever heard in my life. We knew he was hit but didn't know if the shot killed him."

The couple went back to bed, and according to Barbara, "shook the rest of the night." The bear had been up on their porches for a month or more, and anxiety and stress had been building in their minds. Justifiably, Barbara had been afraid to go outside the residence at night. That night, Barbara said they were especially nervous because they didn't know if there was a wounded grizzly just outside their door.

Bill had not wanted to shoot the grizzly but he felt it finally left him no choice. Grizzlies were not protected then, and Bill's action was clearly in self-defense. But Bill had compassion for grizzlies and shot the bear only as a last resort.

Rain fell heavily the rest of that night, so Bill couldn't follow the grizzly's trail the next morning. Days passed, and the grizzly didn't come back on Wednesday or Thursday like he always did. Bill concluded that the grizzly "must have checked out someplace along the line."

Bill and his crew had to shoot only one other grizzly during his time at Schafer. A small black bear had been coming around the station and was spending time on the porch of the ranger's residence, brazenly getting into garbage and food and showing no fear of humans. One night, Bill heard something on the back porch. He looked out and saw the little black bear.

"I had an old .45 pistol," said Bill. "I was looking for shells for it, because I decided to open the door and shoot him through the screen door."

After Bill loaded the pistol he looked out again but the bear had disappeared. Bill called over to the station and told Ken Bell, the packer, that there was a bear on its way over. It was just that little troublesome black bear, Bill told him. He asked the packer to shoot the bear because it had become too bold and could be a danger to the crew or to visitors.

Bill looked out the window of the residence cabin and watched the packer walk out of the cookhouse. Ken aimed and fired.

"I walked out," Bill said, "and asked, did you get him? And he said, 'yeah I shot him and he ran off.' I said, it was just a little black bear, wasn't it? He said 'no it wasn't a little black bear, he was as high as that rail on your woodshed,' which was pretty high. Well, I said, I only saw a little black bear."

About a week later, a man riding on the trail near the residence asked Bill if the swamp near the powder cache always smelled so bad in the fall. Bill told him that, no, he didn't remember that it smelled bad, but maybe there's something dead there. The two men went over and searched the area. They found the dead grizzly that Ken had shot. The bear had made it about 200 yards across a little swampy meadow and died. The huge grizzly's head measured 12 inches between the ears, and its claws were nearly six inches long.

Although Barbara described these encounters with bears as "hair-raising experiences," much of life around Schafer was calm and enjoyable for her. When the station workers were gone for the day, Barbara had a routine she followed. Each afternoon she would radio out and give a weather report. She cooked for the crews and often had dinner ready when they returned in the evening. Several times each week she cooked a big roast so it was in the oven and ready for the men. The station received fresh groceries once a week, transported in by small fixed wing plane. The airstrip served as a major lifeline for supplies and mail.

Like the rangers before him, Bill was intrigued by the stories about the mysterious cave at the base of Union peak. Ranger and history buff Charlie Shaw told Bill where to find the cave, but Bill said it was "all full of rocks" when he visited it; and that it would have been a "major chore" to uncover the cave's entrance. Bill found what he believed was a man-made hole that had been camouflaged on the ledges above the cave, and he thought it could be used as a hiding place for loot or furs. It appeared that whoever dug the shaft dumped the dirt into the creek below. The shaft was sunk 30 feet into the ground, and although it looked like it could join the cave, Bill could not find a connection.

The shaft and cave that Bill described could be in a different location, perhaps lower on the mountain, than the one described by Art Whitney. Art didn't believe that the cave he found would be a practical place to hide anything because it was hard to get to, being hundreds of feet in elevation above Schafer Creek and several miles from the river.

Charlie Shaw, the ranger at Schafer in 1943 and 1944, visited a cave on Union Mountain and wrote that the cave had "the appearance of having been inhabited—smoky ceiling at the entrance." Shaw said the cave had never been studied, and when he last visited it in 1944, its entrance was mostly closed by talus rock.

The mystery of the Union Mountain caves drew the interest of both early and later rangers at Schafer Meadows. Did early pioneers William Schafer or Slippery Bill Morrison use the caves for concealing furs, loot or themselves? Did early people use these caves even before these old-timers wandered in the upper Middle Fork? It's unlikely these questions will be answered soon. The caves are remote, and by most accounts are probably closed by rockslides and talus by now. They haven't been visited for perhaps half a century. The mystery intrigues me, but I'm not sure if I'll ever have the energy or time to try and solve it. To reach the cliffs and begin to search, you must first hike 15 miles from the Morrison Creek trailhead, cross the Middle Fork, hike several miles up Schafer Creek, and then scramble up the cliffs to the series of ledges. Flying in to Schafer airstrip is an option, but that would make it too easy and wouldn't seem right. For now, the mystery of the Union

Mountain caves remains safely in the realm of legend.

During his patrols, Bill Chilton, like other rangers, crossed paths with the likable "renegade trapper" Joe Halley from time to time. Bill noted that Halley had one camp at Whistler Creek and another at Morrison Creek. Halley didn't like people asking him questions. He mostly blew off Bill when Bill ran into him.

"He was a character," said Bill. "I got kind of a kick out him, because he didn't like people to snoop around. If you came into his camp he'd feed you or give you a cup of coffee or whatever, but he didn't want you looking at anything." A classic poacher, Joe didn't take game laws seriously, and he violated them just about all the time he was in the wilderness.

One day, Bill met a man hunting along Morrison Creek near the mouth of Crescent Creek in the early fall. The man was watching a mineral lick, waiting for an elk to walk out so he could shoot it. The man said Joe Halley had packed him in there and told him he should be able to find an elk there.

"The elk season wasn't even open in that area, and he was 15 or 20 miles from the nearest open area," Bill said. "I was riding a big horse and this guy wasn't very big. So I put him up behind me and we rode the eight or ten miles into Joe's camp on Whistler Creek. We rode into camp, and I got right on Joe's case. Joe just laughed, he wasn't concerned at all."

Joe Halley trapped for decades in the Morrison drainage, even though fur trapping was off limits in the wilderness during much of the time he was in there. Joe was able to mostly evade the law though, and only once did a ranger ever catch Joe red-handed with illegal furs.

That time, making a quick decision under pressure, Joe showed wit and resourcefulness. Joe and a partner were packing out a nice bale of beaver. When they had reached the head of Morrison Creek, they looked across the ridge and saw Fred Neitzling, who was the ranger from Essex, and a game warden heading their way. Neitzling saw Joe hurriedly shove a few things in his packsack, and then head down the drainage.

The lawmen caught up with Joe after a few miles. He was sitting by a small fire and offered the men some tea. Suspecting what Joe had been up to, they kicked the fire away and found a kit beaver hide and a damaged beaver hide that he had buried in the snow under the fire. The lawmen escorted Joe out of the wilderness and when they reached the rails, Neitzling flagged down a train. They took Joe into Kalispell, where he saw the judge and paid a $30 fine for poaching beaver.

But Joe Halley had the last laugh. That next morning his partner mushed out of Morrison Creek with a toboggan loaded down with the prime beaver they had trapped. Joe's partner had stashed the bale of beaver, and Joe had served as a decoy to lure the lawmen away from their real fur cache.

Legal fur trapping was reinstated in the Middle Fork during Bill Chilton's

first years in the backcountry.
Bill rode over to Halley's camp
to inform him of the upcoming
trapping season and to ask Joe if he
was going to put in for a beaver-
trapping permit. "I guess I should,"
Joe replied. "I've been waiting 40
years to trap a legal beaver in here."
Even Bill had to laugh at that one.

The state issued beaver trapping
permits for three sections of the
Middle Fork. These areas included
Bear Creek to Granite Creek,
Granite to Schafer Meadows, and
Schafer to the headwaters. Trappers
were limited to a quota of 33 beaver
in each area. Bill Chilton says that
Phil Buck and Floyd Coverdell

Bill and Carol Ann at the Schafer airstrip in late summer, 1957. Within a month, the Chiltons would fly out of the remote Middle Fork for the last time. Bill and Barbara Chilton Collection.

had the section from Granite to Schafer. The men caught their limit of 33
beaver, many of them in the meadows near the airstrip at Schafer. This was
an advantage for the Forest Service, because keeping the beaver thinned out
prevented flooding. During spring, water backed up by the beaver dams
flowed over the airstrip and made for dangerous landings. The trappers
skinned the beaver in the woods. Bill enjoyed watching the trappers flesh
the hides in the bunkhouse. A departing plane transported the men's beaver
pelts out of the wilderness, while they rode out and picked up their gear at
Granite Cabin. Joe Halley never applied for or received a permit. He kept
on trapping as long as he could, under his own "quota system."

In the fall of 1957, Bill prepared to leave Schafer as the alternate ranger
for the last time. He would go on to a long and productive career, serving
decades with the Forest Service around the Flathead. Bill and Barbara closed
the shutters, drained the water systems, and closed up the ranger residence,
the station building, and the bunkhouse.

The couple heard the whine of the Travelaire and watched Bob Robertson
pilot the plane around to the east side of the airstrip for the approach. Bob
brought the plane in for a perfect touch-down. Barbara gathered up Carol
Ann, who was nearly 4 years old, and they buckled into the plane's seats.
The seat and rear door had been removed from the back of the plane, so Bill
crawled in with their dog, Copper, and sat on the floor among some of their
personal gear.

The plane roared down the runway and lifted over the trees, swinging
southwest along Union Mountain. Bill could look out the opening where

the rear door had been. He took a long look at the country he'd grown to love. Gaining elevation, the plane pointed south up Schafer Creek, heading for Whitcomb Peak and the South Fork Divide, eventually landing at Spotted Bear.

The ranger and his wife had come to Schafer Meadows as newlyweds and began their family there. They were lucky. They had lived safely for an idyllic handful of years away from civilization in the middle of what was to become the Great Bear Wilderness. Their little girl had spent wonderful summers where little girls were unheard of. Bill had put his heart into his work at Schafer, and he would have stayed on there; but a permanent, year-around job nearer civilization would be more practical for his family. Art returned to the Middle Fork for inspection trips after the 1964 flood, but he never stayed again at Schafer for long.

Now, like William Schafer, Slippery Bill Morrison, and the rangers before and after him, Bill Chilton had become part of the history and legend of the heart of the Middle Fork.

Chapter 7
GRIZZLY ATTACK ON MOUNT PENROSE
C. B. Penrose's grizzly hunt and
the naming of the Great Bear Wilderness

More than a century ago, Philadelphia Surgeon and Boone and Crockett Club Member C.B. Penrose shot a white grizzly in a high, untracked backcountry basin below the mountain that now bears his name. This adventurer's gunshot set in motion a chain of fate, bad luck, and violence that came together in the naming of Middle Fork mountains and streams, and by extension, the Great Bear Wilderness.

The 250,000-acre Great Bear Wilderness is a massive chunk of land that stretches 52 miles from Kootenai Creek near the town of West Glacier, southeast to Trilobite, Elk and Dean Ridges on the northern boundary of the Bob Marshall Wilderness. For the first 25 of these miles, the Great Bear is about 3-6 miles wide as the raven flies. Along this stretch, the Great Bear is bound by Glacier National Park and the Middle Fork Flathead River on the east, and the Flathead Range and South Fork of the Flathead River on the west. For the next 27 or so miles of its length, it averages about 16 miles wide, sharing a 25-mile boundary with the 1.2 million-acre Bob Marshall at its southeast terminus.

Lands of the Great Bear are drained by the Middle Fork of the Flathead River, which flows for about 30 miles along its east and north perimeter, from West Glacier to Bear Creek followed by U. S. Highway 2. At Bear Creek, U. S. Highway 2 bends east to Marias Pass, and the Middle Fork extends 40 miles upstream through the interior of the Great Bear and then the Bob Marshall. It shouldn't surprise anyone that the untamed Middle Fork is considered to be Montana's wildest river.

To give you an idea of how big it is, and how rugged it is, I don't think the best hiker in Montana could traverse the Great Bear north to south along the spine of the mountains in less than a month. That's partly because of size of the area, and the fact that it's dissected by dozens and dozens of

Charles Bingham Penrose, from an oil painting. C. B. was a fine surgeon, a courageous man, a hunting fanatic and a wildlife advocate. C. B. was also the president of the Pennsylvania Game Commission from 1911 until 1924, and the president of the Philadelphia Zoological Society. Courtesy of the Pennsylvania Game Commission.

heavily timbered, steep creek drainages running east to west from the Flathead Range. But it's mostly because it's one of the steepest, rockiest, brushiest areas in the state with tangles of downed trees, alder, Pacific yew, and devil's club that can be nearly impossible to negotiate. Believe me, I have lots of personal experience with this.

A word about devil's club is probably in order here, because the Middle Fork country is almost defined by it. Also, this nasty shrub and the other plants that make up the impenetrable brush of the Middle Fork country affected the events that led to the naming of the Great Bear. Devil's club has large leaves that look a lot like the leaves of the thimbleberry. The leaves of the devil's club, though, have prominent spines on their undersides and veins. Worst of all, from the plant there extends long, brown, spine-covered clubs, hence its name. On steep slopes it's tempting to grab one of these clubs for balance but few gloves are tough enough to repel the spines. I love devil's club in a way because it's such a part of the Middle Fork, and this plant, along with alder, nettles and a few others, definitely is part of the reason that the country is still lightly traveled.

My love-hate relationship with devil's club and alder in the Middle Fork country began decades ago. I'm glad I can't remember all the times I lost a trail for some reason or tried to drop cross-country from a high mountain lake to a lower trail to "save time," and became entangled in alder and devil's club. It's tempting to do this because the country above about 6,500 feet in elevation is fairly open and brush free. You look down- slope a few thousand feet and think, "that doesn't look too bad from here." But more often than not after you drop part way down you end up eight or ten feet above the actual ground surface, sliding down the alder branches as they bend down-slope.

I remember dropping out of trail-less Sheep Lakes with my friend Dale Sommerfield one September. We had reached the upper lake at about 7,000 feet in elevation after four hours of climbing and then hiking along a relatively open ridge from the backside. We easily "collected" (with hook and line of course) a sample of gullible westslope cutthroat trout for genetic testing at the upper lake, and then dropped over the side of the cirque to follow the outlet down about 1,000 feet in elevation to the lower lake.

This drop wasn't terrible, although it was a lot brushier than it looked. After we collected our sample at the lower lake, we realized that we were kind of stuck. So rather than going out the way we'd come in, we decided to use gravity and drop down directly to Sheep Creek which had a "trail" along its length. We had both done things like this lots of times, but I guess we were trying to test the definition of insanity. I realized we fit the definition again when, about a quarter of a mile into the drop, I was crawling from a downed snag to the next alder branch while clinging to a devil's club. I don't think our feet touched the actual ground much during the entire descent.

I used to get upset when the Forest Service trail crews would cut brush along one of my favorite trails in the Middle Fork country because it encouraged more hikers to enter the area. I found out that I didn't have to worry too much, though, because trail clearing in this country with its tenacious vegetation only lasts a few years.

The Great Bear Wilderness, of course, is named after the great bear, Ursus arctos. The Great Bear Wilderness has always been prime grizzly country. Gordon Pouliott, who lived for decades near Nyack on the wilderness perimeter, told me he once had special steel bars made for all the windows in his house to keep grizzlies out. Once he had to shoot a big male that was ransacking canned food on his screened-in porch. He shot the big grizzly right through his living room window.

Gordon killed a number of grizzlies on his property, sometimes under questionable circumstances. Gordon explained that the Great Bear, being sandwiched between the Flathead Range and Glacier National Park, was a prime grizzly travel corridor. I think the state and federal bear biologists would probably agree with him. Gordon was considered by some to be a local authority on grizzlies, having been featured in *Life* magazine and other publications. He was a colorful local historian and we talked from time to time about how grizzly bears figured in the naming of Great Bear Creek.

Back in 1907, the entire area of northwest Montana was lightly traveled and mostly wilderness. A small party of topographical surveyors of the U. S. Geological Survey, led by Arthur Alvord Stiles, was the first group of officials to survey what is now the Great Bear Wilderness and the South and Middle Forks of the Flathead Drainage. From the passes, Stiles and his party could look east from the top of the Flathead Range and see the spectacular country that would be designated three years later as Glacier National Park. Stiles referred to the steep, rugged expanse of mountains he was surveying as a "God forsaken region" with "high and rugged mountain peaks, snowfields, and living glaciers, wholly uninhabited except by the wild animals, and well nigh inaccessible save in the dead of winter when some adventurous soul of doubtful judgment might make his way thither on snowshoes."

Stiles was right in his assessment about winter travel. Travel in the brush zone of these mountains is much easier with 10 feet of snow cover, as long as the avalanche danger isn't bad. One spring, my friend Mitch Richeal and I skied up past Skiumah Lake, and scaled the cirque above it, not far from the top of the range where Stiles and his party had crossed. It was steep, but not bad at all because the snow was set up firmly. During the snow-free period, though, it would be nearly impossible to get through the alder. When you look at it in the summer from a distance, the hillside looks like a vast green carpet with lines of conifers here and there. The only problem is when you experience it up close, the carpet is about 12 feet thick with alder, pacific yew, and devil's club.

Stiles and his party were equipped with camping equipment and map-making instruments, all transported by a pack-train of mules. The party cut a small trail as they traveled; he believed that theirs was the first pack outfit that had ever entered the area and he was probably correct.

The survey party entered from the west side of the Flathead Range near the present town of Hungry Horse, and traveled upstream about 25 miles in the South Fork of the Flathead Drainage to the Middle Fork Divide. Stiles and his party most likely following the Emery Creek-Hungry Horse Creek drainages and then the ridge between Margaret and Tiger Creeks to reach the top of the divide that separates the South and Middle Forks of the Flathead River.

The Penrose brothers, part of a prominent Philadelphia family, accompanied the survey party into the backcountry. It's hard to imagine a more influential and adventurous trio of brothers. Dr. Charles B. Penrose, 45, was a respected Philadelphia surgeon and a governor-appointed member of the Pennsylvania Game Commission. Bois Penrose, 47, was an influential U. S. Senator from Pennsylvania who lived in Washington, DC. Both of these men were among the 100 original regular members of the Boone and Crockett Club and friends of President Theodore Roosevelt, even though Bois and Roosevelt disagreed on politics from time to time. Another brother, Spencer Penrose, 42, of Colorado, was along for the adventure. Spencer was a millionaire many times over, gaining his fortune in mining and real estate. He built his Colorado fortune on a loan from Bois. At age 27, a Harvard graduate but down on his luck from womanizing and irresponsibility, he had wired his older brother and asked for $10,000 to sink into the Cash on Delivery Mine in Colorado Springs. Instead, Bois wired him $150 for the train fare back to Pennsylvania. Undaunted, Spencer invested that money in the mine and it became the basis for his great wealth.

The Penroses had been traveling (in style, no doubt) around the Lewis and Clark Forest Preserve where the going was relatively easy, using packhorses on maintained trails. Charles, who was probably the more serious hunter of the three, decided he wanted the adventure of hunting big game in this untracked wilderness. So, using their influence, the Penroses hooked up with the U. S. Geological

This is the glacial basin where Penrose and Stiles tied their horses and began their hunt. Mt. Penrose rises above the basin in the top left of the photo. Author Photo.

Survey party, and according to Stiles, "were conducted well up among the snow-capped peaks of the range." As it turned out, when it was all said and done, Charles got way more adventure than he expected or wanted.

We've all had experiences that we wish we could rewind and play back differently. If Charles Penrose could do that for his actions on the evening of September 1, 1907, I'll bet he would.

The Penrose brothers were camped that evening a short distance from the survey party near the top of the Flathead Range on the edge of the present Great Bear Wilderness. The country here at 7,000 feet in elevation drops off in both directions from the range backbone in steep and rocky ridges with high elevation basins of more moderate terrain. The area of the survey camp was mostly open because of its elevation and because it had burned in the past. Think of it as a north-to-south running spine of pretty alpine country and rugged peaks about half a mile wide, with more or less impenetrable steep, alder and devil club- choked approaches from the east and west, and you've got the picture.

Back at the survey camp, Stiles had some extra time on his hands. It was about four o'clock in the afternoon, and the weather hadn't been ideal for surveying and mapping. So, eager to please his important guests, Stiles rode over and offered to take Senator Penrose out for a hunt in a spot not far away where the surveyors had probably established a small "spike camp." But Senator Bois Penrose and his younger brother were too tired from their recent long, rigorous climb, so they declined. Dr. Charles Penrose, who was in great shape compared to his brothers, eagerly volunteered to go with Stiles to the basin where members of the party had seen game about a mile and a half northwest along the spine of the range. It doesn't happen very often, but in this case being in great shape got Charles into a lot of trouble.

Stiles and Penrose mounted their horses and negotiated the broken, relatively open country around the head of the drainage, and then by way of a small saddle to the pretty little basin. The basin sat at about 6,500 feet in elevation below a big mountain that rose another 1,500 feet above it. The two men tied their mounts to stunted, krummholz conifers. Then they separated, looking for game around opposite sides of a small ridge in the basin.

Everything must have seemed just right: the views were spectacular, there wasn't another party around for maybe 50 miles, and the hunting was wide open with no rules and limits (that anyone would enforce). This was 100 years after Lewis and Clark, but these two men had to feel some of the same freedom that they had.

Penrose walked for about half a mile along the rocky ridge through scattered snags dead from past fires, and through beargrass, stunted trees, and alpine meadows. Above the basin, he hunted across a slide that held masses of boulders. Suddenly, he saw a light-colored grizzly bear approaching him from about 75 yards. The bear hadn't seen him because it had been nosing the ground. Penrose took aim with his 7mm Mauser and fired a shot at the bear. Penrose fired twice more as the bear stumbled and rolled about 200 yards down the ridge. The grizzly's body finally came to a stop by a small creek.

Penrose made his way down the ridge along the edge of the boulder slide. He reached the little creek and admired the dead bear, the "whitest" grizzly he had ever seen. The bear appeared to be a yearling and a yearling grizzly can look pretty big without a larger bear to compare it with.

The doctor was elated. What a trophy he would have to take back to his home in Philadelphia. He leaned his gun on a rock and began to take out his knife to skin the grizzly. Then, his eye caught movement on the ridge across the creek just 30 yards away. Looking up, Penrose saw two more white grizzlies, a large sow and a yearling, probably the sibling of the bear he had just killed. The hair on the sow's back bristled, she growled, and then

After Penrose shot a yearling grizzly, he bent down and prepared to skin his trophy. His eye caught movement and he looked up to see a large adult grizzly across the little creek. The grizzly charged immediately. Courtesy of Montana Fish, Wildlife & Parks, Derek Reich.

charged full speed at the startled doctor. The sow charged Penrose like a dog, keeping its head low, and boring in on this lower body. In an instant, the doctor's hunt had changed from really good to really bad.

Grabbing his rifle, Penrose shot at the bear twice as it charged towards him. One of these bullets broke the bear's hind leg near the paw. Penrose was able to shoot the bear in the left shoulder just as the bear pounced on him.

The 170-grain bullets from the Mauser didn't seem to affect the bear. The big grizzly grabbed the doctor's left thigh in her teeth and shook him "like a terrier does a rat." Penrose fell backward into the creek with the grizzly clamped onto his leg. The bear then bit and crushed his left wrist, dropped that, and bit and shook his left breast area. Suddenly, the bear stopped mauling the doctor, but stood over him growling. After playing dead for a few seconds, Penrose grabbed for his gun again, which was lying beside him near the stream. The movement drew a renewed attack from the grizzly. The bear bit through the doctor's felt hat and into the scalp, then bit Penrose's face so severely that one of the bear's canines penetrated the doctor's cheek and snapped off one of his teeth. The bear stopped the attack and this time, Penrose lay still.

The huge sow crossed the creek and walked up on the bank on the opposite side about 20 yards away. She leaned against a small, stunted tree and slumped over. Penrose could see blood oozing from a wound on the sow's left hip and realized that one of his shots had wounded her mortally. Unfortunately for the doctor, the bear had plenty of energy to nearly kill him before she became weak from loss of blood.

Penrose thought that the grizzly had attacked him in revenge because he had killed the yearling bear. The doctor recalled how grizzlies had often charged men of the Lewis and Clark expedition 100 years earlier, before they had learned to fear man. Penrose reasoned correctly that these grizzlies he encountered had likely never seen a man before, so the sow did not hesitate to attack him. The doctor found, just as the early explorers had, that grizzlies are not easy to stop with a firearm. Meriwether Lewis described the grizzly as a "turrible" looking animal, which we found verry hard to kill," after he and one of his men fired 10 balls into a large male bear before it finally died.

As Penrose sat up, covered in blood, he saw that the third bear was still close by. Amazingly, in spite of his severe injuries and worsening shock, the doctor was able to pick up the Mauser, aim, and squeeze the trigger. This time the hammer clicked on an empty chamber. The doctor felt his pockets for more shells but his remaining ammunition had been lost in the struggle. Although the gun didn't fire, lucky for Penrose the third bear growled, turned, and loped away. The entire episode had lasted only moments.

Meanwhile back on the other side of the basin, Stiles had seen a "fine buck deer." Stiles began to back away from the buck. He planned to find Penrose and bring him back to shoot it. Then, Stiles heard Penrose's first shots and thinking that the doctor had bagged game, he turned to shoot the mule deer himself. But when more gunshots echoed from Penrose's direction Stiles became alarmed and hurried over to find the doctor. It took him about 5 or 10 minutes to reach the other side of the ridge where Penrose had shot the bears. As Stiles came around a "jumbled mass of boulders," he was shocked by what he saw.

Stiles said that he saw the doctor in shock, "wandering aimlessly around in the canyon bed." Penrose had lost his gun and his hat. His coat was gone and his pants were torn in pieces. The doctor's head and neck were covered with blood and he held his left arm in his bloody right hand. The pitiful man moaned, "Water, water."

Stiles ran to the small stream on the other side of the rocks and brought a cowboy hat full of water to the thirsty doctor. As the injured man drank, Stiles could see water pouring through a gash in his right cheek. Penrose told Stiles that he was "all in," and that he had "a fight with a bear."

Ragged strips of flesh hung from a long, two-inch wide gash on the doctor's left thigh. One of the bear's teeth had ripped his throat, and five gaping punctures marked his chest. Penrose's left wrist was twisted and broken with bones protruding from the "quivering flesh." His scalp was torn. Tearing strips of cotton signal cloth, and using simple first aid items he had with him, Stiles bandaged the worst of the doctor's wounds. From the doctor's description and from looking quickly over the scene of the disaster, Stiles got a good idea of what had happened.

The two men slowly made their way back to the horses. In their minds, they began to face reality. The doctor had sustained life-threatening injuries, and they were in the middle of an untracked wilderness. Stiles knew that it would be almost impossible to transport Penrose out of the wilderness in time to save him, given the doctor's trauma and blood loss.

Stiles wrapped his "cow boy slicker" around the doctor, and helped him up on his horse. Stiles mounted Penrose's horse and led the horse carrying the injured man over the 1-1/2 trail-less miles back towards the Penrose party's camp. The doctor bravely tried to hide his tremendous pain. Stiles hid his dismay and growing sense of doom about the doctor's chances. After much difficulty they reached the canvas teepees just as the evening light faded.

The doctor's disastrous condition stunned the men anxiously waiting at the camp. Bois and Spencer Penrose probably started rehearsing in their minds how they were going to explain how they had allowed their prominent brother to be killed in the wilds of Montana. Most of us have experienced this: It's just human nature to start thinking the worst when someone we care about is lost or seriously injured.

Stiles was elected to perform the amateur surgery on the doctor. Ironically, Penrose had earlier published a much-cited article on antiseptic surgery, and was considered an expert on the subject. In Stiles, Penrose was lucky that such a calm and capable man was available and willing to take on such a responsibility. The men built a large, bright fire of pitch pine to provide light and warmth, and laid the doctor on a ground cloth. Luckily, the doctor had brought along a surgical kit on the trip, and he was cognizant enough to direct Stiles on how to stitch and patch up his wounds. Penrose injected himself with a "quarter of a grain of morphia." Stiles applied bichloride of mercury on each wound to slow the infection that would inevitably come to the bites and tears.

Finally, Stiles examined the doctor's crushed left wrist and huddled with the other men to decide how to treat it. They agreed that the best approach would be to extract the bone shards, which stuck out at various angles. Penrose told Stiles to have at it, thinking he could endure the pain without anesthetics. But as Stiles began, the doctor passed out from the intense pain. The men changed their minds after that, and simply bound up the wrist again in signal cloth and plaster. It was one o'clock in the morning according to Stiles's watch. Stiles realized that any further medical work would have

Stiles and his party brought C. B. Penrose down from Mt. Penrose and through the impenetrable alder, devils club, and Pacific yew of the Rescue Creek Drainage. Author Photo.

to be done by a real surgeon, if they could get Penrose out of the wilderness alive.

The men helped the doctor into a sleeping bag and carried him to a tent. At this point, Bois and Spencer Penrose could no longer bear to watch the suffering of their brother and they "retired to another tent." Stiles lay down near the suffering man to wait until dawn.

Stiles couldn't sleep. He knew the doctor's wounds would probably become infected; predator bites almost always do. He could not imagine how they would transport the doctor back over the range and down the South Fork, the way they had come in. It would require a climb of 600 feet in elevation on foot to gain the spine of the ridge by which they had entered the area, then a long pack down the ridge and along the South Fork of the Flathead. He calculated correctly that it would take two days at least to cover the 25 rugged miles and reach civilization and the railroad following that route. He knew that Penrose couldn't last, and by the second day they would be "packing out a dead body." If they could get the doctor to the railroad more quickly he had a chance to live, because he could be transported east to a hospital.

During that long night Stiles asked himself over and over again how they would ever manage to get Dr. Penrose out of the rugged mountains. Before dawn Stiles had his inspiration. He decided to "run a hazard" and take an unheard-of route. The rescue party would plunge down-slope to the east through the thick vegetation and cliffs on the opposite side of the range to reach the Middle Fork Flathead River and the railroad that ran along it. The distance in that direction was only about five miles, but nearly 4,000 feet of treacherous elevation had to be negotiated. Few in the party thought it could be done with horses but Stiles insisted, hoping that "providence might point the way." The party made preparations to start at dawn.

The Penroses were lucky to have such a decisive and daring man in charge of their fate. Stiles stayed calm under incredible pressure. Imagine how he felt. He had taken on a hunt a prominent man, a friend of President

Nyack Station, circa early 1900s. The sign behind the "mail grabber" reads: "Western Union Telegraph Office." After the 14-hour trip down Rescue Creek, the rescue party reached this tiny station with the injured C. B. Penrose. Bois and Spencer Penrose loaded their brother on the eastbound train the next morning and accompanied him to the Mayo Clinic. Betty Robertson Schurr Collection.

Theodore Roosevelt, and practically got him killed. He had performed amateur operations on his injuries, and now he had to negotiate a route with the severely injured man that no one in his party thought was possible.

At first light Stiles and the little rescue party left the camp and crossed the pass into the head of Rescue Creek. Stiles' large black horse again carried the injured doctor. Bois and Spencer Penrose walked on either side of the horse to support their brother. Bill Hague, the party's best guide, led the way, leading two packhorses with equipment, food, and water. Two young members of the survey party, boys from the east coast, wielded axes to clear a route for the horses to follow. The men had to cover much of the distance on foot, while leading the horses.

In this manner the party cut and climbed their way through the buckbrush and timber, fighting their way down nearly 1,000 feet in elevation for each mile of distance. The party followed a stream drainage most of the way, challenged by "slide rock, fallen timber, snow banks, and underbrush," according to Penrose's later account.

By dark, to Stiles' great relief, they reached the bottom of the Middle Fork canyon and the railroad. Stiles said he could not have "cut another tree, or broken another brush."

Gordon Pouliott lived at Nyack just two miles from the mouth of Rescue Creek. He shot this grizzly as it was tearing up canned food on his screened-in porch. Gordon was an amateur historian and had plenty of experience with Middle Fork grizzlies. He was particularly interested in the Penrose incident. Courtesy of Gordon Pouliott.

The party quickly mounted and traveled two miles west along the tracks to reach the little station house at the remote siding of Nyack. Stiles and his party arrived about 9 p.m., almost exactly 14 hours after they left the high camp. Nyack's entire population was on hand: the stationmaster and his wife, who prepared dinner for the hungry, exhausted travelers.

The next morning, the men flagged down the eastbound Great Northern Limited, which the Penroses gratefully boarded. Stiles was relieved. His gamble had worked: Penrose was now in good hands and headed to the Mayo Hospital in Minnesota.

Stiles knew that it would be folly to head back to the high survey camp the way they had just descended. So he and his small party may have headed northwest down the Middle Fork of the Flathead to their original point of entry into the wilderness near the junction of the South Fork.

That day, while Charles Penrose and his brothers were chugging their way east, a few of the men from the high camp rode over to the little basin where the mauling took place. The men found that the first bear killed by the doctor was indeed a yearling, and was most likely leading its sibling and mother along the ridge when Penrose shot it. The doctor had not seen the adult and sibling before he shot the first yearling; they were screened from his view by the rocks and uneven country.

The men skinned and examined the sow and saw that she had been shot twice. One bullet entered near her left shoulder and emerged from the left hip. This bullet probably severed the femoral artery and turned out to be the mortal wound. The other bullet broke the lower part of the sow's hind leg. They estimated the weight of the sow at about 300 pounds.

After several days Charles Penrose arrived in Rochester, Minnesota and was admitted to the Mayo Hospital, where he underwent several operations to treat his injuries. Being a surgeon himself, Penrose later listed his injuries in detail in a description he wrote for the Boone and Crockett Club:

"I had thirty tooth wounds," he began. "The muscles of the thigh were crushed and lacerated; the wrist joint was opened, several of the small bones were crushed, and the scaphoid bone was bitten in two; one fragment projecting from the wound; the median nerve was severed at the wrist; the hand had been perforated by teeth in several places; the breast, head, cheek, and neck were bitten..."

Penrose must have realized that, in more ways than one, Stiles saved his life. Several months later he presented Stiles with a new, German-made Mauser rifle. On the rifle stock was engraved: "Arthur Stiles, from C. B. Penrose."

Years later, in an article written for the Boone and Crockett Club, Penrose downplayed the severity of his predicament. He claimed that he felt no pain during the mauling or for a while afterward. By his later, face-saving account, he himself performed much of the initial operations on his injuries during those three hours that awful night at 7,000 feet. This just doesn't seem plausible. Although Penrose was quite a brave patient, Stiles clearly must have done most of the initial treating of the doctor's wounds helped by whatever direction Penrose could give in his difficult condition.

As far as I could tell, Dr. C. B. Penrose never returned to Montana. I thought that he became too busy recovering from his tangle with the grizzly, continuing his surgical practice, and serving as President of the Philadelphia Zoo. Maybe the near-death experience of being mauled by the great bear played on his mind and kept him out of the high country, even with all of his bravado. But recently, by chance, I came upon an article in, of all publications, the *New York Times*, dated September 4, 1910 entitled, "Penrose in Forest Fires." The article was filed from Colorado Springs. Spencer Penrose on returning home from another Montana hunting trip with his brothers must have contacted the newspaper in that town and gave them the story, and the *Times* picked it up. The brief article tells the story: "Senator Boise Penrose of Pennsylvania and his two brothers, Dr. C. B. Penrose of Philadelphia and Spencer Penrose of this city, were hemmed in by forest fires in Montana, where they had gone on a hunting trip, and were compelled to spend several days cut off entirely from communication with the outside world before they got through the flames by a system of 'back driving.' Spencer Penrose brought this news here yesterday on his return from Montana. According to Mr. Penrose, several men lost their lives in the fires near the Penrose camp."

The three Penrose brothers had managed to get themselves in another life-threatening pickle. They came to Montana on a hunting trip at the height of the largest forest fire disaster, in terms of acres burned and lives lost, in the history of the western United States. The brothers seemed to have a knack for getting themselves into trouble on their hunting trips.

In spite of their fate-tempting ways, the Penrose brothers survived and went on to continue their lives of fame and wealth. Bois Penrose was never defeated in a reelection campaign for his senate seat, even defeating the famed conservationist and Roosevelt-associate Gifford Pinchot in 1914. Bois controlled the Republican organization in Pennsylvania until his death in 1921. Charles recovered from his grizzly-inflicted injuries with little permanent effect. He remained a highly regarded surgeon, founded the Pennsylvania Board of Health, and became President of the Philadelphia Zoo, and President of the Pennsylvania Game Commission. He died in 1925. Spencer and his wife developed the city of Colorado Springs, constructed the Pikes Peak Highway, and founded the Cheyenne Mountain Zoo. Spencer lived lavishly and was said to have expenses of $200,000 per month; the legacy of his great wealth continued after his death in 1939 through various foundations that fund social and environmental causes, including one reportedly worth $500 million.

Stiles continued his career as a topographer around the west, including Montana and Texas. He was a major author of the official 1914 topographic map of Glacier National Park and the surrounding backcountry, where he named many of the features.

The Stiles/Penrose trip was a watershed event in the Middle Fork drainage, literally putting the area on the map. The incident influenced Stiles as he assigned names to the area's features, and the influence of Senator Bois Penrose probably added weight to the Geological Survey's acceptance of these names. C.B. Penrose was mauled in a high basin southeast of Great Bear Mountain. To the northeast is the rugged canyon of Great Bear Creek. Stiles performed much physical care on the doctor between Mt. Penrose and Nyack Mountain. The desperate trek down through the alder and devil's club on the east side of the Flathead Range followed Rescue Creek. The three blond bears turned out to be the inspiration not only for some of these features, but eventually of the Great Bear Wilderness established much later.

I've spent time in these drainages over the years with my children, trapping marten in the canyons of Rescue, Skiumah, and Great Bear Creeks. I think often of Penrose and Stiles and feel as though I'm treading on hallowed ground. The great white bear in the high basin left her mark on Penrose and made history. And thanks to Arthur Stiles, the Geological Survey man, Penrose left his mark on the Great Bear.

Chapter 8:
GLACIER'S MYSTERY VALLEY
Nyack Flats, Glacier Park Rangers, and Betty The Trapper

Early Explorers arrive at the Flats

Nyack Flats is an anomaly in the canyon-bound Middle Fork of the Flathead River. After rushing 20 miles downstream from Bear Creek, the river, crowded by canyon walls, emerges like an animal set free from a trap into the most expansive flood plain in its entire drainage. The Middle Fork languishes back and forth for five miles across a mile-wide plain underlain by millennia of gravel deposition.

The sudden change in the river's gradient sends water gushing through the gravels in the form of a giant, subterranean river, with some of the water percolating to the gravel surface in upwelling springs. The channel of Nyack Creek, a major tributary of the Middle Fork, emerges from the high mountains of Glacier National Park and discharges into the same flat. The underground flow of Nyack Creek collides with and joins the Middle Fork's subterranean river.

This hydrologic complex is a central point for bull trout migrating upstream from Flathead Lake to spawn, and for native westslope cutthroat trout and mountain whitefish. For millennia, these springs have drawn these cold-loving species from Flathead Lake to this special place. In late summer, huge bull trout congregate in the flats, enter Nyack Creek, and swim upstream seven miles to a 40-foot falls. Then, they drop back downstream to gravely tails of runs and build nests the size of a pickup-truck bed. The female is driven by instinct to build these nests by lying on her side and thrashing her body and tail against the stream bottom, moving up to a ton of gravel over about a one-week period. Grizzly bears, Native Americans, and settlers have all been drawn up the drainage following the bull trout. Fish up to three feet long, vulnerable in clear shallow water, are irresistible to humans seeking food.

Early explorers of the drainage were perplexed when they reached Nyack

Nyack Flats and the Middle Fork of the Flathead River near the mouth of Nyack Creek, taken September 29, 2006, from the Glacier National Park side. The mountain in the rear center divides Skiumah Creek and Great Bear Creek drainages. Author photo.

Flats. The huge U-shaped glacier-carved canyon of Nyack Creek joins the Middle Fork canyon, forming one of most striking geological features in the drainage. From this vantage point the canyon of Nyack Creek can look larger and more flat-bottomed than the upper Middle Fork Canyon. The two wide canyons at this point confused more than one explorer who turned up Nyack Creek attempting to find a main pass over the Continental Divide.

In 1853, Washington Territory Governor Isaac Stevens, who was in charge of the transcontinental railroad survey's northern route, commissioned Engineer A. W. Tinkham to explore and find a pass suitable for railroad passage through the Rocky Mountains. Tinkham and his party set forth in October, traveling upstream along the lower Flathead River to Flathead Lake. The party then made its way around the 28-mile long lake, and upstream for 40 miles along the upper Flathead River toward the forks. Tinkham reported that no trail existed upstream of Badrock Canyon, the country consisting of woods and lots of downed timber. After passing the mouth of the South Fork, the survey party continued upstream for six miles, reaching the junction of the North and Middle Forks. At this junction, Tinkham turned up the Middle Fork and followed the low, clear river east and south for 15 miles to Nyack Flats. Here, the engineer was fooled by the yawning canyon of Nyack Creek, thinking it would lead to a supposed low pass across the Continental Divide known even then as Marias Pass.

As the party followed the valley bottom of Nyack Creek, they were impressed with the low gradient, beautiful gravel-bottomed stream flowing between spectacular glacier-carved peaks rising 5,000 feet above the floodplain. But their satisfaction turned to concern when the steam's gradient picked up and they encountered a 40-foot high waterfall and series of cascades only seven miles upstream from the Middle Fork. As Tinkham continued up Nyack Creek he began to see that no low pass would be found in this drainage. Finally, at 18 miles upstream the party stood at 7,600 feet in elevation atop a wall-like pass (now known as Cut Bank Pass) across the Continental Divide with an equally steep and rocky 3000-foot descent down the east side to the Two Medicine River.

Although the pass was named Marias in the initial reports, Tinkham had to know that this was not the fabled low pass through the Rockies and would prove worthless as a railroad route. In a later report it was actually suggested that a tunnel might be built through the Divide wall at the elevation of about 5,500 feet. But the writer added, realistically "as the branch of the Flathead [Nyack Creek] falls 2,170 feet in seventeen miles, this route is not likely to be used." Nearly five decades later, the actual Marias Pass was located 15 miles to the south and provided a pass more than 2,000 feet lower in elevation and well-suited for rail travel.

After the Tinkham expedition, the Nyack Flats area was little visited or noticed by explorers and settlers. Thirty years after Tinkham's trip, in 1883, a small party led by explorer Raphael Pumpelly traveled upstream along the same route Tinkham followed. The party, which included William Logan, who would later become the first superintendent of Glacier National Park, was surveying areas north of the Northern Pacific Railroad line that was being built south of Flathead Lake. The Pumpelly party also turned up Nyack Creek and crossed Cut Bank Pass.

Early Settlers and Betty the Trapper

Nothing more of note happened in terms of exploration or interest in the Nyack Flats area until 1891, when the railroad was completed down the Middle Fork from Marias Pass, through Nyack Flats, and on to the Flathead Valley. The little Nyack Flat languished almost undiscovered for decades. It's stunning to think of how late settlers moved into the Middle Fork, it being one of the last areas to remain a frontier in the lower 48 states.

After the railroad was completed through the Flats, the Great Northern established the little siding of Nyack on the upstream end. Because of the gentle nature and suitability of the land for settlement, it was obvious that services would be needed.

Nyack Residents in the 1920s. L to R, back row: Mrs. Jack McDonald, Gladys Bell, Roy Bolton (?) Glacier National Park Guard Jack McDonald; Lottie Robertson. L to R, front row: Louis McDonald, Larry Bell, Clara McDonald, George Robertson, Bill Robertson. Betty Robertson Schurr Collection.

The Nyack country was young, like the geologically young river that wound across its wide, glacial gravel bars. George Robertson, who worked as a telegrapher at the Fielding siding on Bear Creek, moved his wife Carlotta and family to Nyack in about 1915 to run the siding there. The Robertsons soon became the most prominent and influential family in the area, operating both the railroad siding and the general store.

In 1925, the first girl was born to a settler in Nyack Flats. As much as anyone, Betty Robertson reflected the adventurous and independent tradition of her family. But like the rugged country that she pioneered, Betty had a rough start.

In the summer of 1928, three-year-old Betty was playing with her older brother, Gordon, in a canvas wall tent towards the Middle Fork from the family's homestead, store and hotel. Gordon, his younger brother Don, and his older brother Bob, lived in the tent during the summer, enjoying the feeling of camping out and allowing more room in the house for the rest of the family, including Betty, her older sister Virginia, and her parents, John and Margaret, and her grandparents. Little Betty would often play with her brothers in their tent while Margaret was at work on household chores or in

Betty at about age 3 at Nyack, ca. 1928. Betty Robertson Schurr Collection.

the store or hotel. On this warm, sunny day, Betty's "Grandma Lottie" was hanging out laundry behind the store.

The brothers were allowed to have a gun, a .35 Remington caliber rifle, to scare off the bums that would sometimes hop off the train at the Nyack siding. But John Robertson was safety minded—he did not allow the boys to have any ammunition. The rifle was just for show.

That afternoon, as he often did, Gordon was playing in the tent with his little sister. Betty looked up to Gordon because he treated her gently and he included her in his big-boy games. On this afternoon, he and little Betty were eating graham crackers and playing trick-shot with the rifle. The first rule of gun safety is to treat every gun as if it were loaded. Lots of people who ignored that rule have been killed. Gordon wasn't thinking of the possibility that the gun might be loaded. But unbeknownst to him, Bob had been riding across the river fishing the day before and had found one .35 Remington shell. Bob had brought the live round back to the tent and loaded it into the rifle.

"Hold up that graham cracker and I'll shoot it out of your hand," Gordon said to Betty. Gordon sat on a cot and Betty sat at the table by the door and tent flap. Betty smiled, held up the cracker and laid her head down on the table, pretending that a bullet would be coming her way and that she better duck to avoid it. It's a good thing she did. Gordon squeezed the trigger and was bowled over by the loud report of large caliber rifle in the confines of the wall tent. The 200-grain bullet, traveling 2,100 feet per second, struck Betty's little finger and blew most of it off. Blood gushed quickly like an artesian well and soaked the graham cracker that she still clutched until it became soft and crumpled. The slug had skimmed across the top of her head and burned a furrow along her scalp. The bullet missed taking off the top of her skull by inches.

Carlotta jumped at the boom of the rifle. She flinched as the bullet, traveling through the tent flap, narrowly missed her and blew a hole in the sheet she was hanging up on the clothesline.

Gordon ran to the house screaming and terrified. He was horrified to find that part of Betty's little finger was shot off. Betty's mother, Margaret, later called it "a terrible shock, but a lucky escape." The family rushed Betty to Belton on the railroad tracks via a motorized track car, then on to the hospital in Kalispell. Betty was in shock and didn't realize what had happened to her, partly because the nerve in her finger had been destroyed. Dr. Brassett operated on Betty. He was forced to amputate most of what was left of her finger.

This incident was a source of great sadness for Betty's mother.

Betty's brother Bob outside their "big house" with a nice whitetail. Betty says she ate so much venison that she "grew a tail." Betty Robertson Schurr Collection.

Her daughter, only three and barely able to understand she had been maimed for life, had endured a terrible trauma. Her young son was racked with guilt and would have to live with the memory of that terrible day for the rest of his life.

Adding to Margaret's anguish, immediately after the accident Betty began to "stammer" when she tried to talk. In careful, flowing handwriting in Betty's baby book, her mother described how she dealt with her daughter's stuttering. Betty was "made to quit talking when her stammering commenced." This seems like an unfortunate and painful way to have to treat a young girl, but it worked. Margaret reported that Betty "soon quit (stuttering) altogether, fortunately."

After her tough start in life, Betty grew to have the confidence of a frontier girl who could fish, trap, and hunt as well as the boys. By the time she was in 7th grade, Betty trapped the Skiumah Creek drainage in what is now the Great Bear Wilderness. And like Slippery Bill a few decades before her, she didn't want company. When she trapped alone, she didn't have to divide the proceeds from the fur she took. Her dad had taught her to trap while she was

Virginia and "Fishing Genius" Gordon at the water tank overflow pond. Betty Robertson Schurr collection

in grade school. But as a typical teenager yearning for independence, after she learned how to trap, she wanted her dad to stay away from her trapline.

So 13-year old Betty Robertson took one of the most remote drainages on the south side of the Middle Fork for her trapping grounds. Skiumah enters the Middle Fork just downstream from Rescue Creek, spilling out of the mountains into the upper end of Nyack Flats. Betty's dad could look directly into the drainage from the Robertson homestead. The back window of their house faced the trailhead, so John could be on the lookout for his daughter's return from the canyon in the evening after she checked her trap line.

Displaying the natural wisdom of a young girl who knew what she wanted, Betty chose her trapping area well. The Skiumah Creek drainage is classic marten habitat. Huge 300-year-old spruce and larch trees rise above a vegetation complex of Pacific Yew, alder, devil's club and downed timber. This mosaic of vegetation provides cover for marten in the form of abundant snow tunnels on the ground layer and well-protected resting areas in the tall virgin timber. Where you have snow tunnels, you have mice and voles; where you have big timber, you have abundant rocky mountain red squirrels and squirrel nests used by marten for resting. Mice, voles and squirrels make up the better part of the marten's diet, so Skiumah Creek canyon is like an all-you-can-eat buffet for marten and their smaller cousins, the ermine.

Betty laid about a dozen sets in a two-mile stretch of the narrow, steeply rising canyon of Skiumah Creek. She became an expert at trapping marten, coyotes, and ermine (short-tailed weasels), but especially marten. Marten were so valuable (over $100 each in equivalent value) that she fashioned each set just for that species and if she caught a coyote or a weasel, that was fine too. First, she selected a large conifer that shielded a natural depression or covey. Brushing away the snow, she laid the trap in the duff and built up a cubby around it with branches, bark, or fir boughs. She fastened the trap chain securely to the tree. To draw in this enthusiastic carnivore, Betty placed a chunk of bait, usually deer scrap or fish, above the trap and added a dab of secret lure, the recipe passed down from Slippery Bill whom her parents and grandparents knew. Weasel family members like the marten and weasel have noses that can detect scents so well that their sense of smell paints a picture for them in the form of a map to the bait. As humans rely on sight, mustellids rely on their sense of smell. Betty's set was successful when the marten or ermine came in to investigate the wonderful smells, seized the bait, and in doing so placed its foot in the trap and was securely caught.

Betty used size "0" longspring foothold traps, so a captured marten was not killed right away. But because of the high metabolism of this mustellid, death comes relatively quickly, especially in cold weather. A marten caught in a foothold trap will struggle against the trap and usually expire in a matter of hours from a combination of shock and exposure. Often when the trapper checks the set, the marten is found frozen solid. Occasionally, if a marten was still alive, the trapper would strike the marten across the head with a ski pole or axe handle, then compress its chest under a snowshoe or ski until the animal was dead. In later years, the conibear or body-gripping trap was invented and allowed trappers who used them to achieve a much faster kill of trapped marten.

Betty found that once you set a trap line, it had to be tended no matter what. One calm cold day, despite protests by her father, Betty headed up the canyon to check her traps. The thermometer at their Nyack homestead read 22 degrees below zero. Betty just took it for granted that she would go anyway. As she said later, "Once it gets 10 below or lower it doesn't matter—it's all just cold." To keep from freezing, Betty kept moving on her snowshoes as fast as she could along the two-mile trap line. It was hard to handle the steel traps. Even with gloved hands, she could feel the sharp bite of the frigid steel. Like many trappers of her time, Betty says she never grew to love trapping or view it in a romantic way that many of us trappers do today. But her description of running the trap line that day reflected a deep feeling for the solitude and beauty of the Great Bear country. "It was so beautiful and clear, the sky was so blue, and ice crystals were sparkling in the air," she remembered.

At a partly frozen crossing of Skiumah Creek, Betty halted, wondering

Betty, at high school age, with several marten and coyote pelts; ca. about 1939 or 1940. Betty Robertson Schurr Collection.

how to get her canine trapping companion across. She knew the dog's feet would freeze if he stepped in the water. Finally, Betty unlaced her snowshoes and threw them across the creek channel. Grabbing the dog in her arms, she jumped from icy rock to icy rock across the creek.

On this day, Betty felt the trapper's joy of catching one of the finest marten she'd ever seen. "I caught a big black male marten that made me just step back he was so beautiful," she recalled. "His throat patch was just brilliant orange." True, Betty was no doubt thinking of the marten's economic value. But surely she also felt the sheer beauty and wildness of catching and handling such a fine furbearer that almost no one other than a true trapper will ever see.

I trapped Skiumah and Great Bear drainages nearly 60 years after Betty, but I didn't know that I was retracing her trapline. I spent days in the drainage that resembled Betty's 22 below zero day and had the same thrill of seeing marten hanging in my sets, in air sparkling with hoar frost against a deep blue sky. It was my first year trapping, and we used foothold traps, making sets not unlike the ones Betty made, except they were placed about 3-feet above the ground in trees. My partner, Dale Sommerfield, trapped the Rescue and Wahoo drainages. We did it purely for the excitement and solitude and heritage, and probably didn't take this rare experience for granted like Betty says she did. Although we trapped about 10 marten, we made only a few hundred dollars from the pelts with fur prices as they were in 1996/7. I always find it hard to grasp when I talk to old-time trappers; they almost invariably portray their trapping in a pragmatic, job-like way. I can't help but think, though, that it really meant much more to them.

Betty continued to trap right through her high school years to make money for room and board expenses when she stayed in town during the school year. It was a source of pride for her to provide some of the money to cover her education. It was necessary that she took room and board in town because Nyack was not accessible by road from November until May. Only the railroad provided winter transportation. On weekends, and occasionally in mid-week, she would return to Nyack 30 miles by train to tend her trap line.

In a good trapping season Betty would catch about a dozen marten and a handful of coyotes and weasels. She skinned the furbearers in the family kitchen. Betty skinned the marten carefully because of their value, and placed the pelts sock-like over a thin board that stretched the hide and held its shape. A good marten would stretch about three feet in length from the snout to the tip of the tail. After the skin partly dried, she turned the pelt and put it back on the board with the luxuriant fur facing out.

Betty often caught weasels or ermine on her trapline, but they only brought about a dollar or so on the market despite sporting beautiful, snow-white fur. Once a weasel was caught in her trap, it took that trap out of commission for catching marten, so Betty didn't get too excited about catching weasels. Betty could skin a weasel in a few minutes, by "jerking the pelt right off." These foot-long furbearers are then placed on a small board skin side out to dry. The pelts are not turned fur side out.

As did other trappers, Betty found the weasel musk nearly as strong as skunk but not as objectionable. It's almost impossible to skin a weasel without hitting its scent glands. You have to go through a lot of baby powder and shaving cream to get the smell of weasel musk off your hands.

Betty became skilled at putting up the pelts, and the dark-colored, thick furred Middle Fork marten brought good prices. "I bought a horse with my fur money one year," she recalls. If anyone in town smirked at a high school girl trapping, it didn't bother Betty. "I'd tell them, 'Here's a dime, go call somebody who cares.'"

She seemed to balance her raw trapping life with her civilized life in town during the week. She had a boyfriend from a local ranch, so she must have had to work hard to keep clean. Most trappers who handle bait and lure can be smelled at some distance. Take my word for it, you can wash until you think you are clean, but after being around lure all day your sense of smell is not very astute. For lure, Betty used beaver castor and anise oil (whoops, there goes her secret), and let's just say it's harder to rid yourself of that smell than it is to mask the smell of gasoline. You might smell clean to another trapper, but probably not to non-trappers.

Betty had the natural love for wildlife that people feel when they live in their midst. One of the hardest things to explain to others is how you can trap and kill an animal that you deeply respect and admire. Betty demonstrated her concern for wildlife over and over by doing what comes naturally to humans: keeping and nurturing wildlife as pets. Regulations prohibit this practice nowadays, but back in the 1930s it was routine and taken for granted.

One day on her trap line, Betty came around the corner of the trail at the big bend where the trail curves around the steep ridge to the east of the creek and heads straight up the canyon. At the big bend is a huge fir tree hundreds of years old. Many marten have been caught there before and since; it's on a natural route they follow up and down the drainage. This day, though, Betty was surprised to find a lighter-colored, much larger animal, had been caught in her trap. And it was alive and alert.

The little number 0 trap held the coyote by two toes. Betty approached the wary animal, and felt compassion for it. She grabbed a downed limb and struck the coyote on the head, but not too hard. She removed the unconscious canid's paw from the trap. She cut off a length of her bootlace and tied the coyote's jaw shut. She held him firmly in her arms and packed him a mile and 800 feet in descent back down to the house at Nyack. Betty's dad put a little sack with flour over the damaged foot and it healed completely over time. Although Betty kept the wild canid like a pet dog, it never acted like one. She brought him inside at times, and often kept him chained outside where he had access to a shelter. Even after a year, the animal was still shy and retreating. "He was always a coyote," says Betty. Finally, she felt sorry for the animal, unhooked his collar, and let him go.

Along with the coyote, one of Betty's favorite pets was a young marten. Marten "cubs" are born in the spring and are at first dependent on the mother. If a litter of marten is found, it would be easy to lift one and take it home. Betty and her siblings had a number of young marten that they bottle-fed and released. One in particular endeared itself to Betty and it was a family pet for several years. When he was small, he made his home in a kitchen drawer. As he got older and larger, the screened in porch made a good headquarters for the marten, but he was allowed to spend time in the house as well. "He was pretty wild and nervous though," she recalled, "and we couldn't teach him to stay off the table when we were eating dinner."

The marten's demise came when he got too involved in the food chain around the homestead. The Robertsons had a prize canary in a cage inside their home. One day, Betty found a small owl on the road so she took it home. It wasn't long before the owl pinned the canary against the side of its cage and killed it. Then, not much later, the marten grabbed the owl and snapped its neck. Finally, one day the same summer the marten got out and the dogs ran it down. The marten put up a terrific fight. That completed the food chain.

The bears Betty and family kept for pets didn't have to worry about anything eating them, especially after they grew to be big. From time to time, the Great Northern train would inadvertently kill a sow black bear with cubs. When this happened, the Robertsons got the cubs. One day the train collided with and killed an adult female black bear near the section house, orphaning a brown cub. Betty's father pulled the cub out of a tree and took it home. He became their favorite pet. Cubbins was allowed to headquarter in the house while he was small. He would crawl under the kitchen cupboards and lick Betty's toes when she got close.

Like a typical bear, he began to think of the kitchen as his territory. "Just like the marten, we had to lock up the bear in the bedroom when we ate or he'd end up on the table all the time," Betty remembered.

Cubbins' best animal friend was the Robertson's cat. The cat would chase the bear, then the bear would chase the cat. Betty kept a pillow near a chair, and when she wanted to hold the young bear she put the pillow on her lap and sat the cub on the pillow. This kept the bear's sharp claws from digging into her legs.

The little cub grew into a "huge" chocolate colored adult. He was well fed for one thing, intentionally and unintentionally. Once, Betty and her mom made ice cream in a three- gallon bucket. While the ice cream set up, Betty and her brothers went fishing on the Middle Fork, about a hundred yards from the house. When they came back to eat the ice cream it was gone. Cubbins had eaten all the ice cream, and even licked the beater and inside of the bucket. They found him lying on his back looking contented, staring up at them appreciatively as if he thought they had made the frosty concoction just for him.

The large bear provided a lot of entertainment for the family, although sometimes at the expense of the railroad workers who stopped by. "He was cagey, that bear," Betty recalled. "He would narrow his chain and pretend to be at the end of it."

When the men would approach the bear to feed him something, Cubbins would rush out and knock them down. "We'd hear someone scream and we'd look out the window," said Betty. "We'd chuckle and say, 'Well, the bear got another guy.' He was only playing, really; he never bit anyone."

The Robertsons had Cubbins for years. In the late fall, they dug out a spot in the big sawdust pile from the sawmill. In this tunnel they placed a box lined with straw. Cubbins knew just what to do as the temperatures dropped, and he hibernated in the homemade den. When he awoke each spring, the bear would step up on the porch of the house and let Betty know that spring was here. He was out of the den, and expected to be fed.

Finally, Cubbins met disaster because of his ravenous appetite and a bear's weakness for chickens. The huge bear wasn't satisfied with dog food, table scraps, and ice cream. He was drawn to a neighbor's chicken house. One night, the neighbor shot him.

Betty was sad that Cubbins was gone, but she had plenty of other pets, seemingly going through nearly the entire wildlife species list for the Middle Fork watershed. For a short time she had a tethered moose calf, but the mother came back and chewed the rope and reclaimed her young. Betty had her own deer that spent a lot of time in the house during winter. One of her fond memories is the deer sleeping on the rug in front of the Christmas tree.

Betty Robertson Schurr, February 6, 2006. Author Photo.

Betty's wildlife pet menagerie was diverse, but she drew the line at weasels. Betty found young weasels in a mother's nest once and brought the tiny carnivores into the house. "I put them in a screen cage," she said, "but they were no fun to keep. You couldn't even put your hand close to their cage or the vicious things would go after your fingers. We just couldn't do anything with them."

Betty found what many others have noted: weasels are born killers. When you watch a slinky-like weasel float over the surface of the snow you sense an understated power. Weasels sprint to their prey, bite the rodent or snowshoe hare at the base of the neck, and entwine their body around the prey. Weasels then deliver a killing bite to the skull of the animal and may lap the prey's blood or eat part of the carcass. The weasel's sharp, shear-like teeth are the most highly adapted of any carnivore. The short-tailed weasels or ermine that Betty caught are only about a foot long and weigh in at a quarter of a pound. But pound for pound, weasels pack more meat-shredding power than perhaps any other animal on earth. When you think of the cougar, you think of an awesome predator; but a cougar can't compare to a weasel in relative killing power. For a mountain lion to equal the feat of an ermine killing a snowshoe hare, it would have to down a prey weighing nearly two tons.

As Betty noticed, even young weasels are vicious. It didn't take a scientific study to tell her that weasels were born killers. As a matter of fact, a University of Montana study conducted much later showed that young weasels that were separated from their mothers at birth were just as effective in killing mice as the weasels that were raised by the mother.

On Betty Robertson's 21st birthday, she caught 16 nice "flats" or westslope cutthroat trout on the Middle Fork near her homestead. Betty considered the westslope the prettiest fish that swims.

With all her experience with bears and other carnivores, Betty still felt that weasels were the "most ferocious things that live." She had it right when she said, "If a weasel weighed as much as a coyote, you couldn't go into the woods."

Like other settlers in the Middle Fork, Betty and her family lived off the land. "We lived on fish and venison, everybody did," recalled Betty. "I ate so much venison it was unreal. I ate so much I grew a tail."

Betty and Gordon always got along well and often fished together. Gordon was a fishing fanatic and he rarely failed to catch fish when he went to the river. They often fished from their horses, kicking the animals to get them to wade out into the middle of the river. For westslope cutthroat they used coachman and bumble bee flies. For bull trout Betty used a red and white plug on a spinning line. Gordon developed another method reflecting his fishing genius.

Gordon needed two things for his special Middle Fork bull trout fishing technique: wooden shingles and live mice. First, he would use a rubber band to fasten a live mouse to his large hook which he tied securely to the end of his fishing line. Then, he'd place the mouse and hook on a wooden shingle, pay out his line, and let the shingle float out to the heavy current where the bulls, weighing up to 20 pounds, finned along the stream bottom. When the shingle carrying the mouse reached the honey spot, Gordon jerked the mouse off the shingle. The big predatory bulls, seeing the struggling mouse, couldn't resist the image and rocketed through the water to the bait. Gordon reared back on his stout fishing rod and the fight was on. "Nobody could compare with Gordon when it came to catching bull trout," said

Betty. "Those bulls just went wild over those live mice." So much for the contention of some biologists who believe that migratory bull trout from Flathead Lake mostly stop feeding while in the river.

Sometimes Betty used live grasshoppers along with artificial flies to catch cutthroat trout. While some young people remember their 21st birthday by some conventional milestone, Betty remembers her 21st by a fishing event. "On my 21st birthday I got up, went down to the Middle Fork, and caught 16 nice flats." "Flats" was the name applied to the black-spotted, green-backed native westslope cutthroat trout. They may be the prettiest fish that swims when you see them coming in through the clear waters of the Middle Fork, highlighted by the gleaming glacial gravel. And that gravel—it's hard to explain its beauty. The rocks are red, green, blue, and brown. These are some of the oldest rocks known to man, and the stream has rolled them into shiny, round gems that glow in the sunlight that shines through the transparent water.

Even the Robertson's hunting focused on the Middle Fork. The far side of the river is the boundary for Glacier National Park, so park animals from time to time stepped into or across the river and became fair game. Sometimes Betty and her brothers would help this along a bit. They would cross the river into the Park, go out behind the Nyack Ranger Station, and bugle for elk. If they attracted any elk, they'd ride over behind them and try to chase them towards the river where they were legal game.

The National Park Service Rangers were mostly tolerant of this practice. Once, Betty wounded an elk right across the river from the house. Betty ran into Ranger Joe Heimes and he told her, "I'm going over to the ranger cabin, get out cookies, and put on tea. You go kill this elk and we'll have some tea and cookies when you get done." Betty never did catch up to that particular elk, but she was glad that Joe was understanding about it.

Glacier Park Rangers at Nyack

The national park service rangers and their families in those days became such a integral part of the settlers' community in the area they patrolled that they were almost indistinguishable from the local residents. A procession of rangers were stationed at several ranger stations over the years at Nyack, beginning with Dan Doody, who was hired because he was a mountain man who lived in the area and knew the country well. Doody was appointed as one of the seven original Glacier Park rangers on August 12, 1910, and at first stationed at Fielding. Doody, a recognized outlaw, operated out of his cabins on land he homesteaded within the established boundary of Glacier Park across the Middle Fork in the Nyack area. Park records show him officially established as the Nyack Ranger by 1913. Because of his persistent illegal outfitting and hunting within the Park, Doody was finally fired on March 15, 1916.

The first official ranger station at Nyack was built upstream along the Middle Fork, but the runoff-swelled river damaged it. The Park Service replaced the station in 1934.

Many rangers followed Doody over the years and were stationed at least temporarily at Nyack or patrolled the area occasionally. Records are incomplete, but these rangers included Walter Gibb (Assistant Chief Ranger), Lewis Myers (1918), Emmet Rohel (1919), Clyde Fauley, Sr. (1924-26, 30s), John McDonnell (1923-4 and 1928), Frank Lorence (1925), Hugh Buchanan (1928-29), J.P. Winnington (1928), Henry Doust (1932), Frank Guardipee (1930s), Joe Heimes (1940-1) J. Roy Hutchinson (1947-50), Chauncey Beebe, C. G. Harkins, Ray Newberry (mostly stationed at Paola in the 1930s). The last ranger stationed at Nyack was Bruce Miller in 1951.

Also patrolling the Nyack area on occasion were Tom Whitcraft, Chief Ranger at Lake McDonald from 1930-36; Hugh Buchanan while he was ranger at Lake McDonald, 1930-34, and Walton district ranger in 1935, and 1938-40.

Even though the incomplete records show that rangers came and went, Nyack hosted several of the highest rated all-around rangers in the early days of the Park, including Clyde Fauley, Sr., Joe Heimes, and Hugh Buchanan. Hugh Buchanan put in 30 years with the Park Service, patrolling the Nyack area as the ranger in the late 1920s, and in the 1930s from the Lake McDonald area. His background as a firefighter served him well during the big Middle Fork Fire of 1929. Buchanan, a highly respected ranger among the residents in his district, had an honest and clearly stated outlook on fitting in with the locals, although some people may have thought he was too friendly and lenient.

"The Park Service didn't encourage us to associate with the natives too much," Buchanan said. "But I got along with them—better than most Park personnel, I'd say." Buchanan said that locals lived off the land because they had to. He didn't bother the locals if they shot a deer occasionally for their own use. But if the local residents invited friends up to hunt, that was considered poaching, and Buchanan would try to catch them. He acknowledged that the rangers and the locals had to rely on each other in the raw wilds of the Middle Fork, and staying on friendly terms was common sense. Buchanan became good friends with Josephine Doody, wife of old-time ranger Dan Doody. She lived on the original Doody Homestead within the Park, a few miles downriver from the Nyack Ranger Station. Buchanan treated her kindly and, with a few exceptions (see the next chapter), seemed to mostly tolerate her occasional poaching and persistent moon-shining. In fact, rangers at Nyack often relied on Josephine's homestead as a rendezvous point and contracted with Josephine for use of her horses from time to time. Also the Robertsons helped the rangers cross the river at times in their boat.

This is a photo of early GNP ranger Chauncey Beebe with five mountain lion hides at the old Nyack Ranger Station in 1922. At this time Beebe was probably working as a government predator control hunter. Glacier National Park Historical Collection.

Fur poachers attracted a good deal of attention from Park Rangers, and they considered it serious and not something to look the other way about. Buchanan estimated that at one time up to 500 marten were taken each year on Park Service land in the Middle Fork, mostly in the McDonald Valley. But he noted that rangers were effective in shutting down the illegal furbearer take in the Park.

Poachers and rangers played a game of cat-and-mouse. Poachers would wade up streams with hip boots for miles before setting foot on land again. Another trick was to travel on game trails and try to mix their footprints in with moose, elk and deer. Buchanan said he got wise to their techniques, though. And at times he would get tips about a fur poacher when the poacher would slip up and when he was "liquored up," and boast about his fur take.

Rangers had the advantage over the poachers because they had strategically-spaced patrol cabins, well stocked for winter. Their job in winter was to patrol on snowshoes, so they became very good at it, especially after they got their "snow legs," about three weeks into the season. Rangers competed in the "300-club"—30 days a month, 10 miles a day on snowshoes. In fact, rangers shut down the old trappers so well that many fur poachers were forced to revert to moon-shining to get by. Buchanan said that government revenuers, known as the "dry squad," looked for stills in the Park, but they failed to find them because of their lack of woodsmanship. But Buchanan, who seemed to have a doubtful view of the revenuers, knew the

Glacier National Park Guard Jack McDonald and his wife in the 1920s. Betty Robertson Schurr collection

names of the bootleggers in his district and the location of most of the stills.

Another Nyack Ranger, Clyde Fauley, spent time patrolling past the Doody Homestead to Harrison Lake, which sits between spectacular ridges about four miles upstream on Harrison Creek above the Doody homestead. One winter day in 1929, Fauley nearly died on his snowshoes. The air temperature was frigid, 20 degrees below zero, and he assumed the ice on the lake would be safe. He was making his way along the lake on its snow-covered surface, when suddenly, the ice gave way and he plunged into the ice cold water. Fauley barely kept his shoulders and head above water. In his predicament, there was no way he could remove his snowshoes. He pulled himself along towards shore, breaking the thin ice as he went, his heart beating near its maximum rate. With a tremendous effort he finally reached shore, he moved as fast as his numb legs allowed and stumbled towards the Harrison Lake snowshoe cabin, hoping he could cover the half mile distance before he lost the use of his limbs, or froze to death. The well-conditioned and resourceful ranger reached the cabin, and threw open the door. Using dry materials that were always kept available beside the stoves in these cabins, he was able to start a fire in the stove, warm up, and dry out.

Fauley was lucky; he lived through the ordeal only because he emerged from the water not far from the cabin. He had quite a story to share with the locals and his fellow rangers who were members of the 300-mile snowshoe club. This incident helped make Fauley almost a legend with the locals.

Josephine Doody later told Hugh Buchanan that Fauley was the "best all around ranger" the Park had ever had, saying he was a "good man with courage and stamina." This is high praise coming from the wife of one of the original seven Glacier National Park rangers. Fauley became one of Josephine's favorites, often stopping at her homestead for lunch. For example, on June 31, 1930, he wrote in the ranger journal that he stopped at her place and was treated to a piece of early huckleberry pie.

It's clear from the ranger journals at Nyack, which are available from 1928-31, that rangers also spent a lot of time trapping coyotes and feeding deer and elk. In fact, there was an established feed yard one mile downstream from the station within the Park in a big flat on the south side of Nyack Creek. The thought at the time was simple: kill the "bad animals" (predators) and feed the "good animals." Rangers went out of their way to concentrate deer and elk on the feed yard. On January 27, 1928, the Nyack ranger noted: "Fed deer at St. Marys [this is what they called the Nyack feed yard] and patrolling by trail to Doodys....There are quite a few deer coming in to the old feed yard at Doody Landing, and after the winter is farther along it would be well to scatter hay from this point to the present feed yard. 18 deer, 10 miles travel." The next day, patrolling up the Middle Fork, the ranger found a dead 6-point bull elk with two "bullet holes," that he noted must have been shot from the railroad tracks across the river.

Rangers ran coyote traplines particularly downstream from the station. Horsemeat was packed in to use for bait in the foothold traps in sets designed to fool coyotes into stepping into them. On November 7, 1929, the ranger (probably either Buchanan or Fauley, the writer doesn't identify himself) reported that he caught one coyote and missed one because of a stick that got caught between the trap jaws. He noted that he "had chat with Mrs. Doody," no doubt getting her advice on his trapping operation. Over the next several days, the ranger caught four more coyotes, shot at a coyote, saw bull elk fighting, and had dinner and sometimes lunch with Mrs. Doody, whose homestead was located at the downstream end of the trapline.

The rangers's journal entries in early December show what a major snowstorm can mean to even the toughest ranger trying to get around in the backcountry. Day after day, the snow piled up at the Nyack station until many feet of fresh snow prevented any significant movement for days. "I would like to see the man who could travel four miles on snowshoes here today," he wrote. "Physically impossible to get any distance." The ranger barely made it the short distance to the feed yard at Nyack Creek and back to the station. He also noted that he had a hard day shoveling out the boat and crossing the Middle Fork through the slush ice. John and Bill Robertson helped him "tow the boat up the bank to safe ground." He noted that over 100 deer were concentrated in the area and unable to get around. The

Nyack Ranger Station completed in 1934. Glacier National Park Historical Collection.

telephone wire to the Park Service headquarters in West Glacier was down in several places. He made it to Doody's where her phone wire was still up and "reported difficulties with phone line."

By mid-January, the cold had descended on Nyack. On January 16, Clyde Fauley reported a temperature of minus 28 degrees Fahrenheit; the next day, it plummeted to minus 38 degrees. Fauley regularly covered 12-20 miles each day, recorded wildlife sign, and often had dinner with Josephine. Once Chief Ranger Carter accompanied Fauley on a snowshoe patrol, topping it off with dinner at "Mrs. Doody's." On a trip in early March, Fauley noted that black spotted westl slope cutthroat trout were congregating at the Harrison Lake inlet, but "not spawning yet." He wrote that the ice on the lake "rumbled like thunder" while he was walking on it. He noted seeing a number of bald eagles and golden eagles.

Fauley worked through the summer at the station. He fished the Middle Fork for cutthroat trout, noting on June 28, 1930 that he "caught 3 nice cutthroat trout 2 lb each."

Fauley was popular with the locals, but he didn't completely trust them; he suspected that some hunted within the Park boundaries, especially around Harrison Lake where elk were plentiful. That October, he stopped John Robertson coming down the trail from Harrison Lake, meeting him at Doody's. Fauley "searched his stuff, but all he had was some fish."

He noted seeing 16 elk, mostly bulls in "splendid condition" on a patrol to upper Nyack Creek. Ironically, he borrowed a horse from John Robertson, who must not have been angered by the shakedown Fauley gave him less than a week earlier. When it snowed one day, Fauley noted that it was a "handicap" to hunters who wanted to enter the Park to hunt because they would leave a trail. He obviously suspected that many people hunted inside the Park boundary and he was determined to stop it if he could.

Fauley wasn't opposed to taking fish and wildlife. He just wanted it to be legal. In late October, he noted large numbers of anglers catching spawning whitefish in the Middle Fork. He himself notes that he caught messes of whitefish. He noted that "Robertsons are down there from morning 'till night fishing." In Fauley's last entry, on Christmas Day, 1930, he notes a downriver patrol and a return to the station to devour a Christmas Chicken. "The pet marten was in the back porch today," he added. "and received a Christmas feed."

Frank and Alma Guardipee moved into the Nyack Ranger Station in 1930, following Clyde Fauley. Frank had left a forester job with the Blackfeet Tribe in Browning to take the job of Park Service Ranger. The Guardipees lived at the Nyack Station year-around through the early-mid 1930s. The Guardipees gave a family touch to the remote station. When Frank first started with the Park Service at the station, he protested the fact that he was officially on duty seven days a week. This led to the policy of "in lieu days," or days off for rangers in Glacier. Frank also urged that a new station building and residence be constructed at Nyack to replace the primitive, deteriorating cabin.

In 1933, Alma came out and gave birth to a son in a hospital in Great Falls.

The abandoned Nyack Ranger Station residence, September 29, 2006. Author Photo.

This boy may be the only child ever raised at the station. When the boy was 9 months old, they moved into a new station building. The new station had a nice floor, an inside bath tub, and propane lights. Alma encouraged her son to play outdoors, even in the winter. One winter day, when the boy was 2-1/2 or 3 years old, Alma bundled him up in warm clothes to go outside. Alma went into the station bedroom to get him a scarf, and through the window she saw a "moose looking in the window there," as she remembered later. "Well, I knew he couldn't go outside, not with a moose there, and Frank had gone over to the morning mail." Frank had crossed the Middle Fork in a bucket suspended from a cable that had been built to cross the river.

Alma called the Nyack Post Office on the station phone and told Frank about the moose. "He came back and was very careful getting in the house," she said.

Glacier National Park Ranger Hugh Buchanan and his wife. Betty Robertson Schurr Collection.

The aggressive moose wouldn't leave the station area. His orders wouldn't allow him to shoot the animal, so Frank called headquarters in Belton and requested help. Eventually, several rangers arrived on the train and crossed the river to assist Frank. After attempts to haze the animal failed, the rangers finally shot and killed the moose. It turned out that the moose had an infected leg, and it had an ear clip, which made Alma think that someone may have kept it as a "pet."

Other animals the Guardipees lived with at the station were few. Alma said she allowed a "little rabbit" to live inside the station house with them. One fall day, a weasel chased the rabbit past her and right into the building. The rabbit stayed because "he knew he could get protection" from the weasel and other predators. Only once did a black bear try to enter the station, Alma noted. They rarely saw grizzlies or black bears around the station or on patrols.

The cable and bucket system was a convenient way to cross the Middle Fork, and it offered the only way across during spring runoff. But the system had its drawbacks. The cable was somewhat loose, and many people were uneasy about crossing the river in the bucket suspended below the cable. A 12-foot high platform had to be climbed to reach the cable and bucket. So one day Frank climbed up on the platform with the intent of tightening the cable. He began putting pressure on the cable and it broke, hitting him in the head. Frank was knocked off the platform and suffered a broken leg. Frank was transported to the hospital and Alma came back into town with her 9-month old son while Frank recuperated. The residents of Nyack no doubt assisted Frank and helped him onto the train for the ride into Kalispell.

Frank Guardipee was intent on catching poachers who had been taking elk on the Glacier Park side of the Middle Fork from Nyack upstream to Essex. It was a challenge because of the size of the country and the fact that if the poacher was able to make it to the river, he was home free because the Middle Fork high water mark on the Park side was the boundary. So Frank would run towards any shots he heard on the Glacier Park side of the river. Before Frank left Nyack, he finally apprehended a notorious elk poacher and stood as the main witness at the man's trial in Great Falls. The poacher was convicted and reportedly paid what at the time amounted to a huge fine.

Frank spent most of his time patrolling the large Nyack District, but not as much time feeding game as his predecessors did. Frank didn't see much benefit in feeding and concentrating the animals during the winter. It was during Frank's time at Nyack that the practice of feeding deer and elk was halted. Chief Ranger Tom Whitcraft recognized the potential of disease being passed among the yarded animals, and he ordered the feeding stopped.

After 1951, the Nyack Ranger Station was mostly abandoned and since then the district has been sleepy and lightly patrolled as compared to many other areas of Glacier Park. It was always a lonely place anyway, on the far side of the Middle Fork Flathead River and in a remote stretch of the river.

I've passed by the ranger station site many times over the past quarter-century. Usually, I'm on my way across the flats to survey bull trout spawning in Nyack Creek. Brush, conifers, and cottonwoods are slowly but surely reclaiming the residence building and the barn. Elk, deer, and small mammal tracks can be seen in the dirt floors of the two buildings, clear evidence of the rarity of human presence.

When I've visited the area, either on these fisheries surveys, visiting the Doody Homestead, old ranger station site, or fishing Harrison Lake, I've felt a distinct separation from civilization. The Glacier Park side, after all, is physically separated by a cold, rocky river that can rage up to tens of thousands of cubic feet per second during runoff. Even in the heyday of Nyack siding and the years of active ranger station occupancy, I'm sure the rangers and the other passers-through felt the same sense of isolation.

In the final analysis, I believe that in most people's minds the spectacular and remote Harrison Lake was the central point of the Nyack District. Each ranger made it a priority in his patrols, probably in part because of its beauty and the spectacular ridges rising from its shores. It also didn't hurt that the trail up the drainage to the lake joins the main Boundary Trail right at the hospitable Doody homestead. The journal entries about Harrison Lake that still exist mostly reflect awe and adventure. On December 8, 1928, the ranger (probably Hugh Buchanan) made the 14-mile trip to the upper end of the lake and noted that the inlet stream was open and "alive with approximately 100 mallard and canvasback ducks." He also noted, "the lake was completely covered by ice (which I walked on) excepting the outlet and inlet of Harrison creeks." He added that some of the ducks were feeding on the many whitefish that were spawning in the creeks.

One of the last journal entries for 1928, in late December, mentions another trip to Harrison Lake. The entry clearly illustrates the importance of getting along with the locals. Ranger J. R. Winnington, who had been with the Park Service for just six months, reached the Doody homestead at sundown, just as a warm, winter "chinook" wind rolled down the Middle Fork. He saw "considerable" beaver, coyote and deer sign. Winnington enjoyed a Christmas-season dinner at Josephine's, and probably stayed there overnight. Imagine the stories Josephine told the young ranger about the early days of the Park. Imagine accompanying the young ranger on such a patrol and listening to this incredible woman's stories about the Park.

Josephine must have been almost a mother figure to the mostly young rangers who served at the station, and her hospitality in the middle of a wilderness was important to them, judging on how often they visited her. Although Josephine was not particularly law abiding, she and the rangers shared a mutual respect for each other.

Josephine, an enigmatic and some would say notorious figure, had a complicated relationship with the Glacier Park Rangers and with the local residents. Her life story was mostly a mystery; even good friends said later that they never learned her first name. She wanted to just be called "Doody". Her story rivals any frontier woman's in scope and quirkiness. Let me tell you about it…

Chapter 9:
BOOTLEG LADY OF GLACIER PARK
Josephine Doody does things her way on her remote Glacier Park homestead

I am haunted by a woman who died long before I was born. Frontierswoman Josephine Doody was a quirky figure in the lore of the Middle Fork, and even after years of being driven to research her life, I still find her a mystery.

I became interested in Josephine's story one day in October of 1987 on a hike to Harrison Lake. I waded across the Middle Fork of the Flathead River, cut across the flats and found the Boundary Trail along the Glacier Park side of the river. At the junction of the Harrison Lake Trail, I first saw the remnants of the Doody homestead cabin and outbuildings.

The homestead fronts about a million acres of virtual wilderness. To reach it, you have to cross the clear, swift Middle Fork, which like all mountain rivers in Montana, rushes and ebbs with snowmelt and rainstorms. Rising above the homestead, up the Harrison Creek drainage, lies Harrison Lake and the glaciated peaks of Walton and Thompson. Whoever lived at this homestead had to have relished the backcountry and made an effort to separate themselves from civilization.

I was moved by the thought of someone living in this isolated meadow surrounded by heavy timber within one of the most remote areas of Glacier National Park. I felt compelled to find out more.

When I returned to Kalispell after that trip to Harrison Lake I asked Doris Huffine, a former resident of the Middle Fork, postmaster at Nyack, and a pioneer woman herself, about the homestead. She described the people who had lived there: her friend Josephine Doody and Josephine's husband Dan. She told me things Josephine told her that sounded bizarre and unbelievable, but knowing Doris's objectivity and memory, I felt they had to be true. To start sleuthing Josephine's story, I needed to follow up on the leads that Doris gave me.

For starters, I had to spend more time where Josephine had lived at all

Josephine in front of the Doody's original homestead cabin about 1900. Josephine kept herself well-groomed and wore practical dresses and shifts. Glacier National Park Historical Collection.

seasons of the year. So later that winter, I decided to visit the homestead and ski to Harrison Lake. The day was clear and cold, and the Middle Fork was ice-coated. Leaving my hip boots, I decided to take the chance of skiing across the surface of the ice. I skied down the hillside from the highway and across the railroad tracks. At the river, I carefully double-poled my way across on the ice, which was only a few inches thick in the middle of the channel. It was not reassuring to hear the river rushing and gurgling beneath my skis.

When I reached the Glacier Park side, I skied upstream about a mile along the river and crossed the timbered flat to the homestead. Snow hung like wet cotton on the branches of the fir and spruce that were encroaching on the meadow. The winter sun filtered through trees, casting angles of light on the old homestead building. I was probably the only human for miles within the Park. The solitude was pressing.

The trail from the homestead to Harrison Lake rises steeply at first, and then continues gently, up and down, for several miles to the foot of the lake.

In February 1994 the homestead's chimney and the four walls are still standing. Author Photo.

My skis clattered in and out of elk tracks that pockmarked the crusted snow on the trail. When I reached the lake I was captivated by its beauty in winter. The knife peaks of the range angled thousands of feet above it, cutting white teeth in the deep blue, almost purple, sky. The huge glacially carved basin held the lake just right. No wonder the early day Nyack rangers visited this place again and again.

I skied the two-mile length of the lake to the Park Service cabin near the inlet. Elk tracks and beds were scattered about the frozen surface. Based on all the elk sign, the Doodys would have had little trouble getting all the winter meat they needed. On the ski run, I also crossed three or four sets of mountain lion tracks whose owners appeared to be keeping track of the elk herd. As a hunter, I could identify with that. People said that Josephine and Dan had often hunted lions here with their Airedale dogs. In fact, some people said that Josephine was close to a mountain lion in her temperament.

As I skied too fast back down the bumpy trail, a fir branch snapped me across the chin. My chin was numb from the cold air and I didn't feel much pain. But as I stopped and looked down, I saw my blood on the snow. The mountain lion tracks took on a different meaning for me then.

I reached the homestead and skied around the building. The snow was mostly untracked except for a few marks left by squirrels and snowshoe hares. I unhooked my skis and entered the building under a low, leaning porch awning and looked around inside. Cardboard wallpaper hung in tatters from the living room and kitchen. I carefully walked up a creaking staircase to find four rooms with faded pieces of blue and pink cardboard hanging from the ceiling like stalactites. Packrats had stacked cedar leaves in nearly every corner of the rooms. It was clear that, in its day, this building was elaborate and roomy, especially given its location.

I went outside into the fading light and fastened on my skis for the trip back downriver. Skiing around the building towards the front porch, I crossed a set of tracks that I'm pretty sure were not there when I entered the building. Maybe I'd missed them, but I don't think so. The animal appeared to have exited the ground level window when I went in from the back porch.

These fresh tracks were clearly those of a mountain lion. I considered this a sign that chasing after Josephine's story was going to be interesting.

Josephine Gaines was born somewhere in Macon County, Georgia in 1854. Her birth date isn't certain. In her obituary in January 1936, she is listed as 82 years of age, consistent with that birth date. But census records show she may have actually been born in 1848. So she either lied about her age, or the census takers back in Georgia got it wrong.

Josephine was a member of a well-off family who owned a plantation. She told Doris Huffine that she had been suckled by a slave lady. She had been educated in good schools.

She told Doris that as a girl, she had come west in the 1870s on a wagon train, traveling with a young man with whom she had probably eloped. She said that their party came upon a site where another party had been massacred by Indians. She was sickened by the sight of human heads stuck on posts.

After reaching Colorado, Josephine somehow lost her man and turned to prostitution in the saloons, dancehalls, and brothels of the tough western frontier towns. Her wit, direct style, attractive features, and Georgia accent endeared her to the railroad workers and miners. But something went terribly wrong. Josephine shot and killed a man in Pueblo, beginning what would be a lifetime of conflict with the law. Josephine claimed self-defense, and lawmen scheduled a trial. But with help, she fled north on the rails before the trial could be held.

Josephine landed in the raucous town of McCarthyville in 1890 during the boom period of railroad construction over Marias Pass. Now in her thirties, men were still drawn to Josephine's shapely figure and pretty face. Sadly, out of desperation she became addicted to opium supplied by the Chinese railroad workers. So far, Josephine's thirty-odd years had been mostly filled with despair, admittedly brought about in part by her own bad choices.

But Josephine had shown time and again that she was a survivor. McCarthyville proved to be a perfect place for her to hide from the law and continue her "career" as a saloon girl (she later told Doris that she was a "dancer.") Her fiery personality was known and appreciated around the railroad camp. She also had a big heart and compassion for the men who paid for her services. Fed up with the treatment of sick railroad workers in the town's sorry "hospital," Josephine once threatened a railroad official at gunpoint, demanding that he hire a real doctor. She would always be known as someone who didn't hesitate to reach for a gun.

Finally, as the boomtown began to die, Josephine's luck changed. She met a local prospector and trapper who had traveled north from Colorado years

earlier. Dan Doody worked for the railroad construction company and probably spent time in town doing business with Josephine. He fell for her and he wanted her all to himself. He was a few years younger than Josephine, but he figured he wasn't getting any younger, and women were scarce in the wilderness of Northwest Montana. He had claimed some land in Nyack Flats across the Middle Fork of the Flathead River and had built a cabin there. Dan thought that Josephine would fit in just right.

Dan needed a woman, and he believed that Josephine needed to get out from her self-destructive vocation. Dan was sure about it, but Josephine needed some hands-on convincing.

Dan Doody probably near Fielding and Marias Pass in 1904. Glacier National Park Historical Collection..

Dan knew that it wouldn't be easy to get Josephine out of McCarthyville, out of her opium habit, and into his cabin surrounded by wilderness. He knew what he needed to do and how to do it. He couldn't take the chance that Josephine would say no, so he kidnapped her.

One night he grabbed the small but wiry woman, who was high on dope, and tied her to a mule. Over the course of a few difficult days he was able to transport her along Bear Creek, down along the Middle Fork of the Flathead River and across Nyack Flats to his remote cabin and land about 25 miles southwest of McCarthyville.

At first, Dan thought that his plan to save Josephine and marry her had been a bad idea. Josephine raged at him and repeatedly said that she hated him. He had to lock her in a small cabin in order to break her of the addiction. Unpleasant weeks passed, but eventually Josephine admitted that Dan had saved her life. Josephine said that they got married that year but it must have been a "frontier marriage," because no official record of it exists.

Dan had taken action and found himself a woman. He had judged

Josephine Doody loved to fish for cutthroat trout with a long cane pole. Betty Robertson Schurr says this is an old photo of Josephine. She's fishing the Middle Fork. Betty Robertson Schurr Collection.

correctly to act quickly or be womanless. For the next seven years of her life on the homestead across the river, Josephine never saw another woman.

The railroad town below Marias Pass died after the rails were completed west to Kalispell. Only a few prospectors and trappers remained in the remote valley of the Middle Fork. The Doodys were the only people living on the far side of the river.

Josephine found that frontier life on the homestead suited her. Their 160 acres were surrounded by four million acres of wilderness, broken only by the thin rails of the Great Northern Railroad located across the Middle Fork. They were separated from civilization, and had their own large tributary, Harrison Creek, which entered the Middle Fork just upstream. Not far up the canyon was Harrison Lake. Westslope cutthroat, bull trout and mountain whitefish abounded in all these clean, cold waters. Grizzlies, elk, moose, deer, and furbearers roamed their land. All the bounty of this wilderness, everything they needed to live, was close at hand. They had this all to themselves. It's impossible today to imagine what this kind of freedom must have been like. Josephine especially liked to fish the clear waters of the Middle Fork for the cutthroat and bull trout. She developed a lifelong skill and love for catching and eating these vibrant native species.

Dan had designed the homestead buildings with a lodge function in mind, planning to outfit friends and hunters that he might attract from the railroad.

Josephine Doody at the homestead with a stringer of native trout from the Middle Fork. Betty Robertson Schurr Collection.

In the main cabin a large square room dominated the interior. To conserve space, he fashioned two log alcoves along one side for beds, and another alcove for his beloved Airedale dogs. The Doodys used these dogs for protection and ran bears and mountain lions with them when they could. The cabins were located on the edge of a small clearing among the old-growth spruce, cedar and fir. Within a few years, Dan added a guest cabin and built a breezeway connecting the two structures. His illegal outfitting camp was now complete.

Josephine came to love the isolated life on the far side of the Middle Fork, but her past still haunted the couple's happy existence. Lawmen from Colorado were looking for her and telegraphing north to lawmen in Montana. Dan knew he could beat the lawmen because of his knowledge of the country, and because no trainmen would ever give away Josephine's whereabouts.

Up the ridge across Harrison Creek, about a mile north of the homestead, Dan built a small, tight cabin. This cabin was hidden among the timber on the edge of a large cut bank nearly 1,000 feet above the Middle Fork and a long way from any water source. Clearly, this structure was more than a simple trapper's line cabin. It was built for comfort and for hiding. It measured fifteen feet square, with a stone fireplace fit into a corner. Josephine could look out its only window to the river floodplain below. It's rumored that she fled to this cabin or possibly another cabin upriver anytime law officers were rumored to be in the area looking for her.

The Doodys had the confidence of the railway men, and the train was the only practical way to reach the Nyack area of the Middle Fork. This made it nearly impossible for an officer to arrive unannounced and apprehend Josephine.

Dan hosted hunters from all over the country on his 160-acre homestead. From his cabins, he could access millions of acres of wilderness where hunters could find deer, moose, elk, black bear and grizzlies. He didn't have to worry about rangers or game wardens.

Dan, who had worked on the railway at Marias Pass, was highly regarded by officials of the Great Northern Railroad. Jim Hill, the prominent founder of Great Northern, reportedly accompanied Dan on hunting and fishing forays to Harrison Lake. On one fall hunting trip Hill became injured and Dan had to rescue him, hauling him in a toboggan down to the river and across in a rowboat to a waiting train. In gratitude, Hill ordered trainmen throughout his company to stop whenever the Doodys needed a ride or anything else. Hill actually established a stop known as Doody Siding across from the homestead. The "siding" was in the middle of nowhere and was established solely for the Doodys and people visiting them. Hill would stop in his private coach, and Dan would take him and his guests across the river for a few days of hunting.

The Hills had a long relationship with Dan. Dan squired one of Hill's associates, a prominent photographer and artist, around the park on horseback. The photos and paintings from these trips adorned the coaches of the Great Northern trains to promote the beauty of the new national park.

Congress designated over one million acres of northwest Montana as Glacier National Park on May 11, 1910. The Middle Fork of the Flathead River formed the southeast boundary, incorporating the Doody homestead within the Park. Major William R. Logan was hired as Glacier's first superintendent on August 8, 1910, along with Assistant Superintendent Henry Hutchings. In one of Logan's first acts as superintendent he asked Dan, one of the best-known mountain men in northwest Montana, to become a Glacier Park Ranger. Dan accepted the appointment on August 12 and according to the Park records appears to have been the very first Park ranger hired. His area included the entire Middle Fork of the Flathead drainage extending upstream to Fielding and Marias Pass.

Dan was joined by five more rangers: Billy Burns, Joe Cosley, Frank Doll, Frank Pierce, and Dad Randals. An official early photo shows the six rangers on horseback, with handlebar-mustached Dan staring at the camera from under a big-brimmed hat. Logan had chosen the best known, toughest mountain men familiar with each area of what was now a national park. The original rangers were independent but did not fit the strict mode of law officers. They had lived free too long for that.

Dan accepted the appointment, the prestige, and the limited pay of the position; but he didn't accept the government's designation for his part of the Middle Fork. He and Josephine went on hunting and trapping and hosting guests as if nothing had changed. They were going to live off the land they had pioneered for the last 20 years no matter what designation the government gave it. Dan believed he had a certain immunity. After all, he was now the ranger, and he surely wasn't going to turn himself in.

Dan, Josephine, and one of their beloved dogs in front of their original homestead cabin across the Middle Fork of the Flathead River. Glacier National Park Historical Collection.

Dan had a special technique, a combination of hunting and trapping, which he used at times to bag grizzly bears for especially important hunters. He would tie up a stinking carcass of a deer, and then set bear traps in areas where the bears would approach. Dan checked the traps each morning. When a grizzly had been caught in a trap, Dan was ready for the hunter. He would return to his cabins where the hunter was enjoying a leisurely breakfast, and take the hunter out "searching" for a bear. As they approached the trapped grizzly, the animal would rear up and Dan would instruct the hunter to shoot until it was down. Dan would then say, "Let's go back to the cabin and have a bite to make sure this grizzly has time to die. They are real dangerous to approach when they are wounded." Later, the bear would be brought in and skinned, supposedly with the hunter not knowing (or maybe not caring) that he had shot a trapped bear. Dan had the reputation of killing every bear he saw, black or grizzly. This seems inexplicable considering his love of nature and animals that he demonstrated in other ways.

Dan's relationship with the Park Service deteriorated as his reputation for lawlessness grew. Despite his cavalier attitude towards the law, he managed to get himself reappointed as a park ranger six times. Records show him as gaining ranger appointments in 1910, 1911, 1912, 1913, 1914, 1915, and early 1916. He was "terminated" on March 15, 1916 for unstated reasons that were probably obvious to everyone.

Mountain lion hunting was a passion and an attraction for the Doodys, who kept Airedale dogs that were carefully trained to run and tree the big cats. This was one type of hunting that Josephine enjoyed. She liked the thrill of seeing her beloved dogs excitedly chasing a cougar, then being able to watch the 150-pound cat's behavior while it snarled down at them from the branches of a big fir tree. In photos, it's easy to see that the dogs, with their own alcove in the main cabin, were an important part of the Doody's family.

Dan prided himself in being the most accomplished woodsman and mountain man in northwest Montana. But he found out that he couldn't always guarantee the safety of hunters who accompanied him. Unfortunately, his own wife was the victim of a lion hunt gone badly. One big male cat jumped down from the tree where it had sought refuge and attacked one of the Airedales. Josephine foolishly tried to help the dog, and the lion got a few licks in on her before it escaped. Josephine was scratched in the neck and face and bled profusely. From this she bore scars for the rest of her life.

Photos of Josephine at the homestead cabin show a clean, strong woman built wiry and thin, with large hands. Her face was still attractive in a rugged, outdoors way. She wore her hair pulled back tightly with a long ponytail. Her jaw was square and her eyes were keen and intense. In several different photos, she wore a similar work dress with a shift over it. Any man of that time living in this remote part of Montana would most likely agree that Dan was lucky. He had himself a fine looking woman who looked younger than her age, and on top of that, she was willing to live a wilderness life.

As the years went by, Josephine and Dan developed a high value source of income that was perfectly suited to their remote homestead. The dictionary defines bootleg liquor or moonshine as "alcoholic liquor unlawfully made, sold, or transported, without registration or payment of taxes." You couldn't get a better description of what the Doodys did: they made it, they transported it across the river, and they sold it to the trainmen for distribution. And Josephine took particular pleasure in it. After all, the product was highly sought after by men. She could get good money for something that cost her almost nothing, and she could stiff the government, all at the same time. It had similar characteristics of her former profession, and in her mind, it was perfect.

Josephine's moonshine had the highest reputation for quality, produced from the rushing glacial waters of Harrison Creek. The Doodys had three stills housed in small log sheds scattered through the timber on their homestead and they produced gallons and gallons of the white lightning from their own special grain-mash recipe. Josephine sold it by the pint jar, quart jar, or gallon jug.

The railroad siding across the river provided the means for distributing the hooch. A train operator would halt the train (which would be a serious offense except at the Doody siding, where it was winked at) and signal the number of quarts of moonshine by the number of toots on the train whistle. The transaction took place at a prearranged schedule, so that Josephine could have a supply ready in the timber across the river. The trainmen pulled the whistle, and soon a small figure would appear out of the timber and climb into a small rowboat. Josephine was expert at rowing with the bow pointed upstream so as not to lose ground in the current. If the river flow was too high, the sale would have to wait.

The train operators would grab the bow of Josephine's boat when it touched shore below the tracks. Josepine would exchange the mountain dew for cash or credit. Josephine would thank them in a melodious southern drawl, with a little good-natured banter thrown in. She knew how to handle men, of course. And according to those who knew her she could "talk like a muleskinner" which delighted the trainmen. Sometimes the trainmen left the train "parked" at the siding and had dinner at Josephine's, a practice that would have gotten them fired at any other stop along the Great Northern rail line. With the help and cooperation of the trainmen, the Doodys seem to have avoided being busted by the law for their relatively large-scale bootleg operation. There is no record of them being caught by a ranger or "revenuer" during the period that Dan was alive.

Residents were allowed a 5-year grace period to file patents on their homesteads after the Park was formed in 1910. Dan filed his homestead patent on the 160 acres near the mouth of Harrison Creek on November 11, 1914. He and Josephine had reached their 60s, and were in apparent good health despite the rugged lives they had led.

Four years after Dan signed his homestead papers, his health began to take a dive. Because of his condition, a number of men were hired to help the Doodys with their operations across the river. Their pay was room and board, a little moonshine, and limited cash supplied by the moonshine.

By 1919 Dan recognized that his heart was weakening fast, so he transferred the homestead deed to Josephine. A few years later he walked out of the main cabin one day to do chores but died of a heart attack instead.

A January 19, 1921 obitiuary described Dan's death in dramatic fashion: "Death came to him suddenly, but not unexpected. A serious heart trouble for some time made it necessary to give up much of his usual activity, and he realized that the end was not far off. On the morning of January 17 he was in his usual good spirits and apparent health. As he stood giving directions to his men for the work of the day he suddenly sank, and as one of the workmen placed his arm to support him, he remarked that the end had come, and in a moment he had gone, peacefully and quietly."

When asked about Dan's death by the coroner, Josephine was succinct. "Dan dropped dead while out in the yard doing chores," she said, and that sentence appeared on his death certificate.

Dan's 800-word obituary reflected his prominence as a mountain man, calling him "every inch a man" and "one of the best known men in northwest Montana." It mentioned his trapping, prospecting, outfitting, ranger service, and his friendship to railroad presidents and section men. "Scores of people" and "flowers in profusion" attested to his popularity.

Josephine had lost her man again, but in her mid-sixties, she still had lots of energy. She was determined to stay on the wilderness homestead and run it smoothly, with the help of a few men. All evidence points to her success in doing so, although her choices of men turned out to be questionable in a case or two.

On February 5, 1921, Josephine crossed the Middle Fork on the ice, flagged down the train, and rode the 40 miles to Kalispell. At the Flathead County courthouse she witnessed the recording of the homestead deed, officially establishing her ownership.

For the next decade as she aged gracefully into her 70s, Josephine ran the homestead with a special efficiency. Her moonshine business flourished. She was a favorite with many of the Park rangers who patrolled around her 160 acres. And amazingly, she had a much larger dwelling built for herself, her friends, and visitors who came to fish and hunt. Obviously, she knew men well and was good at getting them to do what she wanted.

Chris Vale, who had worked for Dan, became Josephine's foreman and moved into the main dwelling with her when it was completed. The building contained two stories, with multiple rooms for guests and workers. Vale hosted fishing parties to Harrison Lake, but since rangers now occasionally patrolled across the river, the illicit hunting outfitting was scaled down, and then eliminated. Josephine had to get along with the rangers who started patrolling the Nyack area once the first ranger station was built in the early 1920s.

People in the Park Service and others were well aware of Josephine's moonshine business, but did little about it. Jack McDonald, a Park guard at Nyack, was a good friend. He helped her keep the operation under wraps, and by some accounts, actually helped transport the hooch.

Park Service packer Richard "Tiny" Powell, brother of western artist Ace Powell, often packed extra supplies down from the Harrison Lake ranger cabin to deliver to Josephine in the fall. Josephine liked Tiny and from time to time had him over for dinner and a swig of moonshine. Tiny had vivid memories of Josephine's big gold nugget earrings that pulled her ears into the shape of a banana.

"She either liked you or she didn't," Tiny remembered later. "She was pretty independent, and she was a good shot. Some rangers steered wide around her place. They were afraid of her." Tiny didn't mind that Josephine shot and butchered deer year-round. "Hugh Buchanan was a ranger who liked her," he said. "If she poached deer or elk, he didn't see it." Later, Josephine listed Hugh as one of the best rangers in the Park Service. She also admired ranger Clyde Fauley who was stationed for a time at Nyack Ranger Station. Clyde's son, Clyde Jr., recalls having Thanksgiving dinner at Josephine's homestead when he was a boy. Josephine had the reputation of being a good cook, but Clyde remembers that on one occasion she burned the gravy. Clyde remembers that he and other kids called her "Old Lady Doody."

Josephine's moonshining finally caught up with her in 1928, when her friends in the Park Service had little choice but to assist federal officers on a raid of her homestead. Rangers called these men "revenuers" or the "dry squad." In the ranger journal for the Nyack Ranger Station for Saturday, February 18, 1928, the ranger (not identified, but probably her pal Hugh) described the takedown. The ranger had visited the deer feeding station and stopped to see Josephine on his way back to the ranger station. He had little choice but to cooperate with the federal men.

"...I stopped at Mrs. Doody's on my way home and soon after leaving the house I met McDonald and two federal men. They wanted me as a witness as they said they were going to search the place. They talked with her a few minutes and then proceeded to a small cabin about 500 or 1,000 feet from the house and there found a padlock on the door so one of the men chopped it off and entered, finding a 50 gallon still and all that goes with it, 12 barrels of mash and 17-1/2 gal moon, and destroyed all but a sample. They found three deer hides which were behind the house or cabin which they told me they knew nothing, so I took them to headquarters. On the trail from the house to the boat landing they found two stills, one 25—and one 20 gal. About 50 feet from the boat under a log was a one gal jug of whisky making a total of 18-1/2 gal of moon."

The ranger's description illustrates the size of Josephine's bootleg operation, and her energy and cheek. Josephine, about age 74, had not scaled back the bootlegging, but had actually increased production. She was making large quantities of moonshine amidst all the Park Service patrols and regulations. That takes careful management.

Ironically, it was Jack McDonald who led the revenuers on the raid of Josephine's place. McDonald was rumored to not only wink at her bootleg business, but based on more than one source he actually helped her from time to time. It's likely that because of orders from Park headquarters in Belton, he had no choice but to lead the federal men to her place.

Wes Bell, who, as a young man and resident of Nyack, knew Josephine well, chuckled at the thought of revenuers thinking they were getting the drop on her "secret" moonshine operation. "Everybody knew about it," Bell said. "The train men used to leave the whole train parked at Doody Siding, and cross the river to get the moonshine. Sometimes they would eat there, but moonshine was the main attraction." Wes described the cable crossing built across the Middle Fork south of Harrison Creek that provided another way to access the Doodys at high water flows. "I crossed it once with Louie McDonald, Jack's son, when I was nine or ten. It was

Harrison Lake was an important location in the Nyack Valley, and was visited by the Doodys and Glacier Park Rangers in summer and winter. Josephine's homestead was located at the junction of the trail to the lake and the river trail. Author Photo.

a square box. You coasted about half-way across the river, and then pulled yourself the rest of the way. It wasn't easy."

Josephine often hosted Nyack residents at her homestead. Bob Robertson remembers one Thanksgiving when his entire family, including little Betty, rode a horse-drawn sleigh to Doody Landing. They rode the cable car across the Middle Fork, then walked the trail through the snow to the deep-woods homestead.

Once, Wes, Bob Robertson, and another boy came down from a fishing trip at Harrison Lake and found Josephine at the cable crossing. "Josephine wouldn't let us use the cable car because she was mad at Robertson," Wes remembered. "She could be rough when she wanted to be." The boys were forced to use an old leaky boat to get across and were nearly swept down the river. Wes also suspected that Josephine might have been mad at him because he had caught one of her pet cats in a trap.

Two days after Josephine's bust, the ranger was back at her place, "running section lines of her property" and patrolling back to the Nyack Ranger Station. He had taken the train from Nyack to Belton and then traveled the 14 miles on the boundary trail back to Nyack along the Park side of the Middle Fork. Maybe he steered wide around her 160 acres that day until he could find out how mad she was at him for helping in the federal raid. At any rate, by early spring the ranger was patrolling to Harrison

Lake and spending the night at Josephine's, so they must have reached an understanding or a truce.

In fact, Josephine's homestead quite often served as a waypoint and friendly stopover for rangers on patrol. Many entries in the journals for the Nyack Station mention eating dinner at Josephine's, leaving horses there, or renting horses from her. It's hard, then, to understand why the Park Service threatened at one point to remove her line-phone that connected her to the Nyack station and downriver to Park headquarters in West Glacier. Supposedly Josephine refused to start paying $20 per month as requested by the service. Maybe a new bureaucrat in the headquarters had this idea, but he was quickly stuffed when Josephine called the assistant chief ranger.

"If you unhook my phone," Josephine fumed to him, "Every SOB who wants to go to Harrison Lake is going to have to steer clear around my 160 acres." Josephine knew that to reach the Harrison Trail junction from either direction on the boundary trail without crossing her homestead, riders or hikers would have to stumble and climb for a quarter mile or more through downed timber and buckbrush. The switchboard gal, "Bud" Henderson, remembered this incident and said she was quickly ordered to keep Josephine's phone line connected without a monthly charge.

Josephine maintained her friendship with the Hills of Great Northern fame. Louis Hill, Jim Hill's son and president of Great Northern, occasionally stayed at her place and fished Harrison Lake. Hill made sure that Josephine could get on the train in either direction any time she wanted. All she had to do was call her friend Bud at the switchboard in Belton, eight miles downriver, and let her know she wanted a train, either eastbound or westbound, to stop at Doody Siding. Bud would forward the message upriver to Essex Station if the train was coming from the east. Once, a new dispatcher named Ole confidently refused to order the train to stop at Doody Siding, saying "Nobody can stop a train like that." A more experienced trainman informed him that he would be fired if he didn't stop the train at the siding.

As she reached her late 70s, Josephine was bent and hunched forward at the shoulders. She was never tall in the first place. As noted by Tiny Powell, "If she stood straight up when she was young she might have been five-two."

Josephine's face showed the effects of 40 winters in the Montana backcountry. Her face was lined "like a dried peach" and large, gold-nugget earrings had pulled her ears into a banana shape. Josephine had to accept that she was getting too old to remain on the isolated homestead across the Middle Fork and all the work that went with it.

In 1931, Josephine reluctantly moved out of the homestead and across the Middle Fork to a small cabin along Deerlick Creek, just a short distance from the railroad tracks and the road that ran along the river. For the first time in her life, Josephine, now 80, lived in a place that was accessible by a car, at least from May to November. She moved one of her stills across the river and stored it in a neighbor's (the Crawford's) root cellar. She never moonshined again, though. She admitted to friends that it was bad.

Josephine's cabin had one room and two cots, one for her and one for Charlie Holland. Holland, a World War I veteran, worked seasonally for the road department. Charlie needed a place to stay and Josephine was alone, so they lived together for convenience. Velma Guy, a neighbor who lived a mile east, thought that Charlie treated Josephine kindly. Charlie worked for Velma's husband, Bert, on the road crew. Others, though, had a different opinion of Charlie Holland. "If Charlie was so great," asked Doris Huffine who visited Josephine often during this period, "how was it he was always partying in Belton, getting drunk?" Doris thought that Charlie was taking advantage of Josephine's kindness.

Josephine kept 40 cats and cooked beans for them daily. Even in her 80s, Josephine went out of her way to help others. She kept a garden and gave potatoes and other food to Mrs. Wingate, who lived about a half-mile east of her little cabin. Mrs. Wingate had seven daughters and they were poor and hungry.

When Doris Huffine and her sister Maxine visited the hunch-backed old woman, they sat together at a little table under a window that looked out over Deerlick Creek with a mountain ridge rising abruptly from the far side of the creek. Josephine told her tales of the early days while the two younger women listened. Doris stopped by often to hear Josephine reminisce. Doris lived at the Stanton Creek Lodge, about 10 miles upriver along the Middle Fork, and in her Model A Ford drove right by the little cabin on her way to Belton. She would often take Josephine something to eat. Josephine gave the Huffines one of the grizzly hides that had been on the wall of her homestead to display at the Huffines' Stanton Creek Lodge.

Doris said that most people were afraid to stop at the old woman's house because of her reputation of being volatile and hasty with a gun. "She was a spitfire kind of monkey," remembered Doris. "She was tough and I mean tough. She was worse than any man if she wanted to cuss you out. Maxine and I were real careful with her."

The few residents of Nyack Flats helped Josephine. Velma Guy and her young children were favorites of Josephine. Velma's most vivid memory of the old woman was her love of fishing. Josephine would walk down to the Middle Fork, perch on a rock, and fish by the hour for cutthroat trout with a bamboo rod. Her favorite ranger, Clyde Fauley Sr., visited her from time to time.

Josephine didn't go to town often. Sometimes friends drove her into Belton or Kalispell, and sometimes she went in with Charlie Holland. One

The homestead in October 1989. The building is shaky, but still mostly standing. Author Photo

of these trips proved to be a disaster. At the time, Highway 2 was a narrow, treacherous road that snaked above the canyon of the Middle Fork of the Flathead River. At one particularly bad spot, the road swung out to the edge of the canyon. Residents called this point on the road, "Shake hands with the Devil." Charlie lost control of his Studebaker and crashed down over the side of the canyon. Josephine's face hit the dashboard and she was badly scarred for the last few years of her life.

Josephine's health had been excellent for 82 years, but her hard life finally caught up with her in January 1936. The old woman contracted pnuemonia and fell seriously ill. Charlie Holland and Mrs. Crawford, a neighbor, were taking care of her. After four days, Charlie decided she needed to go to the hospital in Kalispell. Josephine protested, saying, "Don't even think of moving me! I'll die sure as shootin' if you move me now in this weather." Josephine knew she had a better chance to survive if she stayed put, but she was powerless to stop Charlie from moving her. Things might have been different if she were not so weak and had access to one of her guns.

Charlie ignored her protests and got word to the trainmen to stop at Doody siding. The train was the only transportation in the Middle Fork canyon during winter. Eager to help, the Great Northern men on January 15 stopped the train one last time for Josephine. It was a snowy afternoon, with temperatures dipping below zero. Josephine was loaded on a makeshift stretcher and carried to the train. At Columbia Falls, Josephine was transferred to the "Dinky," a small, rattle-trap passenger train, and then finally transported on to the hospital in Kalispell. She was unconscious when she arrived and never awakened, according to Velma Guy who came in to stay with her.

The next night at 6:30 p.m., Josephine died. Her death certificate lists "Lobar Pneumonia, left" as the cause of death. The certificate was signed by Dr. Albert Brassett, the same doctor who amputated little Betty Robertson's finger about eight years earlier.

In contrast to her husband's prominence and large funeral, few people attended Josephine's funeral two days later and her burial at the Conrad Memorial

Josephine (left), Mrs. Gruber's niece, and Mrs. Ensinine Gruber. The Grubers were Great Northern Railroad magnates. This photo was taken late in Josephine's life. National Park Service Photo, courtesy of Glacier National Park.

Cemetery. Velma Guy and Tiny Powell, Josephine's old friend from the Park Service, attended. They both remembered that only a handful of people were there. Charlie Holland did not attend. Tiny remembers that her gold nugget earrings that she always wore were gone. He remembered thinking that "somebody must have needed the money pretty bad" to have taken her earrings.

Josephine's obituary was brief and filled with factual errors. She was buried next to Dan, but as I found out when I searched for it, her grave was never marked with a stone.

Charlie Holland got all of Josephine's things, and the deed to the 160-acre homestead across the Middle Fork. Records show that she had transferred the homestead deed to him two years earlier. On the day of Josephine's funeral, Charlie was at the Flathead County Courthouse witnessing the recording of the deed on the homestead to establish his ownership.

True to Doris Huffine's assessment of his character, Charlie lost the 160

Remnants of the hideout cabin perched on the edge of a ridge above the Middle Fork of the Flathead River, October 1989. Author Photo.

acres after only seven months. In the late summer of 1936 he transferred the deed to the Schumachers of Belton to pay off boozing and gambling debts, and then vanished from the area.

The homestead across the Middle Fork is still remote. The 160 acres haven't been altered, although different people hold a deed to some of the acres, and the Park Service now owns a portion. The homestead cabin, which was two shaky stories when I first visited it, is collapsing into the earth. Packrats, marten, mountain lions, grizzlies, elk and deer frequent the meadows and heavy timber around the homestead. The little moonshine root cellars can still be found. Nyack old-timers were confident that sealed moonshine jugs, abandoned and lost during revenuer raids, are still buried here and there around the homestead. Undoubtedly, there are secrets of other kinds buried there that Josephine never revealed.

The existence and location of the hideout cabin has always been murky. I knew that to confirm the credibility of Josephine's stories of her early life with Dan, I had to resolve the questions about this cabin. Some considered it only a legend but I always felt it had to exist. She had described it to Doris Huffine in detail. Whenever I drove along the Middle Fork I looked across the ridges north of Harrison Creek and I wondered.

One October, I visited Gordon Pouliott, who lived at the upper end of Nyack Flats. Gordon was a well-known amateur historian who often searched for clues to the past. Across the river and on the ridge below

Lone Man Mountain, Gordon's son had found a small cabin fitting the description of the hideout cabin. Gordon visited the cabin, which he said was deliberately built to be hard to find, and recorded the artifacts he saw there. He noted shell casings from calibers used in the 1890s and early 1900s, such as the 45-90 and 40-82, glass-blown bottles and soldered tin cans. Based on his own research and oral traditions in the Nyack area, Gordon believed that the cabin did indeed belong to the Doodys.

The October day was unusually warm. When I arrived, Gordon was directing some men in a project to expand his small museum that housed the memorabilia he'd collected over the years. Gordon was a big man. He stood a few inches over six feet and weighed about 190 pounds. He had fought professionally in the heavyweight division after serving with the Marines. Gordon's voice was even more impressive. Even if you were right beside him, he barked at you as if you were 100 yards away.

Gordon walked with me over to a point where we could look across the Middle Fork and see the ridge where the hideout cabin was located. "Right there," he shouted, pointing to a landmark on the mountainside. I remarked that it didn't look very tough to find. Gordon smirked.

I wore hip boots to cross the Middle Fork, then changed to hiking boots and started up the mountainside. Soon I realized it wouldn't be easy finding the landmark that was so prominent from the valley. The timber and brush were thick, and the hillside was divided by small ridges and drainages. I wandered for five hours, jumped a grizzly at 20 yards, and stumbled onto forgotten Half Moon Lake; but I could find no trace of the cabin. Finally I gave up and returned, a little embarrassed, to Gordon's place. "I wasn't going to be surprised if you didn't find it," he said. He offered to go with me next time.

In late October I returned for one more try before snow blanketed the hills. Gordon didn't have time to guide me. Bolstered by more directions from Gordon and my past experience I crossed the river, headed up the mountainside, and found the cabin in less than an hour.

What was left of the cabin was perched about 10 feet from the precipitous edge of a high, steep ridge and cut bank. Thick lodgepole and fir hid the site. There is no source of water even close. The Middle Fork flows along the base of the mountainside 1,000 feet below. The only apparent reason to build a cabin here would be for hiding.

The cabin measured 15 feet by 15 feet, with a stone fireplace filling one corner. In another corner lay a hand-hewn bench and table. The roof was long gone and small trees grew from what was once the cabin's floor. Only the lower three or four logs of the structure remain more or less intact. Fasteners include wooden pegs, square-headed handmade nails, and round-headed nails. According to Gordon, the construction is typical of the late

1800s. This was more than a trapper's shack; in its day, this cabin was carefully built and designed for extensive stays and comfort.

The cabin had been abandoned since the early 1900s, based on the clues found there. No signs of Josephine remain, if she were ever there. Was this the cabin in which Dan Doody locked his "bride" according to the story Josephine told Doris Huffine and her sister Maxine? Did Josephine hide here to thwart lawmen or revenuers?

I carefully searched around the cabin and around the ridge. I found traces of an old trail leading west down the ridge towards Harrison Creek, a mile away. Surely the Doodys at least knew of this cabin.

That's the way it is when you try to piece a story together of someone who died so long ago. With the passage

Clyde Fauley was known as one of the best all-around rangers in the Park. One year he sold enough coyote pelts to buy a new car. Fauley fell through the ice one winter day at Harrison Lake and almost drowned. Clyde Fauley Jr. Collection.

of time, fact and legend become hard to separate. Practically everyone who actually knew Josephine is gone. And now, almost everyone I interviewed in my search for Josephine's story is dead. Some of these folks, like Velma Guy, Bob Robertson, and others, died within months of the time I talked to them. I felt lucky and honored that they passed on their knowledge to me while they could.

Already, even Gordon has been gone for years. Recently, I found a card he sent me in 1996 that I'd forgotten about. His booming voice spoke to me across the years with his written exhortation, "John—SEE ME." I sure wish I could one more time; he was a fine man and a treasure-source of lore about Middle Fork old-timers like Josephine.

I think of Josephine often, as I drive along U. S. Highway 2 through Nyack Flats on my way up the Middle Fork to hike, hunt, trap or fish. I think of the first time I explored Harrison Lake and her homestead on that winter day when a tree branch snapped me across the chin and I bled on the snow near the tracks of a mountain lion. I think of going in the front of the homestead building and seeing the mountain lion track exiting the back through the fresh snow. Over the years, I've visited her homestead many times, alone or with my kids, trying to find inspiration or clues to her story.

When I first started chasing Josephine's story, Doris Huffine's sister Maxine had told me that, in a way, Josephine had really never left her beloved homestead and that she remained there in some form or another. She said that Josephine longed to have her story told so she wouldn't be forgotten. Maxine told me that somehow Josephine had chosen me to tell her story and wouldn't let me rest until I did. Of course, that's superstitious nonsense.

Funny, though, I do feel the urge to ski over to the homestead again this winter. Maybe if I ski around what's left of the cabin and go in quietly I'll finally, in the flesh, really see her this time.

The mountain lion, I mean.

Chapter 10
GLACIER PARK MAVERICK
George Snyder and Other Early Settlers Claim Glacier's Jewel

Lake McDonald and the McDonald Valley

Nearly everyone who's spent time on or around Glacier National Park's Lake McDonald has fallen in love with it. The look from the foot of the lake across this massive sheet of water to the Garden Wall and the Continental Divide is probably the most calming and beautiful view in the park. Ecologist Aldo Leopold wrote that you can't argue about what is most beautiful, but Leopold never saw McDonald and if he did, maybe he would have admitted that this lake is an exception.

In more ways than one Lake McDonald is a mystery right down to the origin of its name. According to L. O. Vaught, the early master of Glacier Park names, the Indians in the Flathead called it "The Big Lake in the Mountains." For a time, the lake may have been called Lake Terry, named for an army officer by Lieutenant John Van Orsdale who visited the lake in 1874 on his way to Nyack Creek and Cut Bank Pass. Another military expedition traveling from the Flathead Valley reached the south shore of the lake in 1883, but they didn't record a name for the lake at the time. This party included the future first Superintendent of Glacier Park, W. R. Logan. Like the earlier expedition, they followed an old Indian trail "abandoned 25 or 30 years ago" upstream along the Middle Fork to Nyack Creek, then over Cut Bank Pass. Logan was the first to document a glacier in the area, later naming it "Pumpelly Glacier."

Some say Lake McDonald drew its name from the swashbuckling Duncan McDonald, who was born in the lower Flathead Valley downstream from Flathead Lake. As the story goes, Duncan was leading a party of Flathead Indians toward a mountain pass in the 1870s when they found out that a Blackfeet party was waiting there to surprise them. McDonald and his companions turned around, headed back down the Middle Fork and avoided the ambush. On their way back to the Flathead Valley, they camped on a beautiful, large lake. On the shoreline near the outlet of that lake, Duncan

McDonald Lake, looking north. Mt. Brown is on the right. Snyder Creek enters at the point on the lake below it near the lake's upper end. Just past Mt. Brown is Mt. Cannon. Mt. Stanton, Vaught, and Heavens Peak stand above the lake on the left. The Garden Wall is in the background. Author Photo, 1999.

supposedly carved "McDonald" on a big cedar. Later, that name was given to the lake by some of the first Euro-Americans to visit it.

Lake McDonald covers more than 6,800 surface acres. It is the largest lake in a national park that is known for its large lakes. If you completely drained the water from all the other large lakes in Glacier and emptied it in a giant graduated cylinder, it wouldn't be half enough to fill Lake McDonald. Lake McDonald holds an astonishing 2,055,376 acre-feet of water.

Shaped like a giant, steep-sided banana-split boat, McDonald is about 9-1/2 miles long following the center of the lake from inlet to outlet. The lake averages about a mile and a quarter wide and has about 22 miles of shoreline.

The lake is seemingly bottomless. McDonald averages 300 feet in depth. Its maximum depth is about as great as any lake you can find, bottoming out at 464 feet. At mid-lake, the water is 400 feet deep for nearly the entire length of the lake. Except for the inlet and outlet areas, the sides of the lake basin drop off at a dizzyingly steep angle. Push out from the shoreline almost anywhere on the lake, take three or four strong swimming strokes, and you're in water over 100 feet deep. If the summer tourists understood this, there likely would be even fewer swimmers on the lake than there are now.

McDonald's huge volume of water is incredibly transparent and pure.

When you drop a small, white and black-striped disk (called a Secchi disk by scientists) in the water and watch it intently as it sinks, you can see it until it drops below 50 feet in depth. This is a year-around average, and is the largest reading of any of the clear large lakes in the park. It's hard to imagine lake water this clear unless you've seen it.

The water in Lake McDonald is clear because there are only tiny amounts of minerals or nutrients dissolved or suspended in it. There are only paltry amounts of calcium, and nutrients like phosphorus and nitrogen. The mostly Pre-Cambrian rock that underlies the drainage gives up only tiny amounts of these substances. And the lake is ice-box cold; just ask anyone who swims in its waters. Each summer my family and I spend time on the lake's beaches. Because of its relatively low elevation (about 3,150 feet above sea level) and protected basin, it's summer-like earlier than most parts of the Park. But the appearance in mid-June is misleading; I enjoyed watching each of my three children, when they were infants, jump and scream when we stuck their little feet in the lake's 40-something degree water. Don't ask me why I did this. I guess it's just a tradition.

The lake is fed by clear and frigid McDonald Creek, the largest tributary system in the Park. The creek's waters originate at over 6,000 feet on the Continental Divide between the Lewis and Livingston mountain ranges. Longfellow, Continental, and Mineral creeks spring out of these high, alpine snowfields to form upper McDonald Creek.

After leaving the alpine, Upper McDonald Creek rushes along under the shadows of the high rocky peaks of Geduhn and Longfellow to the west, and Iceberg and Swiftcurrent to the east. The long, plateau-like Flattop Mountain divides Mineral Creek and Upper McDonald Creek as they tumble south from the Divide. A few miles upstream of the Glacier Wall the two tributaries join, forming the mainstem of McDonald Creek. Then this magnificent cascading creek nearly does a U-turn as it skids along the Glacier Wall, bending first sharply east, then southwest; and then finally forced to straighten and head south between the towering peaks of Heavens, McPartland and Vaught to the west, and Cannon and Bearhat to the east. Stanton and Brown stand as sentinels, as the creek rushes through Sacred Dancing Cascade, and then spills over a final waterfall and into Lake McDonald.

The 9-mile length of Lake McDonald basin is bound by Howe Ridge to the west and Snyder Ridge to the east. The Apgar Mountains to the west and the Belton Hills to the east rise above the foot of the lake.

At the foot of the lake, the subdued, low gradient McDonald Creek leaves the lake and flows for about 2-1/2 miles to join the Middle Fork of the Flathead River. This placid stream bears no resemblance to the rocky fast-flowing mountain stream that enters the lake. As biologists in the Middle

Fork drainage, my crew and I took detailed measurements of the creek width and depth and found it averaged about 100 feet wide and 3-feet deep. There's not another creek in the Glacier or the Middle Fork drainage like it.

Early Settlers Arrive at Lake McDonald

The original Lake McDonald resident probably was a man named McKisson who may have arrived in the mid-1880s. He lived for a time in a small cabin on the west side of the inlet. McKisson lived his lonely life at the head of the lake year-around, trapping marten and lynx in the upper reaches of McDonald Creek amid the old-growth cedar and spruce.

"Dutch John" Elsner was another early arrival at the head of the lake. Dutch John began building a cabin at the small lake now known as Johns Lake, located in a little secluded flat about a half-mile east of the Lake McDonald inlet. It's easy to see why Elsner chose this pretty little spot. Marten in this area were and still are known as the darkest and most valuable marten in the lower 48 states, and there were plenty for the taking. He would be living right in the middle of his marten trapline, beneath huge, virgin western red cedar and grand fir. Dutch John could walk down from his cabin each morning through a little meadow and take in the view of Stanton, Vaught, and Brown as he dipped his water pail into the lake. But other early settlers say that Elsner didn't stay long. John had plenty of marten, lynx, elk, and deer to keep him company, but he soon got lonely. He abandoned his homestead, deciding that the isolated life was not for him.

At the other end of the lake another man, Fred McCrimon, had a mill or timber claim for a time on lower McDonald Creek about a quarter-mile below the lake. Fred officially filed this claim in May of 1891, but he didn't stay long.

These two trappers had been the only temporary residents of the lake before Charlie Howes and Milo Apgar arrived in the area in 1891. As one story goes, Howes and Apgar traveled to the McDonald area in a mule-cart from Great Falls over Marias Pass along the nearly impassable railroad tote road before the railroad was completed into the Flathead Valley. The two men were partners in a store in Great Falls. Another account says that Howes and Apgar arrived in the area via the Camas area of the North Fork.

By 1892, Howes and Apgar had each claimed 160-acre homesteads in the virgin cedar and grand fir at the foot of McDonald Lake. They had grabbed some of the most desirable, level lakeshore land in what was to become Glacier National Park. By the act of filing these claims, the two men demonstrated brilliance in recognizing the potential of these sites.

Lake McDonald and lower McDonald Creek made a perfect stage for the tall, gangly Charlie Howes. Born in Wisconsin 36 years earlier, he had run boats on the Great Lakes and on the coast of Labrador before traveling to

Charlie Howes, here seen with his wife, Maggie, along the shoreline of Lake McDonald near his cabin. Charlie and George Snyder were friends and loose business associates. Charlie supported George in his battles with the Park administration. Maggie was accidentally fatally poisoned at Dow's hotel in the winter of 1919. Photo courtesy of Betty Robertson Schurr.

Montana. In the eyes of most people, Charlie was the finest boatman in the McDonald Valley.

A year or so after Howes and Apgar arrived, French-Canadian Denny Comeau reached Lake McDonald via Metigan Center, Nova Scotia. Comeau claimed a homestead at the head of Lake McDonald on the east shoreline not far from Dutch John's old place. If John had waited a few years, he would have had a neighbor. Comeau built a large claim cabin 18-feet square. Later he was joined in the summer and fall by his wife, Lydia, and several children. Within a few years, Comeau and his family built a larger cabin, established a large garden of hardy plants, and brought in chickens and a cow. Denny was known for his fine string of about a dozen horses he used to squire tourist parties on sightseeing and fishing trips in the drainage.

At about the same time these early settlers arrived, Frank Geduhn established a homestead claim on the west side of the inlet at the head of Lake McDonald. Geduhn, who came west from Michigan, spoke with a German accent and was well known for his fiddle playing. Geduhn built a cabin and lived on his land year-round. He trapped in the upper McDonald Valley, following in the footprints of Dutch John and McKisson, the earliest resident of that parcel. He focused on the dark-furred marten in the upper McDonald Valley. Geduhn became a ranger in the area when the forest reserve was established. Close by, prospector Frank T. McPartland squatted on some land and kept a few small cabins as a starting point for a trail he'd built to mineral claims in upper McDonald Creek. Frank Kelly joined this small group of original settlers, establishing a "camp" and homestead at about the same time further down on the west shoreline of the lake.

George Snyder claimed 160 acres along this point at the mouth of Snyder Creek in the fall of 1894. Prospector Frank McPartland drowned in the lake a few hundred yards out from shore on the right side of the photo. Author Photo, 2007.

To promote the features of the area that would become Glacier National Park and encourage rail travel from the east, officials of the Great Northern Company urged Professor Lyman B. Sperry to explore the McDonald region and report on its potential for tourism. Sperry, a geologist, was asked to determine if any of the rumored active glaciers actually existed in the high mountains. As Great Northern's guest, Sperry rode the train to Belton from the Midwest in 1894. He hired Charlie Howes, whom he called the first settler on McDonald Lake, to tour him around the lake in a rowboat. He found that Howes loved boats and hoped to cater to tourists. Howes was focused on subsistence hunting, fishing, trapping, and fur prices in the area and had not spent much time exploring the upper McDonald Basin for its natural features. In his travels in the mountains around the lake, Howes told Sperry that he had not seen any glaciers. But Sperry saw signs of active glaciers in deposits in upper McDonald Creek. He described what a glacier would look like and asked Howes to keep an eye out for them.

Before he left, Sperry hired Howes to climb the prominent peaks on the east side of the upper lakeshore and look for signs of glaciers. Less than a week after Sperry left the area, Howes contacted him and said that he had reached a ridge near the summit of the large mountain on the upper east lakeshore (Mount Brown), and he had viewed what he thought was a glacier sitting above a beautiful basin which held a jewel of a mountain lake.

By August, Howes had traveled on a faint trapper and prospector trail around the base of the mountain and on up McDonald Creek to the side-canyon that held the lake. He made his way about two miles up the little canyon and emerged from the dense fir and spruce into a U-shaped basin.

The Glacier Hotel, probably 1902. The well dressed group could be George's wedding party, and includes Ida Snyder in a white dress with shawl (#1), George Snyder to her left (#2), Elizabeth Snyder, George's mother (#3), and Edwin Snyder, George's father (#4). Photo courtesy of Krys Peterson, cousin of George Snyder.

Soon, he stood on the shores of the stunning, turquoise, 1-1/2 mile long lake now known as Avalanche. No less than 10 high waterfalls plunged down the bowl of the amphitheater. Sperry was pleased and excited by Howes' report and he made preparations to visit the McDonald Valley again the next year to confirm Howes' discovery.

George Snyder Claims McDonald's Finest Point

George Snyder first came to Lake McDonald in the summer of 1894 as an ambitious 23 year-old. The son of a well-to-do Menomonee, Wisconsin farmer, George rode the train west from Milwaukee, looking to strike it rich in land or minerals. George was a tall man, over 6' 2", and he was bursting with physical prowess. His long neck made him appear even taller than he was. Apparently he was an accomplished bicycle racer in the Midwest. Most importantly, George had lots of ambition and lots of money.

Snyder was handsome with dark hair and mustache; he was articulate, smart, and he brought a certain worldliness to the little collection of settlers. Letters George wrote at the time reflected a good education and large vocabulary. Edwin Snyder, George's father, had plenty of money to build a mansion-like home on seven Menomonee town lots after he retired. Edwin came from a big family, having 10 siblings. But he and his wife had but one child, George, born October 13, 1870, and they lavished attention and money on him. Later, George was joined by an adopted sister and a brother, who

162

died in early childhood.

With Snyder's arrival at Lake McDonald, the first group of original settlers around McDonald Lake was complete.

Asa Powell, who knew Snyder well, once jokingly called George a "remittance man", a person who had been given an independent source of income and sent west by his wealthy family, maybe to cover up a disgrace he had caused. This may have been closer to the truth than Asa knew. Unbeknownst to any

A group gathers on the porch of Snyder's Glacier Hotel in about 1900. Back row, left to right: Denny Comeau, Thomas Jefferson, known as "Uncle Jeff," (with beard) sitting with Ruth Cruger (Eddie Cruger's sister), A.M. Day, Mrs. Lydia Comeau, Mrs. Day. Front row: Eddie Cruger (sitting on steps), Bert Jesmer (cook). Photo Courtesy of the Glacier National Park Historical Collection.

of his Montana friends, George had been quickly married in 1893 and then divorced before he left Wisconsin. George abandoned his first wife, Rose; their little daughter, Grace Elizabeth, was born a few months later. He never mentioned this wife and child to anyone in Montana. He never contacted Rose and Grace after he left, and probably never met his first daughter.

As George rode the west-bound train he carefully looked over the landscape, hoping to see an opportunity. Perhaps he had heard about the McDonald Valley before he left Wisconsin. When the train stopped at the Belton Station (later called West Glacier), he must have decided that this remote wilderness which would become Glacier National Park was the place to stake his future. Once George saw Lake McDonald, he was sure. There was no road in the Middle Fork valley, but the train stop at Belton was only about 2-1/2 miles from the foot of the most beautiful lake he'd ever seen. This was a tourism paradise waiting to happen, and he would be the one to lead it. George had experience with boats back in Wisconsin and he recognized right away that water transportation and touring would be vital in the McDonald Valley.

Most of the level land at the foot of the lake had been claimed by Howes, Apgar, and a few others, so George decided to explore the east shoreline at the upper end of Lake McDonald. To travel up the lake I'm guessing he rented or arranged for a rowboat from Howes or someone else, since only poor trapper trails, possibly first established by the Salish and Kootenai, existed around the lakeshore. As he paddled up the lake, he must have marveled at the surrounding sharp peaks. Then, about a mile short of the lake's inlet, he found it.

A clear, rapid little creek (now called Snyder Creek) entered the lake from the east over a sorted gravel beach at a terraced point. Level land stretched east a quarter-mile to the base of the mountains. The creek drainage led to the Continental Divide, past the massive Sperry Glacier yet to be discovered. A blocky mountain rose 5,300 feet above the site, its ridge extending for three miles south to north. Other peaks (later named Stanton and Vaught) stood four or five thousand feet above the west side of the lake. Snyder could envision the 160 acres along the lakeshore that he would claim, and where his tourist hotel could be built to take full advantage of the land's attributes and priceless views.

But Snyder wasn't the first to explore this place. When he landed at the site, he found that a party had recently camped at the mouth of the creek, but, lucky for George, no one in the party intended to file a claim. The party was led by William Brown, General Solicitor of the Chicago and Alton Railroad. Two members of that party reportedly reached the summit of the 8,500-foot mountain just back of the camp, following in Charlie Howes' footsteps. In honor of the party leader, this peak was named Mt. Brown. The two men must have been experienced climbers, because this mountain wouldn't be considered easy to climb by most people, requiring the climber at one point to inch along for about 20 minutes on huge chunks of rock with serious exposure of 1,000 feet or more on each side. I climbed it with an experienced friend without too much trouble. Later, though, I went back and tried to solo the peak but chickened out instead. In keeping with his vision of this area as a tourist vacationland, George recognized that having a climbable mountain just behind his tourist stop would be good for business.

Those who have dismissed George Snyder as an uncultured opportunist were demonstrated to be wrong. Few old-timers matched his accomplishment of staking the first land claims to this gorgeous point. This is the finest point of land on Lake McDonald and now holds the famous Lake McDonald Lodge.

George Snyder traveled to Kalispell and filed on his homestead. With backing by his father, he began purchasing needed materials and supplies for the hotel he planned to build. He likely spent the winter in Kalispell making preparations to develop his homestead.

George Snyder Brings a Steamer to Lake McDonald and Builds the "Glacier House"

After carefully shopping around, George bought a steamer to transport

George Snyder at the helm of the steamboat F. I. Whitney (right) , docked at Apgar in 1907. That's probably Frank Kelly at the helm of the Emeline. Glacier National Park Historical Collection

supplies and passengers to his homestead, and he planned a tourist stop 9 miles up from the foot of the lake. Again, George had an expansive vision. He wanted a big boat, and he had the backing to buy it. He located a 40-foot steamboat that was running passengers on the north end of Flathead Lake and somehow convinced the owner to sell it to him. That spring of 1895, Great Northern workers positioned the boat on a rail car and transported it the 40 miles to Belton.

After unloading the boat at Belton, Snyder and his crew presumably muscled the boat on rolling logs down to the edge of the Middle Fork, floated it across, and then loaded it on a wagon on the north shore. It's hard to imagine a horse-drawn wagon capable of handling this boat, with its upright boiler. Also, the boat must have weighed many tons. It's possible that the boat was loaded on the wagon near the train station, and then transported across the river on a temporary bridge. Park Service records say the first bridge across the Middle Fork at this point was not built until 1897, but Sperry reports a "substantial bridge" across the river by the summer of 1895. At any rate, once the boat was balanced on a wagon on the north bank of the river, the men tugged and shoved to help the horses negotiate the wagon through the old-growth cedar and along the newly-hacked, narrow "carriage road." Most of the day later, they had succeeded in transporting the huge steamer a little over two miles to the south shore of Lake McDonald.

I'm mystified by this method of getting the steamboat up to Lake McDonald. It would seem much easier to drag the boat to the river, then using lines, poles and perhaps steam power, negotiate the mile or so of river downstream to the mouth of McDonald Creek. From there, a 2-mile trip up this relatively placid and deep stream would bring the boat to the foot of the lake. Perhaps Snyder thought it was too risky to take the boat down the Middle Fork.

Whatever the exact details of this Herculean effort, the ambitious George Snyder had succeeded in placing the first powered boat on any water in what would become Glacier National Park. This moment must have been a triumphant one for this 24 year-old man. He now had a monopoly on major transport of people and materials on the lake, and an unlimited supply of fuel from a forest that had barely seen an axe. Like no one else, George had a firm vision of developing tourism on the lake, and he had the confidence and money to make it happen. To top it off, George christened the steamer the "F I. Whitney," naming it after the chief promoter of tourism for the Great Northern Railway.

George didn't waste any time with his vision. That spring he began building the first hotel on the lake. George's "Glacier House" or Glacier Hotel went up quickly, probably with the help of a paid crew. It's also likely he had help from his neighbor Denny Comeau whose homestead was between Snyder's and the inlet of McDonald Creek. Denny was joined later by his wife Lydia and her four children from a previous marriage. This brood included "Eddie" Cruger, who was 14 years old when Snyder built his hotel. Eddie grew to become skilled in building and in horse packing, and helped around the homesteads. Frank Geduhn, a cabin builder who had a homestead and cabins on the west side of the inlet, probably also pitched in. Snyder built the "hotel" of skillfully cut rough lumber. He added more refined finishings and windows transported up the lake on the "Whitney."

When completed, the two-story Glacier House offered about a half-dozen sleeping rooms. The first floor held a large central room, small dining room, kitchen, and one or two sleeping rooms. A "huge" iron stove provided heat and a means to cook meals. On the second floor, five more guest rooms awaited tourists.

The astute George Snyder chose the spot that turned out to be the access point to Glacier Basin, 6 miles to the east up the Snyder Creek Drainage. From Glacier Basin, a 3-mile scramble is required to reach what has become known as Sperry Glacier, one of the largest in the park. The streams draining the glacial melt-water from Sperry spill mostly into the upper Avalanche Lake Basin. But Snyder Creek carries some of the ice water from Glacier Basin and leads much more directly to the glacier.

A side trip of a few miles up the north branch of Snyder Creek leads to Snyder Lakes. The first lake, only 5 acres in size and 10 feet deep, nonetheless held native westslope cutthroat trout. George visited these lakes and viewed them as one more tourist attraction that could be reached from his strategically located "homestead."

As George wrote in one of his letters to Lyman Sperry, he was "sitting on a gold mine."

Frank McPartland Drowns and the Cattle Queen of Montana is Rescued in Front of Snyder's Hotel

By August of 1895 Snyder's hotel already was the focal point for visiting the upper end of Lake McDonald. Residents and visitors from all around gathered to eat, drink, and gossip. The morning of Monday, August 5, 1895 was no exception. The little hotel was full of locals and visitors, including three of the most colorful characters to ever set foot on the shoreline of Lake McDonald.

The first of these was the grouchy prospector Frank T. McPartland, who along with his two partners had a claim, later known as "Hidden Treasure" on upper McDonald Creek. Frank had a few small cabins near Geduhn's that were used as a base for traveling to the claim. For years before he came to Lake McDonald, the fiery McPartland had prospected on the east side of the Continental Divide, leading a party that made a strike in the Maiden District. He followed rumors of gold around central Montana, and at one point lived like a millionaire after making a promising strike and gaining financial backing of "capitalists" from St. Paul. When that enterprise played out, he was appointed justice of the peace in Maiden Township.

By 1885 McPartland was chasing claims again, this time in the Sweet Grass Hills, then within the Blackfeet Indian Reservation. Frank was likely often on edge in arguments with his mining partners, and in the spring of 1886, he snapped. It probably began innocently enough, with a simple disagreement over drinks with one of his partners, John Moy, over the size and boundaries of the state of Rhode Island. The quarrel rose in pitch until McPartland and Moy were in a full-fledged fight. McPartland got the better of it, and in the process repeatedly cut and stabbed Moy, who died from his wounds. The sheriff arrested Frank and escorted him to a cell at the Choteau County jail.

That fall, lawmen escorted Frank to Miles City to stand trial at the U. S. Court. This was required because Frank allegedly murdered Moy within the boundaries of an Indian reservation. Lucky for Frank, no witnesses appeared for the prosecution; so he was acquitted.

One of Frank's partners in the mining exploration of Upper McDonald Creek who was also at Snyder's that day was probably even more notorious. Mrs. Elizabeth Smith Collins, or Libby Collins, or Mrs. Nat Collins, became widely known as "The Cattle Queen of Montana." Libby was famous for having taken a huge step for women's rights when she became the first woman to ship "beeves" to Chicago and accompany them to the sale. She had to petition railroad officials in St. Paul to allow her to ride along on the train hauling her cattle, because rules prohibited women from riding on such a train. Libby got her way and was able to get about $4 a head for her

Elizabeth "Libby" Smith Collins, known as the "Cattle Queen of Montana" was an early prospector in upper McDonald Creek for a few years beginning in 1895. Her mining partner, Frank McPartland, drowned in the lake that year in front of Snyder's Hotel. Courtesy of Glacier National Park.

beeves. A newspaper article at the time lauded her many achievements, calling her a "lady of whom Montana may well be proud."

But there was probably another side to the Cattle Queen. L. O. Vaught, an author of Glacier Park's early history, concluded that her writings were not reliable, and called her "something of a Calamity Jane".

In Libby's "autobiography", she claimed to have been shot in the knee by Indians, but escaped with her brother by jumping into a cave. She was made captive by another band of Indians, and forced to watch as they beat, decapitated, and murdered other captives, including burning one of them at the stake. She also claimed to have been tomahawked in the neck, spending months in a coma. Finally, the cavalry rescued her, just as she was being forced to run a gauntlet between two rows of Indians ready to beat her to a pulp. In her travels, Libby seemed to encounter every vicious animal that lives in the west. She dodged one mountain lion, and then saved a man who was being attacked by another lion. In this incident, she grabbed the man's revolver from the ground where it lay, and tried to shoot the lion as it gripped the man in a death struggle. The first bullet hit the man in the thigh, but her second shot killed the lion. She bullied a black bear out of a berry patch, and then was treed by it. And, of course, she was caught in a stampede of wild-eyed buffalo, just escaping with her life. Finally, she was shot in the leg above the knee again, this time by an errant bullet from a gambler's six-shooter. She claimed to have spent time in nearly every gold camp in the intermountain west, from Colorado to Montana. Needless to say, there could be a bit of hyperbole in all this. But I think it's safe to say that Libby was a tough, confident, and assertive woman.

Libby and Frank had become acquainted in the Choteau area where they had both been long-term residents. Apparently, Frank discovered the claim in upper McDonald Creek, and then included Libby as a major partner because she could secure backing from businessmen she knew in St. Paul. "Little Lib" as her parents called her, had grown up in a mining family in Colorado. From an early age, she had been possessed by the "gold urge," or as she called it, searching for the mountains' "hidden treasure." Libby served as partial financier and as both the cook and the foreman for the miners who were not known for their social graces. That doesn't sound like an easy job. But she could probably cuss and drink right along with the men, and she'd had plenty of experience doing both.

Also at Snyder's hotel that August 5 was a third partner in the mining venture, Libby's brother, Chandler Smith. Chandler was one of the original residents of Columbia Falls in the Flathead Valley. Chandler had been nervous as the partners and the workers paddled their "crude little boats" on the 400-plus foot-deep lake to Snyder's landing. You see, "Chan" couldn't swim.

The mining operation at "Hidden Treasure" was not going well. Little of value had been found yet. The partners were under pressure to produce results because Libby had convinced financiers to send workers and money to develop the prospect. Because of this, the three were in a foul mood. Snyder and other locals noted that Libby, Chan, and Frank quarreled all day over shots of whiskey. Finally in late afternoon, the three made their way down the terrace from the hotel, gingerly climbed in their boat, and pushed off from shore. Chan, in the middle seat, began rowing the boat towards the inlet and McPartland's cabins, a little over a mile away. Frank was in the prow, and Libby was in the stern.

Soon a row broke out when Frank demanded the whisky jug which Libby held. Chan told Frank to wait until they reached the head of the lake, but Frank persisted. Suddenly, Frank's volcanic temper surfaced again, and he stood up and tried to get past Chan to wrest the jug from Libby. Either Chan hit Frank with an oar, or Frank just fell; and the boat capsized, throwing the three partners into the frigid water. Snyder and the locals at his hotel heard screaming as the three struggled to hold their heads above water.

The rescuers, including Snyder's people and some of the miners who worked for the partners, gathered quickly at the dock. They knew that it wouldn't be possible to get the Cattle Queen into a small boat because of her bulk (she weighed over 300 pounds), so they untied the F. I. Whitney steamboat from the dock, and perhaps in haste began rowing towards the hapless trio as best they could until the engine could be fired up and gain steam.

A few hundred yards out into the lake, Chan Smith clung for his life on the overturned boat. Libby's non-swimming brother watched in horror as she and Frank seemed to be in a death struggle. Frank had panicked, and with the desperate strength of a drowning man, held on to her like a vise. On his belt he had a heavy six-shooter and mining pick. He wore an ammunition belt and heavy hob-nail boots. Add to that his drunken state, and Frank McPartland was like a dead weight dragging down the Cattle Queen.

Twice Libby went down with Frank in this "death struggle," as she described it later, but she managed to get her head above water again. Finally, she unclasped the chain of her Dolman Cloak, which the desperate man was clinging to; and Frank, still grasping the cloak, sank below the surface. Within about three minutes Frank reached his final resting place, probably landing face up in 400 feet of water. His well-preserved skeleton and accoutrements probably still lie in this dark, frigid profundal zone of Lake McDonald, covered only by a thin layer of the glacial silt that builds slowly on the lake bottom.

Libby "treaded water and splashed about" until she reached the boat. She grasped Chan's hands over the capsized craft. Then, according to Libby, based on her experiences on the plains, she let loose a "peculiar distress call or an intonation in my cry which has always been interpreted by those who know me as a call for help." The rescuers redoubled their efforts to reach them.

By the time the F.I. Whitney arrived most likely with Snyder at the helm, Libby and Chan were exhausted, but still clinging to the overturned boat. The rescuers were able to hoist Chan into the Whitney, but could not manage to get the huge Cattle Queen on board. Finally, they tied a rope around her body under her armpits and carefully towed her back to the dock.

George Snyder and the people at the hotel that day were consistent in relating this event to L.O. Vaught, early park visitor and amateur historian; and it's probably very close to what happened. It seems likely that Snyder was along on the rescue, being the owner and main boatman for the Whitney.

Libby's treatment of the event in her autobiography is much more brief and romanticized. But it is consistent with some of the details, and her description of the death struggle is probably right on. "Those acquainted with the immense strength displayed by a drowning person," wrote Libby, "can realize what difficulty was encountered in breaking away from the desperate grasp of the man."

Accounts in the Columbia Falls *Columbian*, and *Kalispell Inter Lake* painted a slightly different picture. The *Columbian* article noted that the well-known prospector Frank McPartland "drowned in Lake Glacier, and Mrs. Nat Collins and Chandler Smith had but narrow escapes." According to the *Columbian*, Frank was trying to save Libby when he went down. Chan then saved Libby by pushing the boat over to her (probably not possible). The *Interlake* article was similar. Both articles noted that McPartland's body had not been recovered.

The day after the drowning, some of Frank's mining associates and others searched the lake surface and shorelines to locate his body. One thing miners had a good supply of is dynamite, and according to Chan, they "dynamited" the lake in a futile attempt to raise his body.

Years later, in a *Columbian* article of old-timer reminiscences, Chan gave yet another description of the drowning in which he claimed to have heroically saved his sister. Chan said nothing of the argument with Frank McPartland, noting that to this day he was unable to account for the "suicidal action" of his mining partner.

After the drowning, Libby, Chan, and their crew continued to work their prospect at the head of McDonald Creek. Within a few weeks, the Cattle Queen nearly drowned again. Libby and Chan were riding along upper McDonald Creek enroute to the claim. As Libby rode her horse across the stream, the horse reared and threw her into the rushing torrent. This 300-pound woman was carried rapidly downstream to the precipice of a "huge water fall," noting that to "be carried over the cliff would mean certain death." At the last possible second, she was able to grasp a submerged branch of a huge tree that had fallen across the stream. Her brother, Chan, crept out on the tree and pulled the Cattle Queen to safety.

George Snyder Helps Lyman Sperry Explore Avalanche Basin and Look for the Big Glacier

That same summer of 1895, Snyder hosted the "Gentleman Explorer," college professor and lecturer Lyman B. Sperry on his trip to explore the lake and basin Howes had discovered the year before. Sperry described his trip in a paper he delivered to a high-brow explorer society and published it in their journal, *Appalachia*. Sperry said that after "crossing a substantial bridge over the rushing waters of the middle fork of the Flathead River," his party struck "at once into a dense forest of fir and cedar. Three short miles brought us to the shores of Lake McDonald." After a long description of the lake, lower McDonald Creek and the shoreline, Sperry describes the area as a good place to stop for a few days, then writes, "if one prefers, he may at once take the trim little steam launch, "F. I. Whitney," and go to the head of the lake, where accommodations may also be had at reasonable rates. The views from the steamer as we sped northward were more than satisfactory…Among the reservoirs of the Rockies, Lake McDonald is clearly the queen."

After a few days of fishing near the head of the lake, Sperry and his little party mounted horses and were guided by the locals (including Frank Geduhn) on a trail they had recently cut out to the lake basin. He describes the gorge below the lake, through which "the waters have cut through a ledge of hard, crimson, jasper quartzite." When Sperry reached the shore of the lake he was overwhelmed by its beauty, noting that "almost unconsciously and instinctively, we lift our hats."

Sperry named the lake "Avalanche", after the two rock and snow avalanches he observed during his visit. Avalanche Lake sits in a spectacular amphitheater, in the cirque and basin below the large glacier Howes had seen the previous year from Mt. Brown. Sperry reported a thriving cutthroat population and good fishing, with large numbers of the "speckled beauties" jumping and "scuddling here and there." Sperry and his party were probably the first to fish the lake, and catch and eat some of these indigenous cutthroats.

In fact the 58-acre lake is home to indigenous westslope cutthroat trout. To prove this, Leo Marnell, the eccentric and likable former biologist for Glacier Park with whom I worked fairly often, took a core from the bottom of Avalanche Lake. This core was sectioned at 1-centimeter intervals and examined as a way of traveling back through time and looking for clues in the lake sediments. Based on the profile of fossilized egg cases of tiny zooplankton, it looks like westslope cutthroat have been feeding on zooplankton in the lake for centuries. So the cutthroat that Lyman and his party caught descended from a fish population that had existed in the lake before Euro-Americans arrived.

The Sperry party named the peaks which stand over the head of the cirque, including Cathedral Dome and Spires, the Sphinx, Sentinel Peak, the Castle, and the Matterhorn, which according to Sperry is a "striking duplicate, on a smaller scale, of the celebrated Alpine peak by that name." Sperry and his party, using instruments brought for the purpose, measured the elevations of high points around the basin. They found that the lowest notch in the horseshoe-shaped wall was 2,400 feet in height. Sperry estimated that Avalanche Lake sat at 3,910 feet in elevation, and that the Matterhorn rose to about 7,910 feet in elevation. Amazingly, Sperry's measurements were only 5-feet in elevation off for the lake, and 24 feet off for the Matterhorn.

Sperry was keen on finding the glacier that Howes had reported seeing in the ramparts above the basin, but the amphitheater around Avalanche Lake frustrated his attempts to scale it. Finally, they were able to reach a notch in the wall at about 7,000 feet in elevation at the base of the Matterhorn. Sperry looked south past the Snyder Lake basin (which he named Horseshoe Basin) to see "nearly the entire surface of Lake McDonald smiling in the sunlight." Still, no route could be found to the area above the headwall to the southeast that reportedly held the glacier. As Sperry wrote, "The mountain peaks and valleys all about Avalanche Basin seem to bristle with taunts of defiance." Unbeknownst to Sperry, the party had reached a point not much more than a mile from the glacier. It seems likely that the summer of 1895 ended without anyone successfully reaching the glacier.

The next spring, Sperry wrote to "Captain" George Snyder regarding preparations for another attempt to further explore Avalanche Basin and find a route to the glacier. In his letter of May 26, 1896, Sperry mentions that Denny Comeau and Frank Geduhn would probably not be able to help because of their schedule. Sperry asks Snyder if he could "furnish the necessary outfit of saddle and pack animals, provisions, tents, etc and take the party for $2.00 per day, deadheading myself as the leader of the party." Sperry, who hardly lacked money, seems like a cheapskate in this offer. Charitably, he notes that Snyder could charge more when the area became more "popular." Sperry specifies dates in July when he and his party will arrive, and adds "Can you see that we are properly taken care of?" Sperry asked George to reply at his earliest convenience and enclosed an addressed envelope.

Looking up towards Glacier Basin and the route to Sperry Glacier. Lyman Sperry contracted with George Snyder and Denny Comeau to help find a route to the glacier. Author Photo, 2007.

That summer, Sperry returned and was successful in reaching the glacier, which was christened "Sperry Glacier;" but he was unhappy with the difficult route his party followed. According to historian L. O. Vaught, the party reached the glacier from Glacier Basin, at the head of Sprague Creek, about six miles from the Glacier Hotel, or possibly from Snyder Lakes Basin. Based on their correspondence, it appeared that George was in the party that reached the glacier.

In August of 1896, after returning to Ohio, Sperry again wrote to Snyder and urged him to find a better route so his photographer could return and document the "moraines and crevasses" of the glacier before the snow came:

"It will be unfortunate if any one who visits the glacier shall be obliged to take the route that we recently took—it is so difficult. I believe that it is possible to find or make a way up the Cliffs at the head of Avalanche Basin between the first and second cascades (counting from the north). If you and

Denny [Denny Comeau] will find a practicable route up there (one up which you can take a photographer and his outfit) and tourists with blankets, I will give you $10.00 cash this fall ($5 each), and will do my best to induce the G. N. folks to hire you to make a permanent trail…"

After offering Snyder and Denny what even then must have been a laughable sum of $5 each to risk their lives for him, Sperry quaintly asked that when they build the trail, they make it "good enough for women."

Hoping to spur George on with visions of lucrative tourism, Sperry added that Mr. Whitney of the Great Northern is "greatly pleased" that a glacier has been found so near Avalanche Basin, and he planned on making special efforts to get tourists to it next season. If the Great Northern photographer could be escorted to the glacier, the photos would be priceless in terms of attracting tourists. He ends the letter with a plea for George to get moving: "Please consult Denny as soon as possible and see if you cannot combine and find (or make) a way to reach the glacier from the Basin. Report to me at once if you succeed as I want to use the fact in an article that I have agreed to prepare for the press. Most cordially yours, L.B. Sperry."

Sperry's letter had the desired effect on George Snyder. Within a few days of receiving Sperry's letter, George and Denny tried but failed to find a practicable route from Avalanche Basin to Sperry Glacier. Apparently referring to the route George and the Sperry party followed earlier in the summer, George reported his failure to find a route in a letter to Sperry. He wrote that the trail would be "so steep in places that some people would get light headed going over it." Snyder then wrote that he and Denny "next tried the way I came down, east of the Matterhorn, but I found that quite an expensive trail to make also, as these rock slides we saw were all very large and it would be very hard to get a trail for horses over them, and from the creek bottom if we followed the creek till the first lake it would then be almost impossible to get to the second lake with horses, on account of a bluff of rocks nearly three hundred feet high between the two lakes." Apparently, George and Denny also attempted to find a practicable route to the glacier from the Snyder Lakes basin located five miles up Snyder Creek from the Glacier Hotel.

Finally, Snyder reported that he and "Uncle Jeff," a popular horseman and packer associated with Snyder's hotel operation, explored the trail "over the Matterhorn and also the trail by which we went to the Glacier this last summer." Apparently George was referring to the route he and the Sperry Party followed through Snyder Lakes Basin, which they called the horseshoe. George wrote that he thought a good foot trail could be made over the latter route. He added in the letter that he'd tried yet again but failed to find a route to the glacier out of the Avalanche Basin. In a reply, Sperry thanked Snyder for the favor and promised to send his letters to Whitney to spur his interest.

George Snyder drove his "touring car" into a wagon team like this one on the old road leading to the entrance to Glacier National Park. The road follows the Middle Fork of the Flathead River across from Belton. This photo was taken in 1925. Glacier National Park Historical Collection.

The next season, a practicable route was found by Sperry and the locals to Sperry Glacier via Glacier Basin. First, horses could negotiate the improved marten-trapping trail six miles up Snyder and Sprague creeks to the basin at 6,300 feet in elevation. There, the horses had to be hobbled, and foot travelers continued on a torturous, switchback trail, back and forth across the wall of the basin, finally passing through Comeau Pass (named for Denny) at 8,000 feet in elevation. Once there, the travelers have reached the west end of the glacier, the main part of which measured nearly 1 ½ miles long and a mile wide. The route from Snyder Lakes Basin (the Horseshoe) explored by George Snyder was never developed but might have proved possible with a lot of trail work.

Lake McDonald Residents Host Early Tourists and Live off the Land

During the next few years, George Snyder and the other settlers in the McDonald Valley catered to a slowly growing number of visitors, still mostly from around Montana. Ed Dow operated a hotel at Belton and a "stage line" from Belton to the foot of Lake McDonald. Frank Geduhn added more cabins to his site at the head of the lake, eventually building his own small, two-story hotel.

F. I. Whitney, in charge of passenger trains for the Great Northern, continued to show intense interest in developing the Lake McDonald area and the Glacier area in general as a tourist playground. In 1897, Whitney sent Walter Raymond, a tour organizer and businessman, to McDonald Lake to look over its value as a tourist attraction. Raymond was also to try out the "amenities" that were offered by the few residents of the lake and make suggestions for improvement. Whitney contacted Snyder and Apgar, and arranged for them to host Raymond and his wife for a short visit.

On a beautiful June day, George and Milo met the couple at the Belton train station. Because of downed timber and lingering snow banks, the road from Belton to the foot of the lake had not been opened for wagon use. Likely apologizing for the inconvenience, the hosts escorted their guests on the 2-1/2 mile walk to the foot of the lake. Raymond noted that the road from Belton to the top of the bluffs on the far (north) side of the Middle Fork was in particularly bad shape, probably rocky and partly washed out. The slender avenue of road through the old growth cedar on to the lake was in better shape.

When the four emerged from the timber at the foot of the lake, the Raymonds must have caught their breath as they took in the spectacular view. Although he doesn't mention it, it's possible that the tour magnate and his wife had a home-cooked lunch at Apgar's. Mrs. Apgar had a reputation for offering the best meals in the McDonald Valley for a reasonable price. She knew this important man was coming and probably put on a great spread for him and his wife.

After a "pleasant sail" up the lake on the Whitney, Raymond and his wife were welcomed at the Glacier Hotel, which Raymond described as "very comfortable." The visitors stayed at Snyder's for 24 hours, entertained by stories of glaciers, mountains, and wildlife. The locals had been well-schooled by Lyman Sperry. They told Raymond that there were seven glaciers north and within a 25-mile radius, and that chunks of one glacier regularly break off and plunge 1,500 feet into a mountain lake below (possibly Grinnell Glacier calving into Grinnell Lake). Raymond noted that there were "good trails from Snyder's to the various glaciers, lakes, and other points of interest."

On the trip back to Belton, Snyder and Apgar assured the tour organizer that they would see to it that the road between the train station and the foot of the lake would be put in proper shape that summer. In a letter to Whitney, Raymond noted that the scenery in the area equals or exceeds anything on the Canadian Pacific Railway, and that he should "make a strong point of the Lake McD country and the more interesting scenery to the north." He concluded that if the road from Belton to the lake is put in good shape, "Snyder and Apgar will provide sufficient hotel accommodations."

George and Milo had passed the test.

The McDonald Lake residents worked together closely, as you might imagine people would when isolated on the fringe of civilization. They often held get-togethers at their lonely establishments. As one of the residents said, "We lived off the country and each other."

Apgars had established a hotel and cabins and hosted "family-style" meals for guests, and at times, for the lake residents. Lots of times, residents fished together for fun and food. One old-time resident claims that Apgars would throw their food scraps in McDonald Creek, in part to get rid of them and in part to feed the fish. "Those fish had stomachs this big around," he claimed. Fishing was great for big bull trout in the fall and for westslope cutthroat just about any time. Another attraction was the fall spawning run of mountain whitefish which congregated in great numbers below the falls on upper McDonald Creek just a half-mile upstream from the lake. These white-fleshed fish could be netted in baskets, and they were excellent when smoked.

Residents also trolled lures behind their boats as they plied the McDonald Lake waters. The anglers wound fishing line around a tin can with wooden handle, so the line could be played out behind the boat as it moved forward. The line was tied to a stout willow pole to fight the fish after it was hooked.

The clever residents of Lake McDonald used boats for just about everything, including the laundry. Denny Comeau and George Snyder perfected the "lazy man's" method of washing clothes. First, the clothes were loaded in a gunnysack, along with a bar of soap. Then the sack was thrown over the side and trailed behind the boat on a rope. By the time the boat traveled the 9 miles to Apgar and the nine miles back to the head of the lake, the clothes were washed and rinsed in pure mountain water.

Residents around the lake counted on George Snyder's steamboat for delivery of freight and supplies. At the head of the lake, Snyder's neighbors Denny and Lydia Comeau had a shallow launch area, and Snyder couldn't actually land the 40-foot steamer and an attached barge at their shoreline. When Snyder had supplies for Comeau's, he would approach the landing, hold the boat in place in deeper water, and pull the cord on his steam-powered whistle. Denny would then row his smaller boat out from the shallows to the steamer and load the supplies. One day when Snyder arrived, Denny was gone on a horse trip. Lydia was busy with the guests and with her new baby, Bea. She asked if one of the guests could row their boat out to meet the steamer, but no one there was willing to try it. So Lydia tried another tact, asking, "Well then, is there anyone here that can hold a baby?" Lydia handed little Bea to the nearest guest, and rowed out to meet the steamer herself. In doing this, Lydia showed why she was known as an "all-around roustabout."

Most residents hunted and trapped, as there were no regulations against it for much of the time before the area became a national park. Charlie Howes and Frank Geduhn were especially active trappers, and like most of the others, focused on marten which were plentiful in the dark, virgin forests of cedar, spruce, and fir around the lake. Many of the original traces of trails were made by marten trappers, including a trace around the east side of the lake and the one up Snyder and Sprague creeks that was eventually improved to Glacier Basin. According to early residents, bears were fewer in number than they are today. Even with all the attractants from the cooking, food scraps and garbage in this remote area, few bear incidents were reported. Bears, both black and grizzly, were much more common after they were protected by the designation of Glacier National Park.

Prospecting Fizzles in the McDonald Drainage

Prospecting soon faded in the district, as miners found that the ancient rock did not hold the riches they hoped it would. The "Hidden Treasure" prospect, officially filed on in 1896 by Libby Collins, her brother Chan, Thomas Jefferson (known as "Uncle Jeff") and others (Mr. Nat Collins' name was on the filing as well), never proved out. According to Libby (Mrs. Nat), beginning in 1895, she and a crew of up to 18 men worked the claim a total of three summers and one winter. Snyder's Hotel must have been a partial base of operations for this crew over these years, given that George's horse packer and guide, "Uncle Jeff" was a co-claimant on the prospect. Uncle Jeff likely helped pack the crew and supplies back and forth from the head of Lake McDonald to the mine site near the headwaters of McDonald Creek. But all the efforts of Libby and her men were in vain. The vein of metal-bearing quartz they had discovered "pinched out" as they followed it deeper into the rock.

When the copper-bearing quartz vein disappeared, the crew lost their enthusiasm. The Cattle Queen said that when the men realized that the small vein had played out, they got nervous and demanded their pay. Mrs. Nat rode the 20 miles back to the head of Lake McDonald and returned with the cash. But this didn't satisfy the men because, "as soon as each one received the full amount due him, the general fear was allayed, and the problem of what to do with their riches was now before them." Worried about robbery, one by one the men came to Libby and asked her to hold his money in safe keeping. Libby was flabbergasted, saying, "this, after they had forced me to go 20 miles to get it!"

Later in the season, a "mining expert" from St. Paul arrived to examine the working and declared that "the vein was lost and the best thing to do was to abandon everything." Interestingly, also in 1896, the Cattle Queen and most of the other Hidden Treasure Claimants also filed on a claim in the Swiftcurrent District, over the Continental Divide from Hidden Treasure. The boom town of Altyn arose there in the late 1890s, but it isn't clear if Libby's group ever worked the claim. With "mining in her blood" Libby eventually headed north during the Alaska gold rush. After her trip to Nome, Libby returned to her ranch in Choteau. According to locals, she continued to come to Belton and visit Snyder's and the other establishments at "Glacier Lake" during summers.

The last claims in the McDonald district were filed in 1899 by N. J. Schroter, one of Libby's "Hidden Treasure" partners. Like the others, these claims failed too, closing the chapter on mining in the McDonald Drainage.

George looks well groomed and well off in this photo. But by the time George was about 60 he had lost everything and moved up the Middle Fork canyon. There he lived in a small cabin near Stanton Creek, living off the land and prospecting. Photo courtesy of Krys Peterson.

Golden Years at the Head of Lake McDonald

The McDonald Lake "community" was tight-knit. Most of them likely joined in the celebration of the birth of Denny and Lydia Comeau's little daughter in 1901 and George Snyder's marriage the following year. On October 22, 1902, when the larch trees around the lake were at the height of their orange color, George married Ida May Walter. George probably met Ida when she came to McDonald Lake on a visit from the Flathead Valley. Maybe Ida had stayed at the Glacier Hotel and liked what she saw, both the Hotel and George, maybe in that order. A photo, probably at the time of the wedding, shows Ida in a white dress, with George in a 3-piece suit towering over her. The couple is standing on the porch of the Glacier Hotel among a group of 17 equally well-dressed friends and guests. Elizabeth and Edwin Snyder, George's parents, stand to George's left.

George's hotel and tourist business was thriving. His "Glacier House" letterhead at the time proclaimed that the resort was located in "the Most Beautiful Spot in the Rockies," and was the starting point for "all places of interest in the Lake McDonald Region, including the Glaciers, Avalanche Basin, Etc." The letterhead included the promise, "Guides, Pack and Saddle Horses always on hand."

One of these guides, Eddie Cruger, had been well trained by his stepfather, and George's fellow homesteader, Denny Comeau. He had become a master horseman and boatman, and was very popular with guests. Genevieve Walsh Gudger, a frequent visitor to Snyder's and Geduhn's at the upper end of Lake McDonald, singled out Snyder's horseman, Uncle Jeff, and young Eddie for making her trips special. She described Uncle Jeff as a "most delightful gentleman, already quite elderly and he was an experienced woodsman who knew every inch of this territory."

Saving her highest praise for the young, handsome Eddie Cruger, Genevieve wrote, "...we always persuaded him [Eddie] to go with us on our trips if we could because everything was made much happier and more interesting by his presence." Eddie taught Genevieve how to "make a fir bough bed, how to cook over a campfire without burning the food to a crisp, how to paddle a canoe, how to climb with the least effort and fatigue, how to watch for and identify the wild creatures, and countless other things."

Eddie became a mainstay at Lake McDonald. For years he packed the Sperry and Vaught parties, who camped near Snyder's place in the summers, into the mountains around the Glacier area. When Great Northern officials visited Lake McDonald, Eddie was often their guide. Eddie specialized in trips to Avalanche Basin and across Howe Ridge to Trout and Arrow Lakes. Some people have a gift in guiding people in the wilderness, acting in part as friend, teacher, counselor, comforter, and protector. Eddie Cruger had that gift, and he inspired trust in visitors who came in contact with him.

It's no wonder that visitors so fondly described the experience at Snyder's resort during these golden years. Snyder's and Geduhn's establishments offered all the basic comforts sought by visitors in an unmatched location. Imagine the excitement of staying in a remote, rustic hotel, exploring just-discovered attractions such as Avalanche Basin and Sperry Glacier. Add to that the incredible fishing for foot-long or better cutthroat, and bull trout up to 20 pounds, and you have a tourism experience second to none.

George Snyder and his staff welcomed visitors as though they were family. A photo of Snyder's porch from 1900 reflects this flavor. Denny Comeau stands to one side of the porch, while to his left, "Uncle Jeff" sits with young Ruth Cruger, Denny's stepdaughter, who is clutching a doll. Sitting on the steps is Ruth's big brother, teenaged Eddie Cruger, a fine looking boy wearing hobnail boots. He looks ready to leap up and help any visitor who would arrive. Next to Eddie wearing an apron and suspenders is Bert Jesmer,

After George Snyder sold his Glacier House on the upper end of Lake McDonald, Lewis had it rebuilt and lavishly furnished. It became the showpiece of the west side of the Park. For years, George ferried passengers from the foot of Lake McDonald to the Lewis Hotel. Joyce O'Neil Collection.

Snyder's professional cook. A slim and determined Lydia Comeau holds a broom and stands in the doorway. This moment, frozen in time, says a lot about the tight-knit group of settlers at the upper end of Lake McDonald.

But a few years later, the little group began to splinter. Sadly, Denny and Lydia Comeau divorced. Lydia kept her half of the homestead, but Denny sold his southern half bordering Snyder's homestead to George. Lydia remained on her homestead during the summers raising Bea and her four other children from a previous marriage. Denny returned to his native Nova Scotia.

At about the same period, in late 1905, L. O. Vaught wrote a letter to George Snyder, asking him if he would be willing to sell the Glacier House and homestead. George replied on February 19, 1906, saying, "In regards to selling my place I really don't care to let it go as it is getting to be a pretty good paying business and shoreline near the head of the lake is going to be a gold mine soon." George noted that he'd received offers of $3 per "front foot" for lots on the shoreline, and that "the parties are coming to select the ground as soon as the snow is gone." He explained that his plan was to sell a few thousand dollars worth of lots, then keep the remainder of the homestead. The talk of the establishment of Glacier National Park probably influenced this rising interest in real estate around Lake McDonald.

But next, foreshadowing what was to come, he tells Vaught that; "if you have anyone in sight that wants to buy, they can have the ranch, hotel, boat, and everything for ten thousand dollars." George acknowledged that the price may seem high, but that it would be a "losing proposition" to take any less.

A few months later, George Snyder's idyllic life at the head of Lake McDonald imploded.

On the heels of Denny and Lydia Comeau's split, on March 6, 1906 George and Ida filed for divorce. George's second marriage had lasted a little over three years. Things continued along in rapid order with Ida kicking it off. Within 20 days, Ida married a Joseph Brown, according to Flathead County records. Possibly related to the split, on May 12, George sold the Glacier House and his homestead to Olive Lewis, wife of well-to-do Flathead Valley fur buyer and businessman John E. Lewis. George had kept his homestead not much longer than it took to "prove up" on it. He wasn't actually issued the patent until a few years later, but the homestead had gone to Olive and John Lewis, who would take it to new heights.

George Snyder Rises Again on his Middle Fork Homestead

But as before, George was well-prepared to recover from these hardships and rise from the ashes. His father and mother had officially filed on a "cash entry" homestead, probably establishing George on it in 1906 with a "quit claim deed." The selection of this homestead was a stroke of genius, just as the selection of the point at the upper end of Lake McDonald had been. The crafty Snyder family had filed on a T-shaped 132.25 acres that tied up the valuable north shoreline of the Middle Fork of the Flathead River for a distance upstream and downstream from Belton. Their land then extended on both sides of the road from the riverbank towards the foot of Lake McDonald. The Snyders had secured the main access to Apgar and McDonald Lake. It also turned out to be the most desirable, level land in the district for locating an administrative headquarters for the future Glacier National Park. With the help of his father, George had done it again.

By the fall of 1906, maybe just to celebrate, George again proposed to Ida, who had recently divorced Mr. Brown. On September 22, George and Ida each sealed their third marriages, two of which had been to each other. A new chapter in George's life was beginning. Soon he had built a "hotel and roadhouse" on the future Park Service administrative site. This operation and his clientele were decidedly different from that at the Glacier House. George's reputation began to decline, and things were aligning to set up a long and contentious "banging of heads" with lawmen and administrators as soon as Glacier National Park was designated in 1910.

George continued to operate the F.I. Whitney on McDonald Lake and eventually began offering trips on the Middle Fork of the Flathead River and lower McDonald Creek. In his boat and hotel operations, he had not been limited by permits or laws before, and he didn't plan to be now. As an aside, maybe to celebrate the designation of Glacier National Park, George and Ida again divorced in 1910 and, predictably, Ida remarried again several months later. George remained a bachelor for a while.

Glacier Park's New Administration Goes after George and his Saloon

Prior to national park designation, property-holders around the lake like Geduhn, Lewis, and Snyder were used to doing pretty much as they pleased at their informal tourist stops. There were no permits and virtually no rules. Forest Reserve Rangers like Frank Geduhn and Frank Liebig lived around Lake McDonald and patrolled the area, but they also trapped and fit in to this tight-knit community. Most of the visitors to Lake McDonald were from the Flathead Valley, while some came from the east on the Great Northern rails. But all this changed radically when the U. S. Congress passed legislation creating the million-acre Glacier National Park on May 11, 1910. All the McDonald Valley old-timers who had enjoyed unbridled freedom now found themselves within the new park boundary and within the control of the U. S. Department of the Interior.

The first year, Glacier Park Superintendent W. R. Logan issue permits to all the operators of boats, stages, hotels, cabins, and horse concessions, no questions asked. He did set rates that he considered affordable for the clientele visiting the park. To Logan's delight, Great Northern by1911 had completed a chalet complex at Belton that could host up to 65 guests, adding to the capacity provided nearby by Ed Dow's hotel. With the designation of Glacier and all the publicity provided by Great Northern, visitation to the McDonald valley skyrocketed. Luckily for Snyder with his little hostel, these thousands of visitors had to pass right by his place on the road from Belton to the foot of Lake McDonald. George was sitting on another gold mine, and he planned to take maximum advantage of it.

In the spring of 1912, to the chagrin of the park administration, George applied to Flathead County for an official license to operate a saloon at his hotel, within the boundaries of Glacier National Park. He had previously served liquor at his hotel and it had developed a seedy reputation. Superintendent Logan passed away in early 1912, so Acting Superintendent Henry Hutchings, Logan's hand-picked clerk, was left to do battle with Snyder. Hutchings had been Logan's assistant when he served as Indian Agent at the Fort Belknap Reservation. As it turned out, Henry was no match for George.

Hutchings scrambled to find a way to stop Snyder from establishing his "road house," telegraphing the Department of Interior in Washington on

March 12 for advice. "George Snyder has applied for saloon license on his place at entrance to new government road Belton to Lake McDonald," Hutchings wrote. "County board meets fifteenth. Shall I appear to oppose it?" The answer came over the wires the next day: Do what you can to prevent Snyder from establishing a saloon sanctioned by the county on patented lands within the national park boundary. Hutchings appeared at the hearing and offered opposition. But Snyder made plans to keep a step ahead of the Acting Superintendent. He set out to collect 20 names on a petition in support of his saloon permit.

On March 19, Hutchings sent a note to the Flathead County Commissioners urging them to deny Snyder's application for a saloon permit, noting, "...it would be degrading to the community to have a saloon run by Mr. Snyder at that place..."

At about the same time, Ed Dow, the hotel owner at Belton who was hardly a Snyder supporter, also sent a note of protest to the county, stating that the saloon "would be a bad thing to have on the road where all the ladies pass. You know that Snyder would be drunk all the time."

Dow filed a counter petition to Snyder's. But the dueling petitions were both deemed invalid. Of the 20 signers of Snyder's petition, only three were actually full time residents or "freeholders" of Belton Township. Of Dow's signers, only one, Dow himself, was a full time resident.

The county commissioners voted 2-1 to grant Snyder the saloon permit.

Acting Superintendent Hutchings had been foiled in his attempt to prevent Snyder from getting his license. On April 11, Hutchings wrote the Secretary of the Interior, cynically noting that "I have the honor to report that George E. Snyder was granted a license for operating a saloon on his land, County Commissioners R. W. Main and Henry Good voting for and Joseph A. Edge against..."

A cocky George Snyder made a trip to Columbia Falls to get supplies and boast about his victory over the federal government. The *Columbian* newspaper carried a story in late April under the title, "Another Resort for Glacier Park." In the story, the editor noted that Snyder had "won his case with the Interior department" and would soon open his saloon. He added that Snyder "has rebuilt the old hotel and has ordered a set of high-class bar fixtures from a Spokane concern." Snyder told him that there would also be a short order restaurant and rooms for "transcient," according to the article. Park officials must have bristled upon reading the article.

By mid-June, R. H. Chapman had taken over the Superintendent's job from Hutchings, who stayed on with the Park in another position. For what he considered the good of the Park, the third Superintendent in a year was determined to take on George Snyder and win. Despite his boasting to the newspaper that he was ready to open, Snyder still did not have his saloon license in hand, because he had not yet paid the permit fee to Flathead County. Others had lined up to protest the license, including the Chamber of Commerce and the Motor Club, but so far to no avail. Finally, Chapman found an angle that he thought was unassailable.

The new Superintendent teamed up with the high-paid lawyers of the Great Northern Railway Company, which operated the Belton Chalets, to thwart Snyder. These lawyers had discovered an obscure law that prevented liquor sales within five miles of any "logging camp, sawmill, mine, stone quarry, or sheep shearing camp," presumably because of worker productivity and safety. Violation of the law was punishable by 60 days in jail, a $100 fine, or both. Luckily for Chapman, the Park was constructing a sawmill at Fish Creek up the west side of Lake McDonald to provide lumber for a planned Park headquarters. Chapman was confident that things would now go the federal government's way.

W.N. Noffsinger, the Great Northern Lawyer, wrote to Chapman on June 15, urging him to complete the construction of the sawmill as quickly as possible so that the law could be used to prosecute Snyder if he established his saloon. Charitably, Noffsinger suggested that Chapman notify Snyder of this intent, perhaps saving both parties a lot of trouble.

But the Glacier Park and Great Northern officials had made a major miscalculation. With careful measurement, it turned out the sawmill was slightly more than five miles from Snyder's hotel site located just into the Park on the bluff along the Middle Fork. Against all odds, the government had lost and George had won, eventually securing his license.

George Holds the Cards on the Park's Administrative Site

During the time George was locking horns with the Park over his saloon operation, he was also negotiating with officials regarding a permanent site for Park Headquarters. That spring of 1912 in a letter to Superintendent R. H. Chapman dated May 29, Ed Dow had offered three acres to the Park for the headquarters site. This land extended from the railroad tracks to the Middle Fork near the south end of the new proposed bridge that would lead directly to the government road on the north side of the river. But Dow's land didn't lie within the Park boundary. George's land was within the boundary and occupied the north side of the river up and downstream, and extended on both sides of the government road to the foot of Lake McDonald. George's land was the obvious choice for the headquarters site.

In a letter under his lawyer's letterhead dated June 3, George made a generous offer to donate five acres of his land "lying on the north side of Flathead River opposite Belton...conditioned, of course, upon the Government locating the permanent and principal administration buildings on the ground donated." Snyder closes by saying that the proposition would be withdrawn "at the expiration of thirty days from date hereof…"

You have to hand it to George. Even though he was locked in a bitter battle with Park officials over his saloon license, he still found it in his heart to offer five acres of the most valuable land in the Park for the headquarters site.

George's offer started Park officials scrambling to discuss it with him. Acting Superintendent Hutchings fired notes back to George's lawyer in Kalispell, Sidney M. Logan, urgently asking him to arrange a meeting between him and George. Soon, R. H. Chapman took over as Superintendent and continued to pursue George's offer. Chapman and Snyder discussed the issue on June 22. George summarized their discussions that day in a lengthy letter again under his lawyer's letterhead. In the letter George makes a specific offer of a 5-acre parcel, but only on the condition that the Park pay him $1,200 for one partly constructed building and pay to have another building moved. The Park officials mulled over George's offer.

In mid-July, Superintendent Chapman sent a letter to the Secretary of the Interior outlining potential choices for a headquarters site. First, he dismissed a site on the east side of the Divide as undesirable. He also discounted the site proposed earlier at Fish Creek on the west side of Lake McDonald because it was too far from the railroad and other transportation. Chapman noted that Snyder's would be the best choice, being located "on the bank of the Middle Fork of the Flathead River directly opposite Belton at the top of the bank where the old County road joins the new Government road and is within the boundary of the Park." But several problems existed. George was unwilling to donate land on the east side of the government road, so his saloon would be located right across from headquarters. And most importantly, Chapman noted that he had "considerable difference over the issue of a liquor license." He added that Snyder was unwilling "to give any assurance as to his willingness to surrender his license." Because of this, Chapman recommended the Dow property on the south side of the Middle Fork, but everyone probably knew that Snyder's was really the best site. Negotiations dragged on and delayed the building of a headquarters for years.

Drunkenness Leads to a Drowning and a Shootout

The following summer, everything that Chapman and the Park officials feared about public drunkenness and George's seedy roadhouse came to pass.

On July 16, a group of loggers in a large boat pushed off from the shore at Belton to float down the Middle Fork to their worksite where they were driving logs. Patrick Burton, a 28-year old lumberjack "whose mind was crazed by an extended drinking spree" suddenly jumped out of the boat at midstream and then "swam and paddled about" before swimming to shore.

Patrick's co-workers tried to coax him back into the boat, but Patrick just reclined on the river bank and went to sleep, so the men continued downriver.

Soon, Charlie Howes' boat floated around the bend. Charlie was transporting two tourists, brothers from the Midwest named Davis, on a fishing trip from Belton to Columbia Falls. Charlie launched his fishing boats from the point of the river at Snyder's Hotel and floated down the Middle Fork past the mouth of McDonald Creek to the junction of the North Fork. The trip continued downstream on the Flathead River past the mouth of the South Fork and on to Columbia Falls. By the time the anglers reached the end point of the 20-mile trip, they had usually caught all the cutthroat and bull trout they wanted or needed. At the docking point, a man met Charlie and helped him transport the boat over to the train station where they heaved the boat onto a the rail car for the return trip to Belton.

Howes was known as the "Belton Boatman" and pioneered the technique of reversing the normal position of the oar man in a rowboat so he was facing downstream. The tall, long-armed Howes used narrow oars with 3-foot paddle sections. By "back-paddling," Charlie could precisely guide the anglers to choice fish-holding spots in the river while avoiding boulders and other obstacles in the swift water.

As Howes' boat came into view, Patrick Burton who was now awake hailed Charlie and asked for a ride across the river. Howes recognized that Patrick was drunk and yelled to him to walk back upstream and cross the river on the bridge.

But Patrick started wading after the boat which was moving rapidly downstream in the current. At that instant, one of the Davis brothers caught his fishing line on a rock and Howes started pulling on the oars, "backing water," so the man could free his line.

The inebriated young lumberjack misinterpreted Charlie's back-rowing, thinking he was holding the boat for him. Patrick "plunged into the swift water" and almost immediately sank below its surface. Sadly, he didn't come up, and the men could see no sign of him. When the boaters passed the work camp over a mile downstream, Charlie notified the foreman about the accident. The foreman immediately headed for Belton and arranged for two of George Locke's boatmen, who headed downstream to try to find Patrick Burton. But Patrick wasn't found that day or the next, despite efforts to raise his body by dynamiting the river.

It's not known for sure if the unfortunate young man's drinking spree had included time at Snyder's saloon, but it seems likely. I'll bet the Park officials thought that it did, and it was exactly the kind of incident they were trying to avoid.

Later that summer on the afternoon of August 18, 1913, George Snyder's saloon was the scene of a "cold-blooded shooting affair" between two drunken friends. A. C. Daly and Frank Ellis had been "batching together" at Snyder's road house for several weeks. Daly had the reputation of being a bad gunslinger. That afternoon, a quarrel broke out between the two men. The argument centered on a dog that Ellis was trying to take care of. The men moved the fight outside to the front of Snyder's saloon building.

Then, according to an article in the *Columbia*n newspaper a few days later, Daly "deliberately pulled out his 45-Colt's revolver and shot Frank Ellis, the bullet entering the stomach." Frank staggered into Snyder's hostel and sank on a bunk. The only witness, Mr. O'Donnell, slipped down the government road towards Lake McDonald.

The article noted that "George Snyder was standing a short distance from the scene and upon hearing the shot went to Belton and reported the affair." When Snyder reached Belton he caught up with Ora Reeves, who, although not a law officer, offered to arrest Daly. Reeves grabbed his revolver and followed George back to the saloon building.

Reeves opened the saloon door and saw Daly standing in the corner with his hands held behind his back. Reeves demanded to know who did the shooting. Daly replied that no shot was fired, but that Frank Ellis had simply fallen, broken a rib, and the jagged edge of the rib had penetrated his stomach. Reeves knew Daly was lying. He went for his gun and got the drop on Daly. He then asked Daly to raise his hands and surrender. Daly grudgingly complied and Reeves took Daly's revolver, which was in his hip pocket.

Reeves marched Daly over to the saloon door and turned him over to a Park Ranger who had just arrived. Ranger Vaught escorted Daly to Belton to wait for the arrival of the sheriff.

With Daly safely in hand, Reeves mounted his horse and headed off in pursuit of the only eyewitness who had been seen heading along the road towards Lake McDonald. Just as Reeves reached Fish Creek on the southwest side of the lake, he saw O'Donnell walking out of the timber where he had been hiding. At first O'Donnell denied that he had witnessed the shooting. But when Reese told him that he could be arrested for the crime, O'Donnell admitted that he had seen Daly shoot Ellis in cold blood.

Reese escorted the witness to Belton. Sheriff Ingraham arrived on the train from Kalispell and took the shooter and the witness to the Flathead County jail. The gut-shot man, Frank Ellis, was taken to the Sister's Hospital in Kalispell where he died of his wounds.

These incidents of drunkenness and tragedy during the summer of 1913 would give Park officials all the fodder they needed to oppose Snyder when he applied for his saloon license the following year.

Ironically, as George Snyder sank into seediness and infamy, his old hotel at the head of Lake McDonald had become the finest tourist spot on the west side of Glacier Park. By the end of the summer of 1913, John Lewis reported that 7,000 tourists had registered at his "Hotel Glacier." The hotel offered rooms for 60 people, a men's club, and a barbershop. As the 1913 season came to a close in October, Lewis began construction on what would become the most lavish and sophisticated new hotel in the Park. This "magnificent hotel" was designed by the prominent Spokane, Washington architectural partnership of Kirtland Cutter and Karl Malmgren: and would include a 3-story, 7,200 square-foot Swiss-chalet structure, with steam heating plant, hydroelectric generation plant on Snyder Creek, and twenty private baths. Snyder's old hotel structure and cabins were moved back from the original site to make room for the new showplace.

Over 500 people attended the opening of the new Lewis's Glacier Hotel in June, 1914. The reviews published in local papers were gushing over the "lady's touch," noting that "Mrs. Lewis has selected with a lavish hand and artistic taste…countless paintings…rich draperies, rugs, and the hundreds of other little things." Frank Kelly was joint owner with Lewis of a "fleet of lake launches" which provided high-class transportation up and down Lake McDonald. Lewis's docks were busy and thriving, with Eddie Cruger and others acting as full time hosts. The Park administrators were satisfied and pleased with the new showpiece, and even more determined to rid the Park of "undesirable elements" like George Snyder and his hostel and saloon business near the Park's entrance.

A Final Battle over Snyder's Saloon

Yet another new Superintendent, James Galen, took up the battle with Snyder in the spring of 1914 when George predictably filed with the county for the annual renewal of his saloon license. Snyder's license under his name had been revoked, so the always-astute entrepreneur filed the request under the name of a buddy, Louis Fournier.

Superintendent Galen was determined to stop Snyder from operating his saloon, pointing to last year's public drunkenness and murder. He directed a storm of protest to the county arguing against the granting of the "retail liquor license" in Fournier's name for the business known as "Snyder's Place" which he called disreputable and undesirable.

In his legal protest, Galen organized his argument in three parts. First, Galen argued that he, as the duly appointed Superintendent of Glacier National Park, had the authority to enforce and preserve order within the Park boundaries. Second, Galen noted that Snyder's Place is located within the Park boundary on the main thoroughfare to Lake McDonald where hundreds of men, women and children visiting the park would find a saloon objectionable. He added that it would be impossible to enforce any government regulations at the saloon, and that the saloon had been the scene of manslaughter. Third and last, Galen said that the application for the saloon license did not contain the names of 20 freeholders who resided within 10 miles of the proposed location.

Some Belton residents fired off a supporting protest and petition to the county. The protesters noted that the saloon "would be extremely objectionable to us and to the people residing in the vicinity thereof and against the best interests of the community."

But Snyder wasn't ready to lie down yet. He argued that the 20 signers of his petition were valid and demonstrated that the community did support his saloon. He had a point. The signers on Louis's (actually George's) petition for a saloon license read like a "who's who" of upstanding original settlers in the McDonald Valley. The supporters included: Frank Geduhn, Charley Howes, John Rogers, Chance Beebe, Eddie Cruger, H. D. Apgar, John Weightman, Will Sibley, Anna Neitzling, and even John E. Lewis. Most likely, all of these independent originals supported Snyder under the principle of the rights of private individuals to conduct business on private lands within the Park without Park control. In the legislation that established Glacier, it's stated that private individuals were entitled to "full use and enjoyment of their land" on valid claims within the Park existing before May 11, 1910. George shared the belief in this principle with the other early settlers of Glacier. At any rate, in spite of his slide towards infamy, George's old close friends stood by him. This makes it likely that you could still find a lot more good than bad in George.

In the end, the government won this particular battle: The County denied George's application. Galen was elated. He had beaten George (who had almost taken on an aura of invincibility) in the arena where the previous Superintendents had failed.

The New National Park Service is not Happy with George Snyder's Boat Operation

Glacier Park officials perhaps became overconfident with this win, and began to underestimate Snyder. Notably, George still had his boat concession, his "hotel", and 132.25 deeded acres of the most strategically located land in the McDonald Valley, land that officials wanted for their headquarters. The Park's battle with Snyder over his saloon license was over, but their war with him over other issues was far from over.

Maybe to bolster his spirits and prove he was still likable, he married Ethel Mae Moore later that summer of 1914. With the saloon battle behind him, he and Ethel focused on his hotel and restaurant, and most of all, his boats.

For a time, George maintained the F.I. Whitney on Lake McDonald. But eventually gas powered boats upstaged his old steamer. Several of these more modern craft operated on the lake, including Frank Kelly's boat.

Determined to continue pioneering, Snyder expanded his boating concession to McDonald Creek and the Middle Fork of the Flathead River for pleasure and fishing trips, loosely associated with Charlie Howes' boating business on the same waters.

In the spring of 1917, the majority of George's prime land on the north side of the river went to the National Park Service (the National Park Service agency had been officially established the year before), after a complex series of land transactions over a period of years. George sold the land, and then got it back several times. Things were complicated by a claim on the land by George's former wife, Ida, and the land went for $7,000 in a sheriff's sale in 1916. Finally, on January 11, 1917, the Director of the National Park Service, Stephen T. Mather, personally paid $16,000 for the land. On April 27, 1917, Mather and his wife, Floy, formally donated the land to Glacier National Park.

George was undergoing a stressful year during this final land sale. His father and biggest supporter, Edwin, died in Wisconsin at age 83. George's mother had died two years earlier. He and Ethel had divorced, and he married Maud Carew that October. It seemed like George was accustomed to living in a perpetual crisis. Who would even want to go through five marriage ceremonies and divorces, considering the personal and legal drawbacks?

Of course the Park officials attempted to bring George's boat operations in line with permitting requirements. In fact, what they were really trying to do was to evict him from the Park once and for all, and George was bright enough to recognize this fact. So things didn't go smoothly at all because, predictably, George chose to blow off the government officials and their rules again.

In the spring of 1918, George applied for a permit to operate two gasoline-powered boats on the Middle fork of the Flathead River, McDonald Creek, and the outlet area of McDonald Lake for "fishing and pleasure trips." His boats included a powerful, loud, 35-foot, 20 passenger, 32-60 horsepower, air-propelled boat, and a 20-foot, 5 passenger, 10 horsepower air propelled boat. By late June, he was granted the permit, signed by none other than Stephen T. Mather, the Director of the new National Park Service (the Service was officially established in August, 1916.). The embattled H. W. Hutchings, who had started the fight years before with Snyder over the saloon license, signed the permit as a witness.

In the permit, the Park Service was careful to limit Snyder's travel on McDonald Lake to the outlet area only, for picking up and dropping off passengers for his river trips. Mather and Glacier Superintendent W. W. Payne had corresponded and agreed that they didn't want George to have free reign on McDonald Lake where he might compete with the much more upscale tourist transport services of Frank Kelly. The Park officials now had a deep distrust of Snyder and his motives, and actually were a little frightened of the private property-rights clout he seemed to have in the county.

George's permit stipulated that he could charge $5 per passenger for a full day of pleasure and fishing on the boats and $2.50 per passenger on shorter trips. There were lots of other rules about inspections and reports. I'm thinking that George took one look at this permit and then ditched it. I doubt that he ever intended to follow these onerous regulations.

Payne wrote to Snyder on July 19 sending him an approved copy of the permit. George had already ignored some of the provisions. Payne wrote:

"It has been brought to my attention that last Sunday you made a trip to Lake McDonald, where you secured a load of passengers, stating that you had a permit to carry passengers from the head of the Lake to Belton. This trip was in no wise a fishing trip, and you should thoroughly understand that you cannot operate on Lake McDonald except for the collection and return to point of collection of parties for trips on McDonald Creek or the Flathead River." Payne closed the letter with a threat to cancel Snyder's concession if he kept it up.

But George did keep it up for the rest of that summer, launching on his lake trips from Charlie Howes' private land at the foot of Lake McDonald. Howes was busy with fishing trips on lower McDonald Creek and the Middle Fork of the Flathead. Charlie often launched his river float trips from a point near George's hotel. The two men got along well even though they competed for tourists to escort on their trips. The services the two offered, though, were different enough to keep this competition to a minimum. Charlie's trips were strictly for fishing, and he was the best, often catching a stringer of bull trout weighing from 12 to 16 pounds.

Maggie Howes is Accidentally Murdered at Dow's Hotel

That winter of 1918/19, tragedy struck the Belton area. Mrs. Bud Henderson was a good friend of Charlie Howes and George Snyder, often taking Charlie back north across the Middle Fork where he docked at Snyder's, and returning to the south side so he could keep a boat on each side. He kept a boat on each side of the river so he could ferry tourists or himself back and forth across the river right at Belton and save the 1-1/4 miles upstream to the bridge and back down the other side of the river.

During the winter, Mrs. Henderson often visited Charlie, who by now was in his 60s, and his much younger, part-Chippewa wife, Maggie. Mrs. Henderson would ski from Belton to Charlie's cabin at the foot of Lake McDonald. Charlie was fun to talk to. He possessed "a keen sense of humor and a sharp wit." He and Maggie were close. But late that winter, the old pioneer was dealt a blow from which Mrs. Henderson said he never recovered.

On Sunday, February 24 1919, Maggie was at Belton working at Dow's Hotel and Restaurant. Right after she ate dinner, Maggie began to feel terrible. She lay down in a bed

Ed Dow's Mercantile and Hotel in the 1920s, near the west entrance of Glacier National Park. This is the site of Maggie Howes' "accidental poisoning." Joyce O'Neil Collection.

and said she felt as if she were going to die. She pleaded for someone to get Charlie to help her. One of the people at the restaurant rang up Diamond "Dimy" Apgar, Milo's youngest son, who was the only one at the McDonald Lake outlet with a phone, and asked him to notify Charlie. Dimy refused, because he and his family were not speaking to Howes. The Apgars and Howes had battled over their land boundaries near the foot of the lake. They finally agreed on a compromise property line, but bad feelings lingered. Because of this feud, the people at Dow's had to find another way to reach Charlie.

Luckily, a Glacier Park Ranger was also at Dow's that night and heard about the problem. He called for someone to pick Charlie up and rush him to Belton. Charlie arrived and ran into the hotel.

"When I got there Mrs. Dow was there," remembered Charlie, "and I ask her how Mrs. H. was and she said she was sleeping fine and I know she lied and rushed in."

Maggie was choking and hacking, but Mrs. Dow tried to cover it up, telling Charlie that Maggie was just snoring. But Charlie knew different, angrily exclaiming, "That's a Death Rattle!"

Charlie put his arm around Maggie's neck, kissed her and shouted "She's dead!"

Later, Charlie said, "I could see right there she was poisoned. Had been given the dope in something." Charlie said he took Maggie into Kalispell and "had her cut open." All her organs were normal and Charlie was convinced he was right about the foul play. He lamented that his wife had "cashed in" before he had, and she had been taken from him by "some foul devil." It's hard to imagine Howes' living around the Dows after this poisoning. And poisoning it was, as the locals soon found out when people started talking.

According to locals, Ed Dow's "no good" stepson had just returned from World War I. The plan was to get Dow drunk, and then have him sign over his land and hotel to the returning "war hero." After Dow signed the transfer, the plan was to poison him by placing the poison in a cup of coffee. Unfortunately for Maggie, she picked up Dow's cup by mistake and downed the coffee, which was laced with strychnine or cyanide. Maggie never had a chance once she drank it.

Newspaper stories in the *Columbian* and Kalispell *Inter Lake* carried brief stories on Maggie's "sudden death," but there was no mention of foul play. The *Columbian* reported that Maggie "was in apparent good health, but during the evening she complained of feeling sick and expired within an hour after going to bed." Charlie said he had Maggie's stomach contents sent to a laboratory in Helena, but no proof of poisoning was ever found.

The Park Service Grabs George's Boats

The harsh spring of 1919 (it snowed four feet the week Maggie died) finally turned into summer, and in spite of his terrible experience, Charlie continued his boat trips from the launch near Snyder's Hotel. And in defiance of federal regulations and with no approved permit, George Snyder continued operating his two "airplane propeller" boats on the river, McDonald Creek, and especially on the lake, launching from Charlie's private dock. The relatively new National Park Service was understandably cautious in exercising their federal authority that Snyder had already tested. But finally, in August of 1919, Glacier Park officials, led by Superintendent W. W. Payne, seized George's boats, including his beloved 35-foot "Louise," from the foot of the lake near Howes' place, and impounded them. Payne also impounded Snyder's floating dock.

Payne probably shouldn't have done that.

Snyder immediately brought suit against Payne for unlawful seizure of private property. After a delay, the case went to trial in Helena before Federal Judge J. Bourquin. The judge ruled that the Glacier Park officials had no right or jurisdiction to seize Snyder's personal property from private inholdings (probably Howes' land) within the National Park. That next spring, Bourquin ordered Payne to return Snyder's boats and dock to the waters of Lake McDonald as soon as possible and for certain within 30 days.

The Park Service panicked. Payne sent notices to major newspapers within a 300-mile radius of Glacier Park announcing that it was not "open season" for private concessions within the boundaries of Glacier. Payne and Mather were worried that the decision would give the impression that the Park Service did not have the power to regulate private property within Park boundaries. They fretted that private inholders were in a "defiant mood," and might even start hunting and trapping in the park without regard to state game laws or federal restrictions.

By mid-June, after correspondence with Snyder's lawyers, Payne returned George's launches and docks "at point where they were taken out of the water." George brazenly resumed operating his boats on Lake McDonald without a permit through that summer of 1920. Snyder then filed suit against Payne. George's case was simple: he asked for damages over the seizure of his boats the previous year.

On December 15, the "Payne trial" took place in Kalispell, with poor W. W. Payne hanging out to dry because he acted within what he thought was his authority as Glacier Park's Superintendent. He was defended by the U. S. Attorney J.H. Toole, who reported that the plaintiff (George Snyder) introduced evidence showing the amount of damage he sustained when the government seized his boats in the summer of 1919. Toole then explained that as defense counsel he "...attempted to set up and prove his (Payne's) official right to seize the boats."

Things went badly for the embattled Superintendent. When Toole tried to introduce proof of Payne's authority, Snyder's lawyers objected and the court sustained the objection. Henry Hutchings, who was again Acting Superintendent, noted in a letter to the National Park Service that the judge "refused to hear the witnesses the United States Attorney called on the grounds that they were Government employees."

Toole embarrassingly reported the results of the trial, stating, "...the jury could do nothing else than return a verdict in favor of the plaintiff. They did so, and fixed the amount of damages at $1,500 and costs."

George had taken on the full force and resources of the federal government and won.

George Goes into the Touring Car Business and Thumbs his Nose at the Park Service

Emboldened by his victory, George pushed the government further. In May of 1921, confronting yet another supervisor, J. Ross Eakin, Snyder bought a "touring car" with the intent to compete with the permitted concessioners such as the Weightmans to haul passengers from Belton to Apgar. Brilliantly, Snyder contacted federal mail officials on the side, who deputized him to carry mail between the two points. Eakin was caught completely off guard, and considering George's reputation as a legal lion, he proceeded with caution. The new Superintendent wrote to Park Service Director Mather in Washington, D.C. and asked what he should do.

Mather still hadn't learned his lesson about Snyder. He scolded Eakin for not being more assertive, reminding him that the road is a government road and the bridge across the Middle Fork is a government bridge. Laughably, he told Eakin to "have a personal talk with Mr. Snyder and explain the situation to him and advise that if he attempts to operate over the Government road or over the Government bridge he will be liable to arrest..."

Eakin was a perceptive man and not prone to rush into a confrontation with George, given the quality of George's lawyers, his recent success in beating the National Park Service (and Payne personally), and the fact that George was a deputized mail carrier. Not wanting to be the next sacrificial lamb, Eakin let George do whatever he wanted with his tour car. The next summer the Park Service collected affidavits from people who Snyder transported without a permit, but they never acted on them. As a U. S. Attorney noted in a letter to the U. S. Attorney General, Snyder had become "execution proof."

Finally, on September 20, 1923, Glacier Park officials got lucky. Snyder was driving his touring car "in excess of 8 miles per hour" and collided with a government horse-drawn wagon driven by Horace Brewster, near the north bridge approach over the Middle Fork. Witnesses said the wagon was pulled over to the side of the road, but a drunken George swerved into it anyway.

George's old nemesis and the park's assistant superintendent, Henry Hutchings, teamed up with Sheriff's Deputy E.M. Swetnam and pursued Snyder to the foot of Lake McDonald. There they found Snyder stalled in the road "locally known as the road to Lewis's Hotel" (now known as the Going-to-the-Sun Road) at Charlie Howes' place. Hutchings turned off the engine of Snyder's car, and they couldn't restart it because George had lost his crank; and the battery was dead. The men pushed the car to the side of the road. In the car, the deputy found "a gallon jug which contained approximately one quart of Moonshine liquor."

Hutchings asked Snyder to go with them, but "he was in such an intoxicated condition that he didn't understand what we meant...." Then, Deputy Swetnam told George he was under arrest, and Snyder got into the lawman's car.

The three men drove back to Dow's place at Belton and had a "luncheon" together. With unconcealed satisfaction, Hutchings wrote that he and Swetnam then "took Mr. Snyder and the jug of liquor to Kalispell, Montana, where I personally turned over the jug of liquor to the Sherriff of Flathead County."

On October 3, Snyder's case was brought before the U. S. Commissioner and charged with reckless driving. It was pointed out that Snyder's reckless driving had nearly caused other serious accidents, and that people who owned cars around Belton were afraid to drive when George was around. Snyder claimed someone unknown to him was driving the car, and they were simply trying to charge the battery and couldn't stop. But this time, the lawyers couldn't save George. The judge found him guilty and meted out a $300 fine and 6 months in the County jail.

Glacier Park Superintendent Eakin was feeling vindicated after the trial. He noted that they could keep the driving-while-intoxicated charge in reserve in case they needed it to "keep him out of the park that much longer." Snyder appealed the case, but the appeal went nowhere. He served his time and requested relief from the fine because he had no money left. Later, adding to George's plight, the U. S. Marshall prosecuted him for transporting illegal liquor within Park boundaries. Snyder pled guilty and was fined $5 along with about $200 in court costs.

The Park Service had finally won the war against George, but it had taken nearly 15 years, thousands of dollars, about a dozen federal lawyers, lots of federal bureaucrats, and six Glacier Park Superintendents to do it. George engaged in more legal battles and battles of will with Glacier Park and National Park administration than anyone in history. He was astonishingly successful in winning most of the battles. But now, downtrodden, nearly penniless, and with a ruined reputation, George finally sold his remaining inholding to the Park and never returned as a concessioner. Ironically, Park officials built their headquarters on the land of their old nemesis, putting George's hotel and outbuildings in service for a time as the government bunkhouse and mess hall.

George Moves up the Middle Fork and Starts a Mini-Gold Rush

Now in his 50s, George was down, way down, but not yet out. By the early 1930s he had squatted about 10 miles up the Middle Fork Canyon along Stanton Creek, a few miles upstream from Nyack. George's little cabin sat on the bank of this mid-sized stream, which is the outlet of Stanton Lake. Stanton Creek holds bull trout and westslope cutthroat trout, and its waters flow ice cold. If nothing else, George selected a pretty spot.

Luckily, George was saved from total poverty when he finally received the remainder of the money from his judgment against former Glacier Park Superintendent W. W. Payne. Believe it or not, it took an act of the U. S. Congress that specifically mentioned George to make this happen. "An act for the relief of W. W. Payne" was passed by the 71st congress on March 4, 1931, more than a decade after George's boats had been seized. It directed the treasury to "pay to George Snyder or his assigns…the amount… not to exceed the sum of $1,800."

After the bill passed Congress, Glacier Park Supervisor E. T. Scoyen repeatedly tried to contact Snyder to get him to submit a claim for the funds he had not yet received. By January 1932, George submitted a detailed statement of costs and interest that had accrued during the previous decade.

Pieces of coal from the hidden vein that Snyder and the Huffines used along Stanton Creek near the edge of the Great Bear Wilderness. Author Photo, 2007.

He dutifully subtracted the money he'd already been paid, and came up with a request for a reasonable $970, which was promptly granted to him after he signed a voucher for the amount. Payne, wherever he was, was finally off the hook; and George had a small living allowance.

The Stanton Creek Lodge and tourist camp was located just to the west of George's cabin. When Dan and Doris Huffine of East Glacier purchased the business and took over the little lodge that spring, they were slow to get to know George. Like most everyone else, they had heard about George's reputation for drunkenness and his penchant to sue people. Doris later regretted how they treated George that first winter. They didn't share their food or help the older man (now 62) during the long months with the railroad existing as the only transportation between November and May.

Finally, in the spring of 1933 after a long and snowy winter and a diet of flour and beans, Snyder shuffled down the still snow-covered road to the lodge. Doris had baked an apple pie and had it outside cooling on the porch. Doris looked up and saw George standing in front of the porch, shaking, with his eyes fixed on the pie. Right away, Doris was filled with compassion and realized her mistake. She had allowed others to set her opinion of a neighbor instead of judging for herself.

Doris cut a piece of pie, put it on a plate, and offered it to the hungry man. Doris remembered that Snyder "… just grabbed it off the plate as if it might escape him, like he would die if he didn't get that pie."

After that day, Doris and Dan became good friends with George and often helped him. For example, they shared a small coal vein located on Stanton Creek not far upstream from Snyder's cabin. Dan would dig sacks of the coal and drag them down the creek bank, then divide the fuel with George. This coal provided a concentrated source of heat for the long winters.

George became a regular story spinner around the small lodge. He knew something about running a tourist lodge, and helped Dan and Doris with his advice. And his stories about early Glacier Park fascinated the young couple and their guests. A true pioneer and with more life experience than 100 average men, George was a walking, talking embodiment of the Middle Fork's history.

Doris felt comfortable enough with George to let him in on her huckleberry picking enterprise. This says a lot, because those of us who have picked these valuable berries know that you don't share your spots with just anybody. On their picking forays, Doris, her sister Maxine, and George drove the narrow road to Gary lookout northwest of the lodge. Once they'd gained the 1,000 feet in elevation, they could work their way south towards Stanton Lake along hillsides ripe with "purple gold."

Doris and Maxine joked about George's huckleberry picking style. Snyder, with "beard down to his belly and belly down below that," was too lazy to bend down and pick the berries. So he would sit down in the patch on a steep hillside and slide through the bushes, ripping them out of the ground and stripping the berries and leaves into his bucket. When they got back to the lodge, they dumped George's buckets into a tub of cold, Stanton Creek water. All the leaves and twigs would float to the top and could be skimmed off leaving the clean berries behind.

The berries were a staple at the lodge restaurant. More importantly, Doris sold the berries to the trainmen at 50 cents a gallon. During these Depression years, these berries yielded an important part of the Huffines' income. And it was probably about the only money the down-and-out George saw.

According to Doris, they had a unique way of storing the huckleberries to keep them fresh. She would pack the berries into jars and bury the jars in the gravels of Stanton Creek near Snyder's cabin. The cold waters flowed through these gravels and kept the berries fresh for months.

With all he'd been through, the enterprising Snyder had not given up on himself. He was already planning on turning the few nickels he got from the purple gold into a fortune, prospecting for yellow gold. He teamed up with local prospector Bill West and started digging prospects in the mountainside a mile northwest of the Stanton Creek Lodge, near Gary Lookout. I'm guessing they found color panning one of the streams draining this mountain and were looking for the source of the gold.

George and Bill dug like badgers. They worked through the fall of 1933, and into the long winter. They had sunk their hole, or adit, deep into the mountain, so they were well below the zone of frozen soil and freezing air temperatures.

That spring, when they had extended their shaft nearly 100 feet into the earth, the men struck what appeared to be the mother lode. Imagine the joy and rush of excitement that gripped these two humble old-timers. At their feet lay a "chunk of quartz loaded with gold."

The men took the sample to Kalispell and confirmed its value. The news of George's and Bill's strike got around. The size of their find was blown out of proportion and a number of prospectors swarmed up the Middle Fork. During this "mini gold rush," prospectors staked 34 claims on the mountain, and the east face down to the highway was "plastered with claims."

But little came of all the digging. Snyder and West dug and dug, but found little encouragement at their prospect beyond that first chunk of promising gold-laden quartz. In late summer, a mining engineer examined the prospects for about a week and concluded that the formation in which West and Snyder had made their strike was "tumbled instead of faulted." He explained that their limited strike was pure luck and there would be no linear mineral vein to follow. George's and Bill's Middle Fork mini-gold rush was over.

George Knocks His Head and Goes to Warm Springs

By the late 1930s, George had moved into Kalispell. Nearing 70, he worked for the Works Progress Administration, a public works program created by President Franklin D. Roosevelt by executive order a few years earlier. This "new deal" program was designed to help unemployed down-and-outers like George.

Unfortunately, in this final chapter of his life George had a terrible accident. He fell off a truck and struck his head. Doris said that she saw him in town, wandering around and disoriented. Sadly, her old friend didn't recognize her.

Authorities eventually responded to George's plight and admitted the old pioneer to the Montana State Hospital at Warm Springs in 1940. Doctors at the institution somewhat wrongly diagnosed George's problem as "senility with psychosis."

George's condition improved and he thrived at the institution because he was more functional than many of the patients. He became a custodian and reportedly treated the other patients kindly. At the time, there were several thousand inmates and a few hundred staff, so higher functioning patients like George were given tasks and responsibilities. Glacier area resident Ace Powell said that when a few old friends from Glacier visited Snyder, the hospital staff told him that George had "visions" of owning tourist hotels in Glacier National Park. The friend told the staff that those were not delusions, but fact. The friends told George that he thought they could spring him from the hospital, but George said he had no friends or family and that the inmates needed him there.

On October 1, 1944, George suffered a massive cerebral hemorrhage, possibly related to his old head injury, and fell into a coma. At 4:45 a.m. on October 17, exactly 50 years after he'd first seen Lake McDonald, George died.

George Snyder was buried along with hundreds of other forgotten people at the Montana State Hospital grounds. A tiny 3x5-inch slat with no name is the only mark that identified his grave. He died penniless, and there was no funeral with old friends on hand to celebrate his life and accomplishments.

The Glacier Park Maverick Beat the Park Service After All

Back in Glacier Park, there was no one left in the administration who thought about George. Lots of the Glacier old-timers who George knew were dead or gone. Most of his friends had no idea where he had gone. It was as if George Snyder had vanished and been forgotten.

But in a big way, George wasn't forgotten. The place names in Glacier National Park stand in tribute to this raucous pioneer. Glacier Park headquarters and the lavish Lake McDonald Lodge both sit on land George originally homesteaded or owned. The massive tour boat the "Desmet" loads tourists at the mouth of Snyder Creek near his old docks, and people leave his old hotel site for hikes to Snyder Lakes, Sperry Glacier, and Snyder Ridge.

Snyde left a huge mark on the Park, but he was never accepted by the Park Service. A U.S. Secretary of the Interior, a U.S. Attorney General, a National Park Service Director, six Glacier Park Superintendents, a host of bureaucrats, and an army of government lawyers had tried for years to evict him from the Park. They finally succeeded, but George left a bigger mark on Glacier than all of them combined.

In the end, and in his own way, I'm guessing that the Glacier Park Maverick was pretty happy with the way things turned out.

EPILOGUE
Wild River Pioneers: Chasing ghosts

The Middle Fork country is spectacular and still mostly remote. In my view, there is no finer river and watershed in the West. And now the old timers who were part of the Middle Fork's history color my sense of its place. Yes, and when I look at the river's clear water, its cutthroat trout, and its peaks, I see the Wild River Pioneers reflected in them.

From the top of the drainage at Marias Pass and Schafer Meadows, to the confluence of the Middle, North and South Forks of the Flathead River, I've chased their stories. And with each story, I've searched for a sense of closure. I wonder about William Schafer, the first trapper in the upper Middle Fork who likely was shot in the back for his furs. He's buried somewhere in the lonely flat at the junction of Lodgepole and Morrison Creek, 10 miles into the Great Bear Wilderness. Over the years I've looked and looked for a pile of rocks or some other clue. His gravesite will probably never be found.

The old town site of McCarthyville still holds many of the pioneers who died during its brief existence. And, if you know where to look there are still lots of reminders that a town existed there more than a century ago. Wooden water pipes wound in metal wire that delivered water to the raucous town now lay in pieces, mostly buried among the trees and meadows on the hillside above the town site. Everything from fancy stoves to cups and saucers and more lay about where they were abandoned. It's obvious that in its heyday, McCarthyville sprawled across the Bear Creek bottom and the hillsides above it. McCarthyville isn't even a ghost town anymore because no buildings or structures are still standing. But on a sunny summer day in 2006, I looked at what remained, imagined the shootouts, and wondered what the toughest town in Montana must have been like for the hundreds and hundreds of people who survived there for the few years of its life.

The remains of Glacier Park Pioneer Frank McPartland are lying in state not far off shore in over 400 feet of water at the upper end of Lake McDonald. Down there in the deep, dark, "profundal zone," his well-preserved bones, clothes, revolver, cartridge belt, mining pick, and hobnail

According to Charlie Shaw, old-time trapper William Schafer is buried somewhere in this remote area of the Great Bear Wilderness near the junction of Morrison and Lodgepole Creeks. Author Photo, 2006.

boots lie covered with eight or ten inches of glacial silt, if the sedimentation rate in McDonald is about the same as in Avalanche Lake. This deep layer of water doesn't "turn over," or exchange with the upper water column. And it's extremely cold. At that depth and pressure, it's about 3-1/2 degrees Centigrade, year-around. There is no light and no photosynthesis; decomposition is extremely slow. There isn't much for bacteria to survive on because in an unproductive lake like McDonald, not much plankton sinks down from the upper water column. Down, way down at the bottom of Lake McDonald, I'll bet the eye sockets of Frank's skull still stare blankly up from the cold darkness towards the surface.

Slippery Bill Morrison's grave is more conventional, marked with a modest headstone in the Conrad Cemetery in Kalispell. Josephine Doody, the Bootleg Lady of Glacier Park, is buried there too, but as I found out, a headstone didn't mark her grave. This will be remedied.

George Snyder, the Glacier Park Maverick, lies at the Montana State Hospital Cemetery, an odd place for such an important Wild River Pioneer to end up. As I followed George's trail, I was surprised that it led to this state mental institution at Warm Springs. After some research and phone conversations with the hospital director, I found that there was an old file on George, but like other old files it had been sent to the Montana Historical Society in Helena. After securing the permission of George's distant cousin,

One of the old wooden water mains that delivered water to McCarthyville. Author photo

Krys Peterson, I requested and received a copy of the file, which had been sealed for more than 60 years. I didn't expect to find much in the file. I was wrong.

George had indeed been committed to the institution on April 3, 1940, at age 70. "Mug shots" included in the file were not flattering. He had shrunk a few inches in his old age, being measured at 5 feet-11 inches and 212 pounds. The bad fall on the ice in Kalispell in November had knocked George unconscious for about five hours, and was considered partly responsible for his "dementia and psychosis" which led to "slovenly personal habits." These factors and his disorientation had led to the doctor's recommendation that he be committed to the state mental institution. George's possessions the day he entered were listed as: "1 pocket knife, 1 smoking pipe, 2 pr glasses, 1 glass case, pkg cig, 1 pkg tobacco, 1 pocket book, 1 cheap pocket watch," and $6.13 in cash. The summary judgment on George's condition was "Indigent." Sadly, this is what this once wealthy, but now pathetic, man had been reduced to.

As I continued looking through the file papers, I was stunned to find a letter dated July 10, 1940 from Dan and Doris Huffine, my wife's great aunt and uncle, the subjects of my first book, *A Woman's Way West*, and George's old huckleberry picking partners at the Stanton Creek Lodge. Based on the correspondence in the file, they were the only two people to have visited George during his stay at the institution. The letter, written in Doris's hand, but attributed to Dan, brims with compassion. Doris asks if they can send him pipe tobacco. Doris mentions that she sent a package of cookies and candy, and writes, "I would appreciate knowing how he is getting along—we saw him there May 1st so we know how he was then." On August 22, Superintendent B. L. Pampel replied to Doris. He wrote that Snyder was up and around, but suffering from arteriosclerosis and general senility. He noted that George's memory "dwelt in the past," that he "seemed not to realize his present location" but seemed happy, enjoying life in his own way.

Indeed, George had visions of a plot by a Kalispell doctor to steal four claims he said he owned in the Middle Fork. He also still imagined himself the owner of Snyder's Hotel and restaurant and listed his residence as Belton. The doctor reported that George shifted back and forth from seeming intelligent to being silly.

As George's stay at the institution dragged on, he underwent long periods of sickness and was often bedridden. The superintendent kept George's daughter, Mrs. Carl Stroenider of Rockford Washington, and Maude Hudson (George's ex-wife) of Willits, California, informed of his condition. His daughter never visited George at the institution. She wrote that George didn't recognize her just before he was committed and so it would be "useless to contact him further." She did ask what she could send him, though.

On October 1, 1944, the superintendent wired George's daughter that George's condition was critical, and followed up with news of George's death from "a stroke of apoplexy" at 4:45 a.m. on October 17. On October 20, George was buried in grave number 10 in cemetery number 6. His daughter had declined to arrange for a burial elsewhere or to pay for embalming, so George was placed in a hole on the institution's grounds alongside hundreds of other forgotten people. Minister Earl Sherman said a few words over him, and then workers shoveled dirt over the grave. George received no headstone and apparently no marker of any kind.

Maintenance Supervisor Bob Suttle of the Montana State Hospital and his staff located George Snyder's burial site among the hundreds of mounds in the institution's Cemetery Number 6. George's final resting place is wildlife-rich mountain valley grassland. Author photo.

For years, I've thought about George and remembered him, and marveled at his persistence and vision. It was an incredible feeling to finally discover what really happened to him and particularly unexpected and spooky to find a letter from my wife's great aunt in an old file that hadn't been opened for more than six decades. Now I feel that chasing George's story had a purpose and accomplished something. The way things turned out, I almost feel that somehow I was directed or at least destined to do it.

I knew that to close George's story, I would have to visit the state hospital and place a headstone at his grave. It seemed appropriate that such an important man in Glacier's history should have some sort of visible marker. I made arrangements with the state hospital maintenance manager for the visit.

On a beautiful spring day, Bob Suttle met me at the institution's main building to take me out to the cemetery. We drove on a little dirt path past bass ponds fed by the waters of the warm springs that gave this place its name. The cemetery grounds are wild grasslands and shrub lands, teaming

Incredibly, Pete Darling located Lena Cunningham's temporary grave marker, placed more than 114 years ago in what is now the Woodlawn Cemetery west of Columbia Falls. The marker was buried about 10 inches under the surface. Author photo

with wildlife. In fact, the state wildlife agency leases the area for hunting and as a state wildlife management area. The peaks of the Anaconda-Pintler Mountains frame the valley to the south. This seemed like a fitting resting place for a person like George Snyder who loved the outdoors.

Bob explained that no actual record of George's grave appeared on the cemetery map. To find George's resting place, they had to measure a distance from a known point and then count the old mounds of people buried in 1944 as best they could to find grave number 11. Ed Johnston and Chuck Fergerson of the maintenance staff met Bob and me at the site. Scattered through the grasslands you could see hundreds of old mounds, some of them with little rusty markers, some with no markers at all. Ed and Chuck had clipped the grasses at George's mound. We set in place George's grave marker, and added some wildflowers I'd picked in the mountains on the way over. Before we left, Ed pointed out some massive whitetail buck tracks on the edge of George's mound. I thought that if you had to be six feet under, this wasn't a bad place at all.

So with the help of Pete Darling, who made the stone, and the maintenance folks at Warm Springs, George Snyder finally has a headstone, one of the few at the institution. Maybe now the Glacier Park Maverick rests in peace.

I thought I'd never find Lena Cunningham's resting place, and it bothered me. Her brutal murder left me wondering. I've studied and imagined her last moments in life. It seemed that she was forgotten, and she needed someone to think about her and the injustice of her sudden death.

I first dug into Lena's story about 15 years ago. I followed leads to old newspaper stories and tried to trace her final path and the murderer's path. On April 28, 1994, the 100th anniversary of the murder, I stood at the spot along the river below the junction of the three forks of the Flathead River, where the killer washed the blood from his hands and clothes. I kept searching for something tangible. I could find no physical link to Lena, no photo, no possession, no artifact, no death certificate or other documents, and no relative. I could find no one who knew anything concrete about her or her murder. Lena seemed more legendary than real.

I finished an early version of Lena's story, but I didn't feel a sense of closure about it. Then one night it struck me. According to old news stories, the young mother was buried west of Columbia Falls a year before the town's cemetery was officially established. But could there be a record of her burial at the site of the cemetery anyway?

Lena Cunningham finally has a headstone at the Woodlawn Cemetery. Author photo

On an April day in 2006 I called Pete Darling, the keeper of the Woodlawn Cemetery on the west end of Columbia Falls. I held on the phone while Pete looked up Lena's name. He came back on the phone and told me that Lena was indeed buried there, and she had a headstone. Could this be too good to be true?

Elated, I dropped what I was doing and drove to the cemetery. When I met Pete there, I found out that his news was too good to be true. Although there was a record of her burial, Pete had looked where Lena was supposed to be and could find no sign of her grave, no headstone, and no marker. I was disappointed but not surprised: a physical link to Lena's story had eluded me for years.

But Pete decided to take another look, this time with a metal detector. Sometimes, he said, evidence of a very old grave could be hidden underground. I followed Pete over to Block 31, near the biggest Ponderosa Pine tree in the cemetery. Pete waved the metal detector back and forth, above the mown green surface of the grass. Suddenly, the detector signaled that something metal lay buried well beneath the sod. He poked a metal rod down into the ground; it struck something solid. Pete dropped to his knees and began digging. I joined him and we both dug with our bare hands. I feared that the hit was probably an old can or a nail.

Then, at about 10 inches below the surface Pete hit a flat piece of metal. To my astonishment it looked like a small plaque. I brushed the dirt off a charming old marker. Clearly visible on a strip of metal was stamped the name: "Lena Cunningham."

I couldn't believe it. Lena's grave marker (a temporary one, Pete explained), placed 112 years ago, lay right before my eyes. Finally, here was a physical link, making Lena's story real. But the marker also told us something sad: Lena never got a gravestone or permanent marker. Evidently, John Cunningham and his children were so devastated by her murder that they soon left their homestead and never returned. After all the fanfare of Lena's large funeral, she and her gravesite were soon forgotten.

Pete and I made plans to be sure that Lena finally got her headstone. Now, she has it, and maybe everyone associated with this tragedy and this poor woman's story will rest a little easier.

Charles Black, Lena's convicted killer, was buried in what was called "Potter's Field." Pete thinks this site is a few hundred yards south of Lena's resting place. Pete is thinking about looking around there someday, to see if he could locate any of the outlaws or paupers that might have been buried there. He thinks that Black might even have a similar temporary marker. But, somehow, I'm not very enthusiastic about learning where Black's final resting place might be.

Just recently, because of a stroke of luck, I found another physical link to Lena's murder that helped me add even more realism to the story. I stopped by the Flathead County Justice Center and asked if there existed a criminal file from the murder case. Why I didn't think of requesting this before, I don't know. Miraculously, the folks at the center were able to locate the file, State of Montana vs. Charles J. Black, by the next day. I felt a sense of awe as Flathead County Deputy Clerk of Court Rae Baker handed me the classic old, tri-fold file. I was holding a file that certainly had been handled by County Attorney Sidney Logan, Sheriff Joe Gangner, and other officials in 1894 and may have been sealed since then, or at least opened rarely. The file contained all original documents, including: the writ of execution for Charles J. Black; three original stays of execution with the gold seal of the State of Montana and signed by Governor John E. Rickards; a 17-page instruction to the jury put together by District Judge Dudley Dubose; Black's lawyers' extensive and credible motion for a new trial, signed by his lawyers and by Black himself; a list of jurors, and more. Also included were about 30 original witness subpoenas personally signed by Sheriff Joe Gangner. The final document in the folder was the original writ of execution, with a handwritten summary signed by Sherriff Joe reporting that he'd hung Charles Black as ordered by the court. I could almost see Joe dipping his pen in the ink well and signing the document, ending the long trail of bringing Black to justice. Reading through this file brought home to me the huge effort Gangner and others had put into the case. No wonder the newspapers of the time praised the sheriff's professionalism.

Sheriff Joe Gangner was haunted by Lena's murder and Black's hanging for the rest of his life. He had saved Black from a lynching, but eight months later he tightened the noose around Black's neck and put a hood over Black's head and hung him. Joe's own life was a mixture of triumph and tragedy. He was perhaps the most successful sheriff in the history of Flathead County when it came to hands-on apprehension of train robbers and murderers. Yet, he was the subject of a witch-hunt by jealous politicians. In his life he and his wife, Eliza, raised four wonderful children. But his life with Eliza wasn't destined to end happily; it ended horribly.

Joe and Eliza had moved south of the Flathead Valley where they raised stock on a ranch in Upper Big Draw, about 30 miles west of Dayton. On April 24 1912, Joe left for his son Fred's ranch, about six miles away. Eliza was at home with her grandson, the son of Annie. It was washday, and Eliza had fired up the cookstove to heat water for the laundry. Suddenly, Eliza looked up to see that the house was on fire. She "put the babe in a safe place" and ran back into the burning house to gather valuables. As she was hurriedly gathering up things in one of the rooms, the draft created by the fire or a falling timber jammed the door against her and she was overcome by the smoke and heat.

A 7mm Mauser cartridge in the "little glacier basin" described by Penrose and Stiles. The head stamp on the decomposing, oxidized casing reads, " UMC 1900" signifying that the shell was manufactured in 1900 by the United Metallic Cartridge Company. Could this be one of the shells fired by Penrose at the white grizzly? Author photo

Eliza's screams attracted a neighbor who was passing by, and he rushed into the burning house. He found Eliza nearly dead, lying on the floor with her clothes on fire. The neighbor was able to carry Eliza out, but she was terribly burned.

Leaving Eliza in good hands, the man rushed to Fred's ranch. Joe and Fred jumped into a wagon and Joe whipped the horses, maybe taking out his grief on the straining animals. The men rushed to Eliza's side and provided whatever comfort they could. A man rushed to the little Flathead lakeshore town of Elmo, and from there phoned Dayton for a doctor and an automobile.

Joe and his son carefully loaded the suffering woman into the car when it arrived and Dr. Dixon administered medical care. Eliza was alive when they reached the hospital in Kalispell, but she was failing fast and in terrible pain. She died at 4:30 a.m. the next morning after hours of "frightful agony." Joe, Fred, and Annie were at Eliza's bedside when she died. How frustrating it must have been for this strong, fine man who had saved so many lives to watch his wife suffer and not be able to help her.

Two days later, people from all over the valley attended Eliza's funeral at St. Matthews Catholic Church in Kalispell. She was laid to rest in nearby Conrad Cemetery. Eliza died at age 49. She left four children. Eliza's relatives must have taken some comfort in knowing that she had saved the life of her infant grandson.

Sheriff Joe, a proven survivor, lived another 15 years after Eliza's death. In mid-January 1927, family members transported a very sick Joe from the ranch in Dixon to the hospital in Missoula. On February 4, at age 65, Joe succumbed to cirrhosis of the liver. Joe's brother Fred, his son Fred, his daughter Annie, and his second wife Mary Pauline were at his bedside when he died. A news article in the *Missoulian* noted that Joe was the first sheriff of Flathead County, and briefly described his role in the shootout with the train robbers up the Middle Fork. His name was misspelled "Gagnier."

Joe was not buried in Kalispell next to his pioneer wife with whom he had come into the Flathead in the spring of 1882 with the first wave of settlers. Ironically, the first sheriff of Flathead County was buried in Saint Mary's Catholic cemetery in Missoula County because of the wishes of his second wife, who didn't want him to be buried near Eliza.

I finally found Joe's final resting place with information from his descendents and calls to Missoula cemeteries. I made arrangements with Mike Hamlin, the "Sexton" of the Old St. Mary's Cemetery in Missoula for a visit. For those of you who were not raised in the Catholic religion or other religions that employ them, Sexton is Latin for "keeper of the dead." The Sexton can have other duties, but Mike's main duties focus on the cemetery.

You won't find a more enthusiastic keeper of the dead than Mike Hamlin. As a youngster, Mike began working at the Old St. Mary's Cemetery for his dad. He took over full time in 1972, and he considers it his calling. He is doing a fine job maintaining the grounds and documenting as much as he can the background of the people buried there. When I arrived, Mike toured me around the cemetery, showing me the gravesites of some of the prominent "residents," like poet Richard Hugo and a former Montana Governor. When we got to Joe Gangner's plot, Mike showed me the little poured cement slab that was partly covered over with sod. We pulled the sod back from the marker and I could read "Joseph Gagnier" imprinted in it. Mike and I talked about getting a headstone "pillow" for Joe, with his name spelled correctly and with the inscription, "First Sheriff of Flathead County." It seems only right for such a prominent pioneer, and I'll be working with Sheriff Joe's descendents to help make it happen.

From the beginning, the story of C. B. Penrose and the white grizzly captured my imagination. I knew that I couldn't rest until I actually stood in that still-remote site in the Great Bear Wilderness where the doctor and the grizzly tangled. When my son, Kevin, a companion, and I explored the little alpine basin a century after the event, searching for that fateful mauling site (and against all odds finding it), I saw a big grizzly scat. The scat was blood red and full of mountain ash berries. Maybe the great bear's descendents had left a mark of ownership for me to see. At least that's what I thought that beautiful afternoon as I walked along the Middle Fork divide in the shadows of Mount Penrose.

As fate had it, Penrose and Stiles left the U. S. Geological Survey camp the evening of September 1, 1907 on what was supposed to be a short hunt, but instead it became a watershed event for the Middle Fork. The two adventurers rode their horses through the pass that turned out to be not only a gateway to a little alpine basin, but also a gateway to history.

The Wild River Pioneers are long gone, but they left their marks. My search for their stories is over for now. But I'll admit that I've unearthed a couple of new leads that I'm going to have to follow. The Middle Fork country is remote, steep, and brushy, so I better ask someone to go with me on my next death march. Sometimes it's hard to find people willing to go along because of the buck-brush and devil's club, but I've found it isn't all that bad if you wear protective clothes and thick gloves.

By the way, what are you doing this weekend?

John Fraley

SOURCES

Chapter 1: Tough Trip over the Lost Pass

An Engineer's Recollections, V, The Discovery of Marias Pass, by John F. Stevens. Engineering News Record, May 9, 1935. In this document and in the one below, Stevens gives the details of his discovery of Marias Pass.

An Engineer's Recollections, by John F. Stevens. Reprinted from the Engineering News Record, 1935, McGraw Hill Publishing Company. This report also covers other aspects of Steven's engineering career.

Buchholz, C. W. 1976. *Man in Glacier.* Glacier Natural History Association, Inc. West Glacier. Buchholz discusses the early exploration of the Marias Pass area near Glacier National Park.

DeVoto, Editor, 1953. *The Journals of Lewis and Clark.* Houghton Mifflin Company, New York and Boston.

John Frank Stevens, *Wikipedia* online Encyclopedia. This contains general information on John F. Stevens.

Kalispell *Daily Interlake*, July 22, 1925. "Statue Unveiled at Summit Yesterday".

The Flathead Story by Charlie Shaw. U. S. Forest Service, Flathead National Forest, 1967. This work contains Shaw's version of important events in the Flathead Drainage, including information on Slippery Bill's cabin on Marias Pass.

The Pioneers, by S. E. Johns. Mimeographed local history, Flathead County Library.

U. S. Geological Survey maps.

Chapter 2: The Middle Fork's Tombstone Town

Administrative History of Glacier National Park, Chapter 1, Discovery and Exploration. Glacier National Park, West Glacier, Montana, May, 1960. This contains some basic information on Marias Pass and McCarthyville.

Demersville *Inter Lake*, December 5, 1890. "A New Town." This news article and the ones below formed the basis for many of the stories associated with McCarthyville.

Demersville *Inter Lake*, January 23, 1891. "McCarthyville gets a Post

Office." Although it is claimed that McCarthyville was granted an official post office, records don't indicate that it did.

Demersville *Inter Lake*, January 30, 1891. "McCarthyville Items." Murder Near McCarthyville.

Demersville *Inter Lake*, February 13, 1891. "Deputies Mumbrue and Evans Return with Two Prisoners Who Are Supposed to be the Murderers."

Demersville *Inter Lake*, April 10, 1891. "Hospital Horrors." This article contains the information about the horrid conditions at the Great Northern "Hospital." I included this and other information in a shorter article I wrote about McCarthyville for True West Magazine published in 1992.

Early Flathead and Tobacco Plains, by Marie C. Shea. A Narrative History of Northwestern Montana, 1977.

Fisheries surveys, Montana Fish, Wildlife & Parks. Fish trapping, Bear, Geifer Creeks, summer 1981; Snorkel surveys of Skyland and Bear Creeks by John Fraley, July 1981. Bull trout nest counts, 1980-2006. Data housed at FWP headquarters in Kalispell.

Muscle, Grit, and Big Dreams: Earliest towns of the upper Flathead Valley, 1872-1891, by Carle O'Neil. In this book, the incorporated towns for the era are described. Although Eugene McCarthy claimed to have secured a post office, and it was reported in the newspaper, it probably was not official. According to the book and according to conversations with Carle, McCarthyville never received an official post office and thus was never an incorporated town.

The Flathead Story, by Charlie Shaw. U. S. Forest Service, Flathead National Forest, 1967.

The pioneers, by S. E. Johns. Mimeographed local history, Flathead County Library.

Chapter 3: Shootout at Bear Creek

Coroner's Inquests, Flathead County Justice Center, for the outlaws Jack Chipman, Samuel Shermer, and Jack White, October 1893.

Kalispell Inter Lake, September 1, 1893: "Cool Piece of Villainy." This article and the series of articles cited below, cover the story of the train robbery, pursuit of the robbers, and White's eventual murder

Kalispell Inter Lake, October 6, 1893: "The Robbers Caught."

Kalispell Inter Lake, October 13, "The Dying Confession."

Kalispell Inter Lake, October 27, 1893: "Is it Murder?"

Kalispell, Montana, and the upper Flathead Valley, by Henry Elwood, Thomas Printing, Kalispell, Montana.

Shooting Research Center. Classic Cartridge Report: Shooting the .45-90 Winchester.

The Columbian, October 5, 1893. "A Red Hot Trail." Articles from *The*

Columbian confirmed information about the train robbery and chase, and in many cases contained the best information about the events. I used this and other sources when I wrote a shorter article on the train robbery in 1994 for *Old West Magazine.*

The Columbian, October 12, 1893. "Shermer Confesses."

The Columbian, October 19, 1893. "Rotten to the Core." This article outlines the malfeasance charges against Sheriff Joe Gangner and other county officials.

The Columbian, October 26, 1893. "White Shot Dead"

The Pioneers, by S. E. Johns, mimeographed history of the Flathead, Flathead County Library. This history contains information about the train robbery and subsequent events.

Chapter 4: Black Murder on the River

The story surrounding Lena Cunningham's murder, the subsequent investigation, the trial, and the hanging of Charles Black is complex and sensational. I worked on the story for about 15 years and spent time along the river trying to visualize the event. With the help of Pete Darling, I finally found Lena's lost grave. At the Flathead County Justice Center I went through the recently discovered criminal file that had likely remained sealed for over a century. I did my best to tell the story as accurately as I could, considering the time that has passed since the event and the multiple accounts of each of its aspects. Readers can pour over the dozens of sources I used and judge for themselves how well I did.

The following news articles give extensive details and analysis of the Lena Cunningham murder, the investigation, the trial, and the hanging of Charles Black. I used what I thought was the best information from each article, and especially used items that were consistent between accounts.

Kalispell *Daily Inter Lake*, May 4, 1894. "A Terrible Crime."

Kalispell *Daily Inter Lake*, August 17, 1894 "Black Found Guilty."

Kalispell *Daily Inter Lake*, August 24, 1894. "To Hang September 28."

Kalispell *Daily Inter Lake*, September 28, 1894. "Will Not Hang Today."

Kalispell *Daily Inter Lake*, December 14, 1894. "Black Will Swing."

Kalispell *Daily Inter Lake*, December 21, 1894. "Charles Black Hung."

The Columbian, May 3, 1894 "An Awful Murder."

The Columbian, August 9, 1894. "The Black Trial."

The Columbian, August 16, 1894. "Black Will Hang."

The Columbian, October 26, 1893. "The First Fire."

The Columbian, short notes, December 7, December 21, 1893, and August 23, December 13, December 20, 1894.

The Columbian, December 27, 1894. "Black is Dead."

The Kalispell Graphic put out a special edition, December 21, 1894, the day of Black's execution. This edition presents a version of the murder and hanging, and background information on Charles Black, alias Calvin Christie.

Criminal File: Charles J. Black vs. the State of Montana. This 2-inch thick file luckily was found one day in mid-February, 2008, when I stopped by the Flathead County Justice Center and asked if it existed. Why I didn't think of asking about this earlier, I don't know. The file contains: Black's writ of execution, three stays of execution signed by Governor John E. Rickards, a 17-page instruction to the jury, Black's lawyers' extensive and credible motion for a new trial, a list of jurors, and more. Also included were about 30 original witness subpoenas personally signed by Sheriff Joe Gangner.

Early Flathead and the Tobacco Plains, by Marie C. Shea, 1977, Flathead County Library. Contains information on early Columbia Falls. Carle O'Neil's book, *Muscle, Grit, and Big Dreams* also contains extensive information on Columbia Falls.

Interviews, April 2006, with Pete Darling of Columbia Falls, curator of the Woodlawn Cemetery. Pete and I found Lena Cunningham's lost grave and marker. Pete also shed light on the nature of temporary markers, chasing ghosts, and the possible location of Black's grave (we might find it yet).

Interviews, May 2006, with Sheriff Joe Gangner's descendents, Mary Sullivan, Mike Dockstader, and 96-year old Effie Dockstader of Bigfork. These folks shed some light on Sheriff Joe Gangner's history.

Kalispell Montana and the Upper Flathead Valley, by Henry Elwood, Thomas Printing, Kalispell, MT. Contains information from the Kalispell Graphic news account of the incident.

The Pioneers, by Sam E. Johns, 1943, Flathead County Library. Contains information on the murder.

Chapter 5: Slippery Bill's Gold

Charlie Shaw, testimony at a hearing on Senate Bill 392, Great Bear Wilderness designation, July 29, 1979, Congressional Record. In this transcript, Shaw tells about Slippery Bill's legendary statement that Bill really did kill William Schafer.

Data Books, John Fraley, Montana Fish, Wildlife & Parks, bull trout nest counts and winter furbearer surveys in the upper Middle Fork Drainage 1980-2006.

Death Certificate, State of Montana, Bureau of Vital Statistics, William H. Morrison. Flathead County registered No. 34. March 6, 1932. This document adds facts to the legendary story of Slippery Bill.

Doris Huffine Papers, notes on Slippery Bill Morrison and the upper Middle Fork, August, 1958. Doris often made notes on her interpretation of the Middle Fork's history after she talked to old-timers. In these, Doris raises the possibility that Bill had a mysterious past and hid loot in the upper Middle Fork near Schafer Meadows.

Flathead County Deed Record No. 206, June 27, 1930, Flathead County Courthouse.

Interviews with Tim Darr, former Great Bear Wilderness hunting guide, Bigfork, MT, April 6 and 25, 2006.

Interviews on April 27 and May 2, 2006 with Don Hauth, U.S. Forest Service backcountry ranger extraordinaire at Schafer Meadows from 1978-1990.

Interviews, various, with conservationist and old-time trapper Bud Moore, 1996-2007. Bud described the method old-time trappers used to trap large areas using strategically-spaced cabins. He conducted such a line in the Lochsa River country of Idaho and wrote about in *The Lochsa Story*, land ethics in the Bitterroot Mountains. Bud also helped me learn old-time fur trapping methods that I used in the Middle Fork over the years. Through my own backcountry marten trapping in some of Slippery Bill's old stomping grounds, I gained a feel of what it must have been like for men like Slippery Bill and William Schafer.

Kalispell *Daily Inter Lake*, March 9, 1932: William H. Morrison, obituary, and services held. This article, along with Slippery Bill's death certificate, supplies accurate details about this legendary character.

The Flathead Story, Charlie Shaw, 1967. U.S. Forest Service, Kalispell, MT

The Pioneers, by S. E. Johns. 1943. Mimeographed copies, Flathead County Library.

Trails of the Past: Historical Overview of the Flathead National Forest, Montana, 1800-1960, Kathryn L. McKay.

Chapter 6: The Heart of the Middle Fork

Interview with Art Whitney, former Schafer Meadows USFS Ranger, July 7, 1999, at Art's home in Bigfork. Art died just four months after this interview. Much of the early history I used in this chapter came from this interview with Art and a few follow-up conversations with him. I recorded the major interview and transcribed it.

Interviews with Bill Chilton, former Schafer Meadows USFS Ranger, and his wife Barbara, July 2006, at the Chiltons' home in Kalispell. Bill supplied much specific detail about his time in the Middle Fork in these interviews and in follow-up conversations. I recorded the major interview and transcribed it.

Interviews on April 27 and May 2, 2006 with Don Hauth, USFS Ranger at Schafer Meadows from 1978-1990. Don's knowledge of the Middle Fork backcountry was a big help in putting some of its history into perspective for me. I got to know Don when I was the fisheries biologist for Montana Fish, Wildlife & Parks

Interview with Tim Darr, former hunting guide in the Middle Fork, April 25, 2006, near Bigfork. Tim had some interesting perspectives on the Middle Fork country and its history.

The Flathead Story, Charlie Shaw, 1967. U.S. Forest Service, Kalispell, MT. Charlie Shaw's information on the early Flathead is considered credible by many. Serving as a Forest Service ranger, Charlie knew many of the Middle Fork characters or heard lore about them.

Chapter 7: Grizzly Attack on Mount Penrose

DeVoto, Bernard, Editor. 1953. *The Journals of Lewis and Clark*. Mariner Books, 1997 edition.

Gifford Pinchot. *Historic Pennsylvania Leaflet No. 39*. Pennsylvania Historical and Museum Commission, Harrisburg. 1976.

List of the 1904 members of the Boone and Crockett Club in *Trail and Campfire, The Book of the Boone and Crockett Club*, edited by George Bird Grinnell and Theodore Roosevelt. Originally published in 1897, reissued in 1988 by the Boone and Crockett Club.

New York Times, September 4, 1910. Penrose in Forest Fires. A brief article telling the story of the Penrose brothers in Montana on a hunting trip during the disastrous 1910 fires.

Noel, T. and C. Norman. *A Pikes Peak Partnership, The Penroses and the Tutts*. Boulder: the University Press of Colorado, 2000. Also, Cripple Creek History Page, Wikipedia.

Penrose, Charles B., M. D. *An Encounter with a Grizzly Bear. Hunting and Conservation, Book of the Boone and Crockett Club*, Yale University Press, 1925, edited by George B. Grinnell and Charles Sheldon.

Pouliot, Gordon, taped interview. Interviewed by John Fraley at Gordon's Nyack home, June 26, 1999.

Stiles, Arthur Alvord. *A Bear Hunt in Montana. National Geographic* (19) 1908.

U. S. Geological Survey. Topographic maps, 7.5-minute series, Nyack, West Glacier.

U. S. Geological Survey. Original Topographic Map of Glacier National Park. 1914 version. Surveyed in 1900-1904 and 1907-1912. Topography by Arthur Stiles and others.

Chapter 8: Glacier's Mystery Valley

Born Killers, article on weasels in *Montana Outdoors*, September/October 1999, by John Fraley. This article contains information on the life history of this vicious little carnivore.

Interview, Betty Robertson Schurr and John Schurr, March 31, 1999. Betty graciously shared her early experiences in the remote Nyack Valley. I recorded and transcribed the interview.

Interview, Betty Robertson Schurr and John Schurr, February 3, 2006. Betty expanded on the earlier interview and answered follow-up questions.

Interview, Clyde Fauley, Jr., May 8, 2007 in Lakeside. Clyde told me about some experiences of his father, Clyde Fauley, Sr., as a Glacier National Park Ranger. Clyde, also a ranger in the Park, remembered Josephine Doody and, as a boy, ate Thanksgiving dinner at her homestead one year.

National Park Service, Glacier National Park Archives, Interview, Hugh Buchanan, 1981. This interview and the ones listed below provide lots of information about the history and experiences of rangers in the Nyack.

National Park Service, Glacier National Park Archives, Interview, Clyde Fauley, Jr., February 28, 2001.

National Park Service, Glacier National Park Archives, Interview, Alma Guardippee 8/1/84.

National Park Service, Glacier National Park Archives, Nyack Ranger Station Journals, 1928-1931. These journals contain many stories of ranger experiences in the Nyack area written in their own words. The most valuable, detailed entry I found was the description of the "busting" of Josephine Doody's bootleg operation on her homestead within the Park. Also, most interestingly, the journals contain many entries showing that most of the rangers had extensive contact with Josephine. This makes sense because her homestead cabin sits within the Park, right at the junction of the trail to Harrison Lake.

Railroad Surveys, 1853-1855, in Vaught Manuscript, Glacier National Park Archives. The Vaught papers are the best early source of Glacier's history, in my opinion.

Robertson Papers, Betty's baby book, courtesy of Betty Robertson Schurr.

The Pioneers, by S. E. Johns, Volume 2, 1943, Flathead County Library.

Trails of the Past, Historical overview of the Flathead National Forest, Montana, By K. L. McKay 1994. Commissioned by the U. S. Forest Service, this report contains information on Forest Service rangers and early history of the agency's activities in the area.

Chapter 9: Bootleg Lady of Glacier Park:

Census records, various, Macon County, Georgia, Courthouse. Contains conflicting information on Josephine Gaines Doody's birthdate.

Death certificate, Josephine Doody, Flathead County, Montana Courthouse.

Death certificate, Dan Doody, Flathead County, Montana Courthouse. Dan and Josephine's death certificates represent the best information for their vital statistics.

Death announcement, Josephine Doody, Kalispell MT *Daily Inter Lake*, January 17, 1936.

Deed records on the Doody homestead from the Flathead County Courthouse, Kalispell, MT. These show the complex ownership history of Josephine's homestead within the Park.

Historical interview with Bud Henderson, August 1975, on file at the Glacier Park Library, West Glacier, MT. "Bud" Henderson knew Josephine as well as anyone during Josephine's later years.

Historical interview with Francis June, February 1979, on file at the Glacier Park Library, West Glacier, MT.

Historical interview with Ralph Thayer, July 1975, on file at the Glacier Park Library, West Glacier, MT.

Interviews with Betty Robertson Schurr, March 1999 and February 2006. Betty was 11 years old when Josephine died, but she remembers the woman in her old age.

Interviews, Doris Huffine and Maxine Conrad, December 1988 through January 1990. Doris and Maxine stopped by to visit with Josephine off and on for years when Josephine lived in a small cabin along Deerlick Creek. Doris, a Middle Fork old-timer, had an incredible memory for detail, as I found out while interviewing her for my first book, *A Woman's Way West*. Josephine seemed to confide in Doris and Maxine above all others and told them the complete story of her early life. I rely on the extensive interviews with Doris and Maxine, which I recorded and transcribed, for much of my information on Josephine. I had learned that if Doris told me something, it was usually correct, at least to the best of her knowledge. A few days before Doris died in January, 1990, she reviewed an early version of Josephine's story I had written for True West magazine (published in 1990) and agreed that it was accurate as far as she knew.

Interview, Lewis Voss, April 1989, Kalispell, MT. I conducted these interviews with Lewis, Velma, Tiny, Wes, and Bob as I chased Josephine's story. I transcribed these interviews. Sadly, all of these old-timers are now gone.

Interview, Velma Guy, April 1989, Kalispell, MT. As a young mother, Velma knew Josephine well although she knew her only as "Mrs. Doody." Velma said that Josephine thought that Velma's children were "just right." I interviewed Velma at the Brendan House care facility in Kalispell. I brought her some flowers, which seemed to please her. She died shortly after our interview.

Interview, Tiny Powell, April 1989, Kalispell, MT. I interviewed Tiny at the Kalispell Livestock Auction. He was a favorite of Josephine.

Interview, Wes Bell, April 1989, Kalispell, MT. Wes said that Josephine didn't like him much, and that she particularly disliked Bob Robertson! As young boys, Wes and Bob sometimes conflicted with the old woman.

Interview, Bob Robertson, April 1989, Nyack, MT. I interviewed Bob by telephone to his home at Nyack.

Interviews and conversations with Gordon Pouliott, fall 1989- summer 2000, Nyack, MT. Gordon allowed me to cross his land to reach the Middle Fork of the Flathead River where I could cross and search for the hideout cabin. He affirmed theories that this cabin was the one mentioned by Bud Henderson, Doris Huffine, and several rangers.

Obituary, Josephine Doody, Kalispell, MT *Daily Inter Lake*, January 20, 1936.

Obituary, Dan Doody, Kalispell MT *Daily Inter Lake*, January 19, 1921.

Chapter 10, Glacier Park Maverick:

Biography of Edwin Snyder and Obituary of Edwin Snyder, Krys Peterson Collection.

Buchholz, C. W. 1976. *Man in Glacier.* Glacier National History Association, Inc. in cooperation with the National Park Service.

Collins, Elizabeth Smith. 1912. *The Cattle Queen of Montana.* Dyer Printing Company, Spokane, Washington.

Columbian Newspaper, Columbia Falls, MT. The following articles in this fine paper formed the basis of many of the subplots in this chapter and corroborated many of the stories garnered from other sources:

--August 8, 1895, Frank McPartland Drowned.

--April 18, 1912, New Improvements in Glacier Park

--April 25, 1912, Another Resort for Glacier Park, Snyder's Saloon

May 30, 1912, Glacier Hotel Opens for Season.

June 12, 1913, Glacier Park is Mecca for Tourists.

--July 17, 1913, Flathead Claims Another Victim: Patrick Burton, a Lumberjack, Goes to a Watery Grave Near Belton.

--August 21, 1913, Shoots Partner After Quarrel at Snyder's Saloon.

--October 2, 1913, Glacier Park Closes a Successful Season.

--June 18, 1914, Crowds Attend Park Opening

--September 14, 1916, Park Administrative Site to Be Built At Belton.

--February 27, 1919, Sudden death of Mrs. Chas. Howe.

--January 9, 1913, Reminiscences of Old-Time Resident.

Death Certificate, George Snyder, Deer Lodge County. George died on October 17, 1944, but his death certificate was filed in 1949. Certificate provided by Krys Peterson, George's cousin.

Ellis, B. K., J. A. Stanford, J. A. Craft, and D. W. Chess. 1992. Monitoring Water Quality of Selected Lakes in Glacier National Park, Montana. Open File Report, Flathead Lake Biological Station, The University of Montana,

Polson. Contains water quality data for McDonald lake and other Park lakes.

Fraley, John J. and Patrick T. Clancey. Downstream Migration of Stained Kokanee Fry in the Flathead River System, Montana. *Northwest Science* 62: 3, 111-117. This and the following publication contain information on lower McDonald Creek.

Fraley, John J. and Patrick J. Graham. 1982. Physical Habitat, Geologic Bedrock Types and Trout Densities in Tributaries of the Flathead River Drainage, Montana, in W. B. Armitage, editor: Acquisition and utilization of aquatic habitat inventory information symposium, Portland Oregon.

The following sources formed the detailed basis for much of this chapter. I owe a huge debt of gratitude to Ann Fagre of Glacier Park for helping me search for these:

Glacier National Park Records 1910-1984, Box 172 file 5: Saloons in the Belton Area. This includes: application for a retail liquor license by Louis Fournier for George Snyder with petition; protests filed by Belton residents and J. L. Galen, Glacier Park Superintendent; various letters from Henry Hutchings, acting Superintendent to Interior Department Officials; letters to the County from Glacier officials; letters from the Interior Department to Hutchings; letters from George Snyder's Lawyers to superintendents of Glacier Park;

Glacier National Park Records, 1910-1984, Box 211, file 6, 1912, Permanent Headquarters. This includes: various letters to and from Ed Dow and George Snyder from Glacier Park Officials regarding their offers to donate land for a permanent headquarters for the Park; letter from Snyder's lawyer to Superintendent Chapman regarding the proposed donation; letter from Chapman to the Secretary of Interior regarding a search for a permanent headquarters site.

Glacier National Park Records, 1910-1984, Box 87-6, 1917-1951, Concessions, George Snyder. This includes: various letters from Superintendent W.W. Payne to Stephen Mather, Director of the National Park Service; letters from U. S. Attorneys to Payne and from Payne to U. S. Attorneys; letters from George Snyder's lawyers to Payne and from Payne to Snyder's lawyers; letter from Payne to newspapers; letter from U. S. Attorney Toole to G. F. Shelton; letters from Snyder and application for boat concession permit; boat concession permit issued to Snyder; affidavits from tourists who rode on Snyder's tour car; affidavit of Complaint by Hutchings and Swetnam regarding Snyder's collision with the Government wagon; letters regarding the accident from the Park Superintendent to U. S. Attorney and replies; letters from Superintendent Scoyen to Snyder regarding his old boat claim settlement and replies from Snyder; Park Service Voucher for Snyder's claim; copy of congress' Act for the relief of W. W. Payne.

History of Apgar. 1951. Compiled by Leona Harrington and the pupils of

Apgar School. Especially useful were sections written by Eddie Cruger and Genevieve Gudger.

L.O. Vaught Papers, 8:1, box 1 files 16 and 18: letter from E.G. Yarret regarding place names in the McDonald Valley, October 23, 1895. Letters from L. B. Sperry to George Snyder, May 26, 1896, August 26, 1896; Letters from George Snyder to L. B. Sperry, October 3 and 14, 1896; reply from Sperry, October 1896; letter from

L.O. Vaught Papers: Letter, Walter Raymond to F. I. Whitney, June 28,1897; letter, handwritten on "Glacier House" letterhead, from George Snyder to L.O. Vaught, February 19, 1906; handwritten letter from Charlie Howes to L. O. Vaught, February 27, 1919; affidavit, early McDonald history, by George E. Snyder as sworn to L. O. Vaught, 1934; notes by Vaught, Kalispell, August 1935; letter by L. O. Vaught re: Collins-McPartland incident, correspondence file, September 30, 1942; excerpts of letters, Vaught B-1 F-16, and notes regarding early settlers at Lake McDonald.

Glacier National Park Administrative History, West Glacier, MT. Administrative report by Glacier Park officials.

Green, Charles. 1962. *Montana Memories*, Volume IV. Blue Print and Letter Co. Printer, Great Falls, MT. On file at the Flathead County Library. A charming book about the Flathead's early history. Helps confirm that George Snyder made a gold strike near Doris and Dan Huffine's Stanton Creek Lodge.

Historical interview with Bea Macomber and Ace Powell, June 4, 1976, on file at the Glacier Park Library, West Glacier, MT

Historical interview with Bea Macomber, Helen Myers and Ace Powell, August and September, 1976, on file at the Glacier Park Library, West Glacier, MT.

Historical interview with Ed Neitzling on file at the Glacier Park Library, West Glacier, MT.

Interviews, Dan and Doris Huffine and Maxine Conrad, 1982-1990. Dan and Doris owned the Stanton Creek Lodge. George Snyder lived in a little cabin nearby in the 1930s. Doris had hilarious stories about her friend George.

Interviews, Lon Johnson, Glacier National Park Cultural Resource Specialist, Winter and Spring, 2007. I also referred to the chain of title for the Edwin Snyder Homestead which was compiled by Lon. Lon was a terrific help and source of knowledge about the history of the McDonald Valley.

Interviews, Krys Peterson, (George Snyder's Cousin) Winter and Spring, 2007.

Interviews, Ed Amberg and Billie Homlund,, Montana State Hospital,

March 2007 regarding George Snyder's 5-year stay.

Kalispell Inter Lake, Newspaper, Kalispell, MT. These articles lent corroboration to some of the stories in this chapter.

August 9, 1895, Drowned at Lake McDonald.

August 9, 1895, Sperry to Return to look for Glaciers.

August 23, 1895, Regarding Frank McPartland drowning, background.

August 23, 1895, Found the Glacier, report of the Sperry Party.

August 30, 1895, Gorgeous Scenes, Sperry party in Avalanche Basin.

February 25, 1919, Mrs. Charles Howe dies.

February 26, 1919, Funeral of Mrs. Howe Held this Afternoon.

Marnell, Leo F. and Dirk Verschuren. 1997. Fossil Zooplankton and the Historical Status of Westslope Cutthroat Trout in a Headwater Lake of Glacier National Park, Montana. Transactions of the American Fisheries Society 126: 21-34. Leo helps prove that westslope cutthroat were indigenous in Avalanche Lake.

Montana State University, Museum of the Rockies, Bozeman, MT. "Glacier National Park Archeological Inventory and Assessment. 1995 Field Season Report. Part III: Historic Land Use" by Kenneth w. Karsmizki, 1997. Report on file at Glacier National Park, West Glacier, MT.

Ober, Michael J. 1973. Enmity and Alliance: Park Service-Concessioner Relations in Glacier National Park, 1892-1961. Master's Thesis, University of Montana. Mike's thesis covers the history of the concessions throughout Glacier Park. This is a fun and interesting read.

Sperry, Lyman B. 1896. Avalanche Basin, Montana Rockies. Appalachia 8: 57-69. In his own words, Lyman describes this gorgeous lake and basin.

U. S. Fish and Wildlife Service 1979. Survey of the Aquatic Resources of Glacier National Park. Water quality information for lakes and bathometric map of Lake McDonald. Technical report on file at Glacier National Park, West Glacier, MT. Contains the map that shows the incredible depth of Lake McDonald.

Epilogue

Criminal File, Flathead County: State of Montana vs. Charles J. Black, Flathead County Justice Center. See notes under sources for Chapter 4.

Death Certificate, Joseph Gangner, Missoula County Recording Division. This was hard to find because I assumed Joe's certificate would be filed in Flathead County.

Interview, Bonnie Ellis, Limnologist at the University of Montana Biological Station on Flathead Lake, May 17, 2007. Bonnie spent eight summers sampling the water column of Lake McDonald. She passed on information on water temperature, oxygen, and the trophic status of the lake in regards to the possible condition of Frank McPartland's remains.

Interview, Mike Hamlin, Sexton of the Old St. Mary's Cemetery in Missoula, MT, June 5, 2007. Mike pointed out Joe Gangner's grave and gave options for a new headstone.

Interview, Bob Suttle, Maintenance Supervisor for the Montana State Hospital, June 7, 2007. Bob shed light on the past nature of burials at the state hospital at Warm Springs.

Interview, Joe Gangner's descendents Mike Dockstader, Effie Dockstader, and Mary Sullivan, Bigfork, MT May, 2006. This information helped me understand Joe a little better. According to their family history, Joe was bothered by Black's hanging and was not convinced that Black was the killer.

Interview, Pete Darling, Woodlawn Cemetery, Columbia Falls, May 2006. Pete and I shared the excitement of finding Lena Cunningham's lost grave marker.

Kalispell Times, weekly newspaper, April 26, 1912. "Mrs. Gangner Loses Life in Burning Ranch House."

Missoulian, February 6, 1927. "Requiem Mass Said For Gagnier Monday."

Missoulian, February 5, 1927, page 1. "First Flathead County Sheriff, Joseph Gagnier, Called by Death."

Montana Historical Society Library. Copy of Montana State Hospital patient file for George Snyder. File contains letters from George's daughter, his former wife, his friends Dan and Doris Huffine, and replies from the superintendent. Also included were medical records, the Superintendent's report, and various telegrams. The report contains two photos of George from when he was committed.

Index

Skiumah Creek, 109, 118
Skyland Creek, 6, 12
Smith, Chandler, 169-171
Snyder Creek, 166, 178
Snyder Lakes, 166, 175
Snyder Ridge, 158
Snyder, Edwin, 162
Snyder, Elizabeth, 162
Snyder, George, 162-201, 203-206
Snyder's Saloon, Hotel and Roadhouse, 186-190
Sommerfield, Dale, 97, 118
South Fork of the Flathead River, 74
Spence, Henry, 174
Sperry Glacier, 164, 175, 180
Sperry, Lyman P., 161, 162, 166, 172-175
Spotted Bear, 68, 74
Sprague Creek, 178
Stanton Creek Lodge, 198, 204
Stanton Creek, 197
Stanton Lake, 197
Stanton Peak, 157
Stevens, John Frank, 3-11
Stiles, Arthur Alvord, 95-109, 211
Strawberry Creek, 65
Stroenider, Mrs. Carl, 205
Summit Creek, 5
Summit Mountain, 6
Suttle, Bob, 205-206
Teakettle Mountain, 35, 38
Three Forks Guard Station burning, 84-85
Three Forks, 70
Tiger Creek, 98
Tinkham, A. W., 111-112
Tom Tom Lake, 79

Toole, J. H. U. S. Attorney, 195
Train robbery, 22, 23
Traplines, 53-59
Trilobite Lakes, 76
Trilobite Range, 76
Two Medicine Pass, 5
Two Medicine River, 2, 3, 5, 112
U. S. Geological Survey, 97, 108
Undersheriff Hickernell, 50
Union Peak, Mountain, 76, 91

Vale, Chris, 145
Van Orsdale, John, 156
Vaught, L. O., 156, 168, 170, 173, 181
Washington Governor Isaac Stevens, 2
Weasel, short-tailed, ermine, 117, 122, 123
West Glacier, 95
West, Bill, 199
Westslope Cutthroat Trout or "flats", 14, 37, 79, 83, 97, 123, 124, 139, 172
Whistler Creek, 55, 68, 92
Whitcomb Peak, 94
Whitcraft, Tom, 94
White, Jack, 24, 29-33
Whitney, Art, 68, 71-80
Wiles, Thomas, 70
Winchester, 45-90 caliber, 28
Woodlawn Cemetery, 207
Wyman, Fred, 69

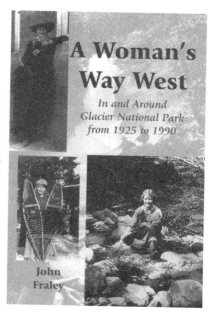
231